How to Make Money from Crypto Trading & Investing for Beginners

Complete Guide on How to Buy & Sell Bitcoin & Altcoins for Profit, DeFi Yield Farming with Cryptocurrency Investments Tips

Lucrative Business Ideas Series
Book 5

Buzzer Joseph

Copyright © 2020 Buzzer Joseph

All Rights Reserved

No part of this book may be reproduced in any form without a written permission from the author. Reviewers are allowed to quote brief passages of the content of this book in their review write-ups.

Legal Disclaimer

The information contained in this book are business advice, for motivating and enlightening entrepreneurs and investors. Most of them worked for the author. But there is no guarantee that it will yield the same result for you.

The author and publisher disclaim any liability arising directly or indirectly from the use of this book.

DEDICATION

This book is dedicated to God for giving me the inspiration to write this book for all entrepreneurs and investors who wish to learn how to successfully trade cryptocurrencies and make money.

Table of Contents

INTRODUCTION 9

CRYPTOCURRENCY ACRONYMS AND TERMINOLOGIES 11

ABOUT BITCOIN 13
    History of Bitcoin 13
    Historical Background of Bitcoin 13
    Bitcoin as an Emerging System for Virtual Payments 14
    A Change in Perception 15
    Bitcoin and Government Regulations 15
    Remarkable Bitcoin Price Movement 17
    Price History of Bitcoin in 2020 18
    Annual Closing Prices and Percentage Return of Bitcoin 18
    Bitcoin Price Forecasts 19
        Bitcoin Price Forecast 1 19
        Bitcoin Price Price Forecast 2 19
    The Mystery behind Satoshi Nakamoto 20
    Bitcoin vs Traditional Currency and Other Cryptocurrencies 22
        Factors that made Bitcoin Different from any Traditional Currency ... 22
        Why you should not Compare USD to Bitcoin 23
    Understanding Bitcoin, Cryptocurrency, and the Blockchain Technology ... 26
        What is a Blockchain? 26
        Blockchain as a Distributed Ledger 26
        The Transparency of Blockchain 27
        Blocks 27
        Bitcoin Nodes vs. Miners 27
        Decentralized Network 28
        Who can Use the Blockchain Technology? 28
        Cryptotechnology 28
        New Functionality Layer 28
    Understanding the Bitcoin Protocol 29
        Bitcoin Addresses 29
        Bitcoin Mining 29
        Consensus Algorithms 30
        Bitcoin Price 30

Blockchain and the Evolution of the Internet 30
   The Sharing Industry 30
   Smart Contracts 31
   Government Services 31
   Record Keeping 31
   Intellectual Property Protection 31
   Internet of Things (IoT) 32
   Management of Online Identity 32
   Information Management 32
   Stock Trading 32
   Crowdfunding 33

Database vs. Blockchain 33

Challenges Facing Bitcoin 34

Why Hackers Request their Victims to Pay Ransom with Bitcoin 35

Various Ways to use Bitcoin 35

Bitcoin as a New Asset Class 36

WHAT ARE ALTCOINS? 38

Some Popular Altcoins 38

ABOUT ETHEREUM 40

Ethereum (ETH) 40
   Why is Ethereum Important? 40
   Why is Ethereum Valuable? 41

BITCOIN INVESTMENT STRATEGIES 43
   Long Term Buying and Holding 43
   Short Term Bitcoin Trading 43
   Bitcoin Mining 43
   Doubling your Bitcoin 44

VARIOUS TYPES OF BITCOIN WALLETS 45
   Online Bitcoin Wallets 45
   Mobile Bitcoin Wallets 46
   Desktop Computer Bitcoin Wallet 46
   Paper Bitcoin Wallet 46
   Hardware Bitcoin Wallet 47

Hot Wallets vs. Cold Wallets 47

Non-Custodial vs. Custodial Wallets 47
   Non-Custodial Wallets 48
   Custodial Wallets 48

LONG TERM BITCOIN INVESTMENT VS. BITCOIN TRADING 49

Investing in Cryptocurrencies for the First Time 49

Some Secured Centralized and Decentralized Exchanges 51

Strategies for Successful Bitcoin Trading 51

Real Life Bitcoin Investment Strategies 52
   Cost Averaging Investment Strategy 52
   Investing a Lump Sum into Bitcoin at a Time 53
   Bitcoin Investing Hedge Fund 53

Best Practices with Bitcoin Investment 55

CRYPTOCURRENCY SECURITY TIPS 57

Strategies Used by Cyber Criminals to Steal your Cryptocurrencies 57
   Malware 57
   Phising 58

Tips to help you Protect your Cryptocurrencies from Getting Hacked 58

How to Recover your Lost Cryptocurrencies 62
   Fund Recovery in Hot Wallets and Exchange Platforms 62
   Fund Recovery in Cold Wallets 63
   Trusted Detective 63

CRYPTOCURRENCY MARKET ANALYSIS & TOOLS 64

Cryptocurrency Fundamental Analysis 64
   Real Life Application of Cryptocurrency Fundamental Analysis 66

Cryptocurrency Technical Analysis 66
   Important Technical Analysis Terms 66
   Essential Technical Analysis Tools/Indicators 70

How News affect the Prices of Assets 74

Best Websites/Tools for Crypto Coins Analysis and News 75

CRYPTOCURRENCY TRADING BASICS 76

Day Trading Guide 76
   Day Trading Advice 76

Bitcoin vs. Stocks 77

Coin vs. Token 78

The Basic Unit of Bitcoin 79
   How to Convert any USD Amount to BTC or Satoshi 79

The Basic Unit of Ethereum 80
    How to Convert any USD Amount to ETH or Gwei 80

The Best Time to Buy Bitcoin 81

The Best Time to Sell Bitcoin 81

How to Track Bitcoin Transactions and Know its Status 81

How to Track Ethereum Transaction and Know its Status 84

How to Choose a Secure Crypto Exchange Platform 86

Recommended Centralized Exchange Platforms 86

Recommended Decentralized Exchange Platforms 87

How to Calculate your Percentage Profit in Short Term Cryptocurrency Trading 88

How to Calculate your Percentage Profit in Long Term Cryptocurrency Trading 88
    Considering Cost Averaging 91

How to Calculate your Cryptocurrency Profit in Excel 92

LEGIT WAYS TO MAKE MONEY WITH CRYPTOCURRENCIES 93

DeFi Yield Farming and Staking 93

Cryptocurrency Trading 94

Crypto Coins Investment 94

Cryptocurrency Affiliate Marketing 94

Bitcoin and Altcoin Mining 94

Freelance Sites that Pay with Cryptocurrencies 95

Micro Job Sites that Pay with Cryptocurrencies 95

CLASSIFICATIONS OF CRYPTOCURRENCIES BASED ON THEIR MARKET CAPITALIZATION 96

Large-Cap Cryptocurrencies 96

Mid-Cap Cryptocurrencies 97

Low or Small-Cap Cryptocurrencies 97

Which Category of Cryptocurrencies are the Best to Invest In? 97

CENTRALIZED CRYPTO EXCHANGE TRADING GUIDE 99

How to Sign Up with Any Exchange Platform 99

Spot Trading vs. Futures and Margin Trading 99

How to Set Two Factor Authentication (2FA) for your Exchange Apps 101

Different Ways to Buy and Sell Cryptocurrencies 101

How to Use KuCoin Exchange App 103
- Mastering KuCoin App Home Interface 103
- KuCoin App User Profile 104
- KuCoin App Security Set Up Guide 104
- How to Use the KCS Pay 80% Fee Feature 107
- How to Change KuCoin App Default Currency 107
- Important KuCoin Pages 107
- How to Transfer Funds between your KuCoin Main Account and Trading Account 116
- How to Deposit Funds into your KuCoin Main Account 117
- How to Withdraw Funds from your KuCoin Main Account 118
- Guide to KuCoin Spot Trading 119
- How to Trade Margined Futures with KuCoin App and the Web Version 120

How to Use Binance Exchange App 121
- Mastering Binance App Home Interface 121
- Binance App User Profile 122
- Binance App Security Set Up Guide 122
- How to Use the BNB Pay 80% Fee Feature 123
- Important Binance Pages 123
- How to Deposit Funds into your Binance Account 131
- How to Withdraw Funds from your Binance Account 131
- Guide to Binance Spot Trading 132
- Guide to Binance Features Trading 133

DECENTRALIZED CRYPTO EXCHANGE TRADING GUIDE 134

Private Key vs. Recovery Phrase 134
- Private Key 134
- Recovery/Mnemonic Phrase 134

How to Use Trust Wallet App 135
- How to Setup a Private ERC20 Wallet using Trust Wallet App 135
- How to Secure your Trust Wallet App 137
- How to Import/Create Multiple Wallets in Trust Wallet App 139
- How to Add/Remove a Token from Trust Wallet App Home Page 139
- How to Deposit and Withdraw Tokens with your Trust Wallet App 140
- How to Trade with Trust Wallet Built-In DEX 143

How to Use ImToken Wallet App 147
- ImToken Security Tips 147
- How to Setup a Private ERC20 Wallet using imToken App 148
- How to Import/Create Multiple Wallets in ImToken Wallet App 151
- How to Add/Remove a Token from ImToken Wallet App Home Page 156
- How to Deposit and Withdraw Tokens with your Trust Wallet App 158
- How to Swap Tokens with ImToken Built-in DEX 160
- How to Access the Recovery Phrase and Private Key of your Wallet in ImToken 161

How to Use WalletConnect with Trust Wallet and ImToken App 164

How to Use the DApp Browser of any Decentralized Wallet App to Trade with any DEX 167

How to Setup and Use Metamask Wallet 171
    How to Install Metamask on PC 171
    Creating a Wallet 171

Uniswap Trading Guide 172

CONCLUSION 173

OTHER BOOKS BY THE AUTHOR 174

CRYPTOCURRENCY INVESTMENT BONUS 176

OTHER FREE HELPFUL RESOURCES 178

INTRODUCTION

Bitcoin and altcoins are already taking over the world economy. With more and more businesses realizing the power of Bitcoin, you will be able to use yours in more places to make purchases in the nearest future. PayPal Inc. joined the cryptocurrency market in October 2020, allowing customers to buy, sell and hold bitcoin and other some other cryptocurrencies using the U.S. digital payments company's online wallets. By 2021, PayPal customers will also be able to use cryptocurrencies to shop at the 26 million merchants on its network. More international companies are preparing to follow suit. This means that the value and price of Bitcoin and some other altcoins will continue to skyrocket. Don't be left out!

Crypto trading and investment are some of the lucrative business ideas that can make you rich within a short period of time. It can also wreck you financially very quickly if not properly guided. That is why you need a grounded knowledge of cryptocurrencies in order to make money in this field.

I have been a cryptocurrency investor since 2016. My goal is to retire young and wealthy, escaping the daily grinds. I taught myself how to trade Bitcoin and other altcoins for profit, both on short term (including day trading) and long term basis. Although I learnt crypto trading the hard way, but that was what made me stronger and successful. It took me years of studies, trial and error to become a consistent online money maker. My main aim of writing this book is to help young investors understand the real-life strategies of succeeding as a cryptocurrency trader within a short period of time. Cryptocurrency trading is not gambling or an online poker game. To be successful in crypto trading, you need the right tools and you need to be motivated, to work hard, and to persevere.

Here are some of the things you will learn from this book, **How to Make Money from Crypto Trading & Investing for Beginners**:

- **All About Bitcoin & Blockchain:** History of Bitcoin & Blockchain, Basic Unit of Bitcoin, Bitcoin Price Forecast, Database vs. Blockchain, Bitcoin Investment Strategies, Various Types of Bitcoin Wallets, Long Term Bitcoin Investment vs. Bitcoin Trading, Real Life Bitcoin Investment Strategies, etc.
- **All About Altcoins:** Some popular Altcoins, All about Ethereum, Basic Unit of Ethereum, etc.
- **Cryptocurrency Security Tips:** Crypto Cyber Crime Strategies, How to Protect & Recover Lost Cryptocurrencies, etc.
- **Cryptocurrency Basics:** Crypto Acronyms & Terms, Legit Ways to Make Money with Cryptocurrencies, DeFi Yield Farming & Staking, Sites that Pay with Cryptocurrencies, Classifications of Cryptocurrencies Based on Market Cap, etc.
- **Cryptocurrency Market Analysis & Tools:** Fundamental Analysis (FA), Technical Analysis (TA), How News affect the Prices of Assets, Best Websites/Tools for Crypto Coins Analysis & News, etc.
- **Cryptocurrency Trading Basics:** Day Trading Guide, Bitcoin vs. Stocks, How to Convert any USD Amount to BTC or Satoshi, How to Convert any USD Amount to ETH or Gwei, Best Time to Buy & Sell Crypto Coins, How to Track BTC & ETH Transactions, How to Choose a Secure Crypto Exchange Platform, Recommended Centralized & Decentralized Exchange Platforms, How to Calculate your Cryptocurrency Profit in Excel, etc.
- **Centralized Crypto Exchange Trading Guide:** How to Sign Up with Any Exchange Platform, Spot Trading vs. Futures and Margin Trading, How to Set Two Factor Authentication (2FA) for your Exchange Apps, Different Ways to Buy and Sell Cryptocurrencies, How to Use KuCoin Exchange App, How to Use Binance Exchange App, etc.
- **Decentralized Crypto Exchange Trading Guide:** Private Key vs. Recovery Phrase, How to Use Trust Wallet App, How to Use ImToken Wallet App, How to Use WalletConnect with Trust Wallet and ImToken

App, How to Trade with any DEX from your Decentralized Wallet App, How to Setup and Use Metamask Wallet, Uniswap Trading Guide, etc.
- **Cryptocurrency Investment Bonus!**

This book equips you with all you need to know in order to be successful as a crypto trader and investor. **Explore this book**, follow the guides and apply the tips. You will surely become financially stable. **Don't forget to share your testimony** once you move to a higher financial level with the help of the tips in this book.

Love from,

Buzzer Joseph

CRYPTOCURRENCY ACRONYMS AND TERMINOLOGIES

Here's some helpful terminologies to anyone starting out on crypto coin trading and investment.

1. **Altcoin:** Any cryptocurrency other than bitcoin. They are the various alternative cryptocurrencies that were launched after Bitcoin's massive success. The term means *alternative coins*: other than bitcoins. They were launched as enhanced substitutes of bitcoin with the claims to overcome some of the pain points of bitcoin.
2. **Ashdraked:** A situation where you lost all your money.
3. **Bag Holder:** A person who buys and hold coins in large quantity hoping to make good profits in the future.
4. **Bear/Bearish:** Negative price movement of coins. Bears/sellers take the market price below by selling crypto. Bearish comes from the bear, who strikes downward with its paws, thus driving prices down.
5. **BTFD:** Buy the Fucking Dip (an indication to buy a coin when it has dumped so hard)
6. **Bull/Bullish:** Positive price movement. Bulls/buyers want to take the market price up by buying the cryptocurrency. Bullish comes from the bull, who strikes upwards with its horns, thus pushing prices higher.
7. **Dildo:** Long green or red candles.
8. **Dump:** To sell off a coin.
9. **Dumping:** Downward price movement of coins.
10. **Bull Run:** A favourable market situation for altcoin traders. The prices of the coins skyrocket, given these traders huge profit. After a bull run, bear run takes over.
11. **Bear Run:** An unfavourable market situation for alt coin traders. The prices of the coins drop a lot, leading to huge loss. After a bull run, bear run takes over.
12. **Blood Bath:** A term used to qualify a bearish market condition, when the prices of alt coins have tanked a lot.
13. **DYOR:** Do Your Own Research.
14. **FA:** This means Fundamental Analysis. Crypto fundamental analysis is a qualitative approach to market information investigation. For instance, you might look at its use cases, the amount of people using it, or the team behind the project. Your goal is to reach a conclusion on whether the asset is overvalued or undervalued. Fundamental analysis will be explained in detail in a section of this book.
15. **TA:** This means Technical Analysis. Crypto technical analysis involves using real-world data to try to predict the future of the market. It involves looking at past statistics of the cryptocurrencies in question, including factors like volume and movement. TA users believe they can predict future price movements based on the past performance of assets. This is achieved by identifying candlestick patterns and studying essential indicators. Technical analysis will be explained in detail in a section of this book.
16. **FOMO:** Fear of Missing Out (A coin is pumping and you get the feeling it's going to pump more, so you buy high)
17. **FUD:** Fear Uncertainty and Doubt.
18. **HODL:** Hold onto Dear Life. Long term traded coins are referred to as Hodl coins.
19. **JOMO:** Joy of Missing Out.
20. **ATH:** All Time High. The highest price a particular coin has attained.
21. **ATL:** All Time Low. The lowest price a particular coin has attained.
22. **Long:** Margin bull position.
23. **MCap/Market Cap:** This means Market Capitalization or simply Market Cap. Market Cap is a useful metric to know the real value of any cryptocurrency. It is a product of the Total Circulating Supply and Price of the coin. It essentially represents the hypothetical cost to buy every single available unit of the crypto asset (assuming no slippage).

24. **Moon:** Continuous upward movement of price of a particular coin.
25. **OTC:** This means Over the Counter. Over-the-counter trading is a trade made directly between two parties and takes place without the mediation of an exchange. It is organized among groups of dealers in a marketplace without a central location. For OTC crypto trades, the two parties trade both crypto-to-crypto or crypto-to-fiat.
26. **Pump:** Upward price movement.
27. **SAJ Candle:** Huge green candle.
28. **Shit Coin:** A coin with no potential value or use.
29. **Short:** Margin bear position.
30. **Swing:** Zig zag price movement (upwards and downwards).
31. **Reverse Indicator:** Someone who is always wrong predicting price movements.
32. **RSI:** This means Relative Strength Index. This is a momentum oscillator used in technical analysis to measure the magnitude of recent price changes to evaluate overbought or oversold conditions in the price of a stock or other asset. For cryptocurrencies, RSI measures the strength and speed of a market's price movement by comparing the current price of a cryptocurrency to its past performance. Since the RSI is a momentum indicator, it shows the rate (momentum) at which the price is changing. This means that if momentum is increasing while the price is rising, the uptrend is strong, and more and more buyers are stepping in. On the other hand, if momentum is decreasing while the price is rising, it may show that sellers soon might take control over the market. The RSI oscillates between zero and 100. Traditionally, the RSI is considered overbought or overvalued when above 70 and oversold or undervalued when below 30.
33. **Whale:** A very wealthy cryptocurrency trader/market mover.
34. **Centralized Exchange (CEx):** Centralized exchanges conduct trades from fiat-to-cryptocurrency or vice versa. They can also be used to conduct trades between two different cryptocurrencies. While this may seem to cover all of the potential transaction types, there is still a market for another type of cryptocurrency exchange as well. There is always a middle man who sets the price bids.
35. **Decentralized Exchange (DEx):** Decentralized exchanges cut out the middle man, generating what is often thought of as a "trustless" environment. These types of exchanges function as peer-to-peer exchanges. Transactions are done entirely based on smart contracts and atomic swaps. Assets are never held by an escrow service. Also, decentralized exchanges allow only payments in cryptocurrencies.
36. **Stablecoins:** A stablecoin is a cryptocurrency that is meant to limit the volatility that investors experience in the cryptosphere. Stablecoins are usually pegged to another asset with a stable value, but they may also be backed by an algorithm. Stable coins can be classified based on the commodity that backs them. The major classes include: Commodity Backed Stablecoins, Fiat Backed Stablecoins, Crypto Backed Stablecoins, Siegniorage Style Stablecoins, etc. Here are some of the best stable coins: Tether (USDT), True USD (TUSD), Paxos Standard (PAX), USD Coin (USDC), Binance USD (BUSD), etc. You can read more about stablecoins at https://www.benzinga.com/money/best-stablecoins-and-4-types-of-stablecoins.

ABOUT BITCOIN

History of Bitcoin

The money that we use every day has three fundamental traits: it is tangible, regulated by a central authority, and it can be faked. Bitcoin embodies none of these traits. It is digital, no one is regulating it, and it is impossible to counterfeit.

Although it is named Bitcoin, there are no actual coins that you can hold if you buy this digital currency. It is free-flowing because there is no one controlling and monitoring its footprints. In addition, it is not affected by the traditional currency factors such as deflation or inflation because market demand completely defines its value.

And finally, you can't reverse Bitcoin transactions. Once you initiate the process, you cannot retract it. The transactions can be done with total concealment of your identity, and the cost is very minimal compared to banks. Slowly, Bitcoin is now becoming as popular as other currency values. But, with no backing from the government, this cryptocurrency is only as relevant as deemed necessary by its users and receivers (consumers and merchants).

Historical Background of Bitcoin

In 2008, Satoshi Nakamoto published a white paper entitled "Bitcoin: A Peer-to-Peer Electronic Cash System," which describes how this cryptocurrency works. After only several months, the first version of Bitcoin was released. The first Bitcoin transaction was recorded between Satoshi Nakamoto and Hal Finney, a known personality in the world of cryptography. The exchange rate between USD and BTC in June 2009 was only 1 BTC = 0.0001 USD. The exchange rate was based on the cost of running a PC to generate Bitcoins.

Very few people were aware of the existence of Bitcoin, and most of them were coders, programmers, and cryptographers who were constantly discussing the promise of the currency of the future in online forums. Eventually, an exclusive forum was created, which has helped coders to easily coordinate with each other to take part in the development of the open-source code through Github.

The Bitcoin protocol was considered as a breakthrough innovation in the field of cryptography, even though it is founded on early innovations. The cypherpunks, a community of experts in cryptography, played a vital role in recognizing the ingenuity of Bitcoin and helped in its development.

By 2010, the ecosystem supporting Bitcoin was mostly used for recording transactions. This is the early phase of the Blockchain technology. Payment processors and wallet services were still non-existent, and there was also no actual user interface. This restricted transactions between people who were aware and had the technical skills to initiate codes for the blockchain. For instance, a programmer in Florida initiated the first commercial Bitcoin transaction - **10,000 BTC for just two pizzas** in the Silicon Valley, coins that are worth over $100 million today..

But the prototype of a market ecosystem started to rise. By the early months of 2010, the first exchange became accessible for anyone who wanted to trade Bitcoins. An article describing Bitcoin was published on Slashdot, a popular technology website, which stirred the interest between early adopters. After this, Mt. Gox launched another platform for exchange, which became a major trading channel for Bitcoins for at least two years.

Buzzer Joseph

Bitcoin as an Emerging System for Virtual Payments

By 2011, Bitcoin started to become an emerging system for virtual payments, even though its usage is still restricted by the aspirations of early followers. The anonymity feature of the cryptocurrency made Bitcoin an enticing channel for digital black markets. It also gave rise to the Silk Road, which was an online store for illegal items (mainly prohibited drugs), which used Bitcoin as a method for payment. Unfortunately, the illicit online platform was among the early introductions of Bitcoin to the public, which has prompted the government to investigate the currency for its involvement in drugs and money laundering.

It also resulted in media coverage with Time, Bloomberg, and Forbes writing about the cryptocurrency. Politicians warned their constituents about Bitcoin, and it also became the subject of academic discourse. Some TV shows also aired episodes covering or mainly focusing about Bitcoin.

By this time, other commercial services also began to emerge. WikiLeaks began accepting donations in the form of Bitcoin. Bitpay, which allows merchants to accept Bitcoin through a phone app, was also launched. More Bitcoin exchanges were open, which allow people to trade BTCs for other cryptocurrencies as well as fiat currencies.

The Bitcoin code also underwent a significant change. Satoshi Nakamoto primarily managed the codebase maintenance, but he has never appeared in public and never talked to anyone from the community, except through online forums. By April 2011, Nakamoto appointed Gavin Andreson to manage the project. Andreson immediately appointed four other cryptographers to help him in maintaining the codebase, and they also developed several structured ways to update the fundamental Bitcoin and Blockchain code. It was also in 2011 that Litecoin was introduced as the first alternative cryptocurrency.

During 2011, the financial markets were doing well, but people were not happy. In September, the Occupy Wall Street began and soon Occupy protests were demonstrated in major cities around the world. The world saw the possibility of living in a world where we don't need to depend on the banking system.

By the year's end, more and more people became ambivalent about using virtual currency. Bitcoin was seen by the public as the currency of the future, while the government perceived it as a tool for purchasing illegal items and for money laundering. By 2012, Bitcoin was riding along the trend for being legitimate in most areas, which had conflicting impact. It became a valuable target for online thieves and hackers. One example is the hacking of Mt. Gox, which has led to the loss of thousands of BTCs.

Black markets using cryptocurrency for payment transactions still operate with an estimated $20 million worth of BTC revolved around Silk Road in 2012. Meanwhile, a popular gambling site, Satoshi Dice, flooded the whole platform with very minimal gambling bets, which ignited a forum on dealing with micro transactions.

In general, the cryptocurrency community was experiencing the effects of having no centralized regulatory body. There were also no allocated funds to help in the development of the core codes, and there are no dedicated places to resolve issues.

As a result, the Bitcoin Foundation was created, which mainly works to conduct education and outreach, represent the currency to the governments of the world, and to manage the fund to develop the technology. Later on, the Bitcoin-central.net, a popular Bitcoin exchange in Europe, was granted licenses similar to banks.

As it attracted the attention of more states, the legality of Bitcoin became a major concern. The public is using it like a fiat currency, trading it similar to a stock or bonds, and downloading it like a digital product. The Silk Road and online gambling was a major concern for governments, and some merchants stopped accepting Bitcoin because of legal issues.

A Change in Perception

Broadly, 2012 was around the time governments saw the potential of a bankless society. Mainstream media such as Forbes published several articles focusing on the use of Bitcoin for international remittances. WordPress began accepting Bitcoin, citing the limitations of conventional payment processors that hinder bloggers outside the US and UK to participate in the blogosphere.

2013 was a year of volatility for Bitcoin where two significant fluctuations in the Bitcoin price were experienced by consumers. The first fluctuation happened in early 2013, when the European Union and Cyprus entered into a bailout deal, which included a levy on bank accounts with huge deposits. This has ignited account holders in Cyprus to purchase large amounts of BTC. As a result, the price of Bitcoin doubled almost overnight, and the Cyprus experience became a precedent for using BTC as a means to conserve currency value.

Bitcoin managed to survive a huge crisis in terms of legitimacy in 2013 when Silk Road was shut down by the federal government and its founder arrested. All assets of Silk Road were seized, and it has resulted in a wider association of Bitcoin to the black market. This led to a fast dropping of price, but it immediately recovered.

In the global arena, governments started to become more serious about Bitcoin. However, not all responses were in favor of the cryptocurrency.

The United States government heavily regulated Mt. Gox as a financial transmitter firm, and moved some of its assets. It also established among the earliest regulations governing the usage of Bitcoin via a guidance report for people who are using, trading, and managing digital currencies. Specifically, the exchanges should comply with the policies of the state on money laundering. The US Senate also called a senate hearing to discuss Bitcoin, and to the surprise of many, Congress declared its position as being open to the long-term potential of Bitcoin.

Meanwhile, after its prior approval, China decided to ban all financial institutions and citizens from using Bitcoin.

The next wave of Bitcoin's volatility happened in November 2013. In only 30 days, the price of Bitcoin jumped from around $100 to more than $1300. This resulted in higher awareness for Bitcoin, and it once again enticed media outlets. In only a short span, Bitcoin moved from an effective virtual currency to a technological breakthrough. The price fell again in the later part of the year, but it never went below $200.

The rise of Bitcoin resulted in the emergence of alternative digital currencies, which are similar cryptocurrencies based on an improved or a separate underlying protocol. The first was Litecoin, which was introduced in 2011, but only after two years, hundreds of alternative coins were introduced in the public. Some are scams, while some became quite successful and are still being traded today, such as Litecoin, Manero, and Ether.

Mt. Gox finally shut down its operations in 2014, which had a large impact on the legitimacy of Bitcoin because the platform had been the most successful and the longest-running exchange for cryptocurrencies. It was the foundation of the community and the whole Bitcoin ecosystem. The shutdown was abrupt, and leaked records revealed that the platform lost around $40 million worth of BTCs. Critics of Bitcoin were quick to declare that Bitcoin was a sham, and it really influenced the ability of the virtual currency to safely operate without any regulation or oversight from a central authority.

Bitcoin and Government Regulations

As a response, the governments began to implement regulations. The tumultuous end of 2013 resulted in the sudden awareness of the people about the volatility of Bitcoin. China ordered their banks to close the accounts of Chinese digital currency exchanges, although the majority of them cited legal flaws to continue their operations.

The IRS mandated that Bitcoin should be taxed like a property, and the state of New York launched its Bitlicense, which is a legal licensing structure for commercial firms who want to receive and accept digital currencies. This was massively criticized by the community because the character of Bitcoin as an unregulated currency was deemed fading.

Meanwhile, Bitcoin gradually seeped into the business world, and many huge retailers started to accept Bitcoin payments. This includes Microsoft, Dell, Newegg, Tiger Direct, and Overstock. PayPal's subsidiary also announced its ongoing integration of Bitcoin on its payment platform.

People also started to see Bitcoin as a digital currency by using the underlying technology for other areas. This resulted in a rise of applications using blockchain beyond the scope of digital currency. This was termed Bitcoin 2.0, in which people can use blockchain technology to keep all forms of data. This included Factom, which built a layer of data over blockchain to enable a secure, verifiable, and simple method of keeping records. Maidsafecoin was also another protocol added to permit distributed storage of files to be added on blockchain, while Ethereum was a platform used by software developers to run projects on a distributed channel.

This signified the emerging notion of what early adopters had envisioned—that the cryptocurrency will become the bedrock of the evolution of the World Wide Web. Today is similar to the 1990s, and in the next few years, the blockchain technology could disrupt everything. The seed was planted, but alongside it, the reality that it will take time.

In spite of these developments, the price of Bitcoin started a gradual decline in 2014, which even plummeted below $200 in early 2015 and was really idle for months. One major cause of the decline was the introduction of new virtual currencies. The market share of Bitcoin declined from 96% to 76% in December 2014. Another factor was the sobering realization that revolutionizing the financial markets will take some time. Despite its idealistic sense of being unregulated, Bitcoin is not above the law, and it can be very complicated to paddle through financial law. Yes, Bitcoin can be disruptive, but it could be a slow disruption.

However, the basic platform continued to operate. There were still attacks every now and then, which included a substantial loss of $5 million worth of BTCs from an important exchange in early 2015.

World governments continued to study the effects of this technology while also reiterating that Bitcoin is not above the law. Silk Road founder, Ross Ulbricht, was sentenced to life imprisonment without parole, and the CEO of Mt. Gox, Mark Karpele, was arrested by Japanese authorities.

The most important shifts were initiated by the banking industry. Many financial executives started talking about distributed ledgers and blockchains instead of the digital currency. Microsoft also introduced its blockchain services, which provided a platform for businesses to try blockchain and explore how they can use it for the various areas of their operations.

This in turn flamed the rising interest in Bitcoin among the general public as well as financial traders and investors. The price of Bitcoin started to increase again as people began realizing that Bitcoin and the blockchain technology has a promise. The protocol of Bitcoin was built to process about seven BTC transactions for every second. The blockchain blocks were not big enough for storage. Bitcoin users realized that it was only a matter of months before the whole blockchain would reach its limit, and if nothing were done, it could affect the growth of the currency.

This resulted in a massive debate on whether to expand the size of the blocks to allow more transactions or to find a new position for the Bitcoin blockchain as a layer for settlement while permitting other services to initiate transactions. Without a governing authority, Bitcoin forums do not follow orders, have no public sanctions, and adhere to no democratic rules. The Bitcoin Foundation started hosting events, and online forums such as Bitcointalk and Reddit became public discussion boards.

The debate was fierce, and no agreement was reached. This was a major blow to the legitimacy of Bitcoin as a currency. People considered Bitcoin's inability to resolve a simple challenge of expanding its size, and wondered if it was capable of dealing with other problems. People also began talking about other alternative currencies that could be as viable as Bitcoin.

In 2016, the popularity of Bitcoin continued to increase with the network exceeding 1 exahash every second. Meanwhile, the Japanese Cabinet recognized cryptocurrencies such as Bitcoin as having the purpose and use of an actual money, and Bidorbuy—the biggest online marketplace in South Africa—started to accept Bitcoin payments for their customers. In Argentina, Uber began accepting Bitcoin payments after the government banned credit card companies from transacting with the company. Another major cyberattack occurred in August 2016 when Bitfinex was hacked that resulted in a loss of $60 million worth of BTCs. Bitcoin ATMs started to emerge around the world with around 800 ATMs worldwide. The Swiss Railway also updated its ticketing system so that riders can purchase tickets using Bitcoin.

By 2017, the number of merchants that are accepting Bitcoin continue to increase. NHK reported that they have recorded around 4.6 expansion rate among online merchants that are accepting Bitcoins. BitPay also announced that their transaction rate tripled, and cited usage of Bitcoin is increasing among B2B companies.

Bitcoin also gained more legitimacy among legacy financial companies and legislative bodies. For instance, Japan finally passed a law to enable Bitcoin as a legal method of payment, and Russia declared its interest to legalize usage of cryptocurrencies in the country. Skandiabanken, the largest online bank in Norway, already started the integration of Bitcoin accounts.

In the first and second quarter of 2017, the price of Bitcoin already exceeded the spot price for an ounce of gold, which was unprecedented. It also hit $2,000 in May 2017. The number of projects in GitHub related to Bitcoin also reached 10,000, while the exchange trading volumes continue to rise. In August 2017, the price of BTC reached $4,400.

Remarkable Bitcoin Price Movement

These are some of the few biggest movement in price of Bitcoin.

April 2013 Crash

In early April 2013, Bitcoin was trading for as much as $237. It fell to $67 overnight. This sharp drop hit the market with a lasting effect, as it took over 6 months for the price to recover to previous levels.

2013 End of Year Rally

Bitcoin recovered fully from the April 2013 crash at the start of November 2017, and this marked the beginning of one of Bitcoin's most notable bull runs. By the end of the month, the price had quadrupled, then it stabilized around the $700 mark by the new year.

February 2014 Crash

Following the currency's recent rally, there was bound to be tension in the Bitcoin price in the first months of 2014. This tension broke out when news aired that cryptocurrency exchange Mt. Gox had been hacked. This dropped the price of Bitcoin from around $800 to below $450.

2017 Bull Market and All Time High

2017 was a great year for Bitcoin price-wise, but the bullish price action went parabolic in the last few months of the year. Between November 1 and December 17, Bitcoin's price skyrocketed from $6,600 to its All Time High (ATH) of over $20,000 — a more than three times increase.

2018 End of Year Dump

Contrary to the previous year, 2018 brought a prolonged bearish price dump for Bitcoin. Following the closure of a 10-month long price wedge, Bitcoin fell from as much as $6,700 to below $3,700 within the single month of November.

June 2019 Bull Rally

Following the dump in November 2018, Bitcoin spent several months slowly creeping up to the $8,000 mark. Then, in the month of June alone, Bitcoin rallied to almost $13,000, eventually stabilizing around $10,000 for the coming months.

Price History of Bitcoin in 2020

As at 31st January 2020, the price of Bitcoin was $9,501.38.

Bitcoin also experienced a dip in price in March and April. By 13th March 2020, Bitcoin dropped to $4,916.78. By 1st April 2020, the price was $6,423.61.

But by August 2020, Bitcoin crossed $12,000.

By ending of September to the beginning of October 2020, Bitcoin price stabilized around $10,500 to $10,700.

The chart below shows the price history of Bitcoin from January 2020 to August 2020, with elaboration on the highest and lowest price hit for each month.

Bitcoin Price History in 2020

MONTH	HIGH	LOW
August 2020	$12,301.19 (August 8, 2020)	$11,063.50 (August 3, 2020)
July 2020	$11,113.66 (July 31, 2020)	$9081.44 (July 6, 2020)
June 2020	$10,211.23 (June 2, 2020)	$9,007.14 (June 28, 2020)
May 2020	$9,999.93 (May 8, 2020)	$8,568.88 (May 12, 2020)
April 2020	$8,784.96 (April 30, 2020)	$6,423.61 (April 1, 2020)
March 2020	$9,160.39 (March 7, 2020)	$4,916.78 (March 13, 2020)
February 2020	$10,630.37 (February 15, 2020)	$8,793.50 (February 27, 2020)
January 2020	$9,501.38 (January 31, 2020)	$6,965.72 (January 3, 2019)

Bitcoin price history in 2020 [Source: bitcoinprice.com]

Annual Closing Prices and Percentage Return of Bitcoin

Below is the annual closing prices of Bitcoin and its ROI from 2013 to 2019.

YEAR	CLOSING PRICE (% RETURN)
2019	$7,233.44 (93%)
2018	$3,743 (-74%)
2017	$14,156 (+1942%)
2016	$693 (+61%)
2015	$430 (+34%)
2014	$320 (-58%)
2013	$754

Bitcoin annual closing price and ROI [Source: bitcoinprice.com]

These dump and quick recovery of the price of Bitcoin proves that it has a very high potential in future.

Bitcoin Price Forecasts

Bitcoin Price Forecast 1

The first notable Bitcoin price forecast was found at https://gov.capital/crypto/bitcoin/. The prediction was that:

- By the end of **2020**, Bitcoin will attain a regular price of **$13310.48**, best possible price of **$15307.052** or a least possible of **$11313.908**.
- By the end of **2021**, Bitcoin will attain a regular price of **$20088.42**, best possible price of **$23101.683** or a least possible of **$17075.157**.
- By the end of **2022**, Bitcoin will attain a regular price of **$32447.06**, best possible price of **$37314.119** or a least possible of **$27580.001**.
- By the end of **2023**, Bitcoin will attain a regular price of **$47653.03**, best possible price of **$54800.9845** or a least possible of **$40505.0755**.
- By the end of **2024**, Bitcoin will attain a regular price of **$62259.77**, best possible price of **$71598.7355** or a least possible of **$52920.8045**.
- By the end of **September 2025**, Bitcoin will attain a regular price of **$70986.22**, best possible price of **$81634.153** or a least possible of **$60338.287**.

Bitcoin Price Price Forecast 2

Another notable Bitcoin price prediction was found in the 10th publication of the CRR (Crypto Research Report) at https://news.bitcoin.com/bitcoin-price-20k-2020-398k-2030/. The article covered a popular valuation method used for Bitcoin's future price forecast, called the "equation of exchange" model.

In this model, the percentage of the Total Addressable Market (TAM) can be used to estimate a crypto asset's implied future price. The model gives a target price that crypto assets should be priced at based on assumptions regarding changes in supply and demand.

In summary, the CRR researchers arrived at future price estimates for BTC, ETH, LTC, BCH, and XLM as summarized below.

Equation of Exchange Forecast of Crypto Asset Prices

	Non discounted utility price predictions				
	Current	2020	2025	2030	2033
Bitcoin	$9,263	$19,044	$341,000	$397,727	$395,270
Ethereum	$208	$331	$3,549	$3,644	$3,441
Litecoin	$44	$83	$1,216	$2,252	$2,299
Bitcoin Cash	$235	$414	$6,690	$13,016	$12,941
Stellar	$0.07	$0.09	$2.40	$7.81	$8.26

Price predictions for bitcoin, bitcoin cash, ethereum, litecoin, and stellar by the CRR team [Source: news.bitcoin.com]

NOTE: Many people have predicted the prices of Bitcoin in the past. Some of their predictions were right, while others were wrong. The essence of these price prediction is to help you feel the future potential of Bitcoin. None of these predictions has 100% guarantee. So make your own research before investing in Bitcoin.

For instance, according to https://bitcoinprice.com/predictions/, Tim Draper, a billionaire venture capitalist, had envisioned Bitcoin to hit $10,000 USD by 2018, which was correct.

Also, Mike Novogratz, a Bitcoin investor correctly predicted Bitcoin's price could rise up to $10,000 by April 2018.

Some other investors who predicted incorrect Bitcoin future prices were:

- John McAfee – $500,000 (by 2020)
- Ran Neuner – $50,000 (by 2019)
- Trace Mayer – $27,395 (by Feb 2018)
- Masterluc – $40,000 to $110,000 (by 2019)
- Mike Novogratz – $40,000 (by 2019)
- Thomas Glucksmann – $50,000 (by 2019)

The Mystery behind Satoshi Nakamoto

A person named Satoshi Nakamoto is credited as the inventor of Bitcoin, but no one has actually seen him. Hence, some people speculate that Satoshi Nakamoto is just a pseudonym used by a person or a group who authored the original white paper in 2008 and developed the first version of Bitcoin in 2009. Take note that the Bitcoin protocol requires people to use a birthday for registration, and it is known that Nakamoto signed up and used April 5 as his birthday.

Even though it can be enticing to go with the imagery of Nakamoto as a quixotic, lone genius who invented Bitcoin from nowhere, this type of innovation can never be created out of thin air. Most inventions, regardless of their "originality", were actually built on pre-existing research. In the case of Bitcoin, there were many precursors such as the Reusable Proof of Work by Hal Finney, Bit-Gold by Nick Szabo, B-Money by Wei Dai, and Hash Cash by Adam Back. These early virtual currencies were created as early as 1990s.

The anonymity behind Bitcoin can be driven by two main motivations. First is of course the privacy. As the cryptocurrency gradually increases its popularity, which now transcends many facets of our global society, its creator will of course become an instant celebrity and will be under the scrutiny of the government and the media.

Second is safety. Considering its first year alone, there were around 33,000 blocks mined, which was rewarded with 50 BTC for every block. The total payout that time was 1.6 Million BTC, which is now worth more than $900 million. Because very few people were aware of the existence of Bitcoin that time, many speculate that most of these blocks were mined by Nakamoto, and so he is now a multi-millionaire. If you are worth $900 million, you can become an easy target for criminals, specifically because Bitcoins are more like cash and less like stocks, wherein the private keys required to authorize the transfer could be printed out then hidden somewhere.

Mainstream media speculated some people to be the actual Satoshi Nakamoto. Top suspects are Vili Lehdonvirta, a well-known economic sociologist, and Michael Clear, an Irish cryptographer. Other media outlets also suggested that Nakamoto could be a group composed of three people—Charles Bry, Vladimir Oksman, and Neal King—who applied for a patent about secure channels of communication prior to the registration of the domain bitcoin.org.

Other suspects include Shinichi Mochizuki (a popular mathematician in Japan), Jed McCaleb (co-founder of Mt.Gox), and Gavin Andresen (Lead Developer of Bitcoin). In 2013, Techcrunch released an interview with cryptography researcher Sky Grey who claimed that Nakamoto is actually Nick Szabo, the creator of Bit-Gold based on textual analysis of the white paper in 2008.

Meanwhile, in 2014, Newsweek published a cover article featuring a 64-year-old Japanese American engineer named Satoshi Nakamoto who is living in California.

There are many other suspects, and all of them deny being the inventor of Bitcoin. But regardless of the anonymity of its creator, one thing is clear: Bitcoin is now an important innovation, which could change our world in the years to come.

Bitcoin vs Traditional Currency and Other Cryptocurrencies

Bitcoin is a breakthrough innovation, and it can actually replace our traditional currencies. But how is this digital currency so different from the money we use today? A $10 bill also has no other value other than what we agree as a society. And if the future society decides it wants to trust the Bitcoin system instead of the dollar model, then it can really become the currency of the future.

In essence, Bitcoin is quite different from the United States Dollars, for example, because it is not backed by the US state. This means that no institution has the power over this currency. The mere fact that the US government requires all payment to be in USD builds a direct demand for it. This demand cannot be easily replicated by cryptocurrencies.

But if we look back at our history, the involvement of a government in the monetary system goes deeper than merely demanding tax payments in its preferred currency. Understanding this history is beneficial for us to understand the possible restrictions of virtual currencies such as Bitcoin. In general, governments have the inherent right to control our financial systems. It is important to take note that the state values the system of seigniorage for its revenue, so it is quite impossible to let this revenue source be replaced by a private money source like Bitcoin.

At present, cryptocurrencies are effectively not relevant if you compare it with the USD, which is a global payment system. However, those who are expecting the expansion of Bitcoin to a global scale are also considering the possibility that Bitcoin will not remain exclusively in the private domain. Once it becomes wide and large, this currency will definitely entice the government as signified by the declaration of the US Senate to be open for the long-term purpose of digital currencies.

Meanwhile, the concept of private currency as a solution to the inefficiencies of the barter system has minimal historical importance. For instance, although people usually believe that precious metals such as silver and gold were used gradually by the private sector as another medium for value exchange, in practice, people are not sure if the metallic component of currency coins are equal to its agreed value.

Coins were only widely accepted as a medium of exchange when governments had standardized its production. The Roman Empire, for example, practiced the currency system. After its downfall, however, people gradually returned to the barter system. Advocates of Bitcoin also believe that the verification and security problems in Bitcoin are less likely to impact a virtual currency. This area is yet to be seen in our future.

Bitcoin enthusiasts have also cited their commitment to limit the supply of digital coins, but currency experts are not completely relying on these claims. They oppose the interest of those who are regulating these currencies, so trusting them may not be the best thing to do.

Factors that made Bitcoin Different from any Traditional Currency

In spite of certain exceptions, there are several factors that make Bitcoin quite different compared to our current financial systems:

Decentralized System

Fiat currencies such as USD, EUR, and JPY are under the regulation of a central government agency, usually through the central bank. Hence, their production can be regulated. The creation and transaction involving Bitcoins are regulated by a code, open source, and will largely depend on the P2P nature of the ecosystem. No central governing body can interfere in the Bitcoin processes.

Value

Take note that a currency is only accepted as a currency if it has an agreed value. Any currency such as the Japanese Yen represents value because the Japanese government, its people, and the international community agree that this currency has value. Bitcoin follows the same principle.

Bitcoin is created through mining. The effort behind the activity provides the currency its value, while the changing demand and supply results in the fluctuation of value.

The concept of work providing value to a currency is known as **POW** (Proof of Work) model. This is also known as proof of stake in other forms of virtual currencies. The Bitcoin ecosystem generates value if the transactions are recorded in the public ledger as producing a block also requires work.

Virtual

Traditional currency is signified by an actual object (bills, coins) to represent value. But Bitcoin is digital, and due to this you can keep the value using a digital wallet. Hence, there is no actual object that can represent Bitcoin.

Pseudonymity

Bitcoin owners keep their assets in a secured wallet. The confirmation of the account holder is kept in an encrypted place that they can control, but not associated to the person's identity. The connection between the Bitcoin and its owner is pseudonymous rather than anonymous as the ledgers can be accessed by anyone. Hence, these ledgers can be used to access data about people who are part of the Bitcoin ecosystem.

Cryptographic

Secure transaction is a main feature of Bitcoin. This feature is used to control the production of coins and to verify transactions.

Adaptive Scaling

Bitcoin is designed to allow one block of transaction to be mined in 10-minute intervals. The algorithm adapts after 2016 blocks, which is about 2 weeks, to make the mining more difficult or easier depending on the time that it took for the blocks to be mined. The mining is easy if it only takes 10 days to mine the blocks. Hence, the system will increase the difficulty.

You should not worry if at this point you are a bit confused about how Bitcoin works. It can be a challenge for beginners to understand these basic concepts of Bitcoin. Moreover, each chapter of this book will help you learn more about Bitcoins until you become more aware on how this cryptocurrency can become the currency of the future.

Why you should not Compare USD to Bitcoin

Two decades ago, when the World Wide Web was only beginning to gain ground, it was in a similar condition as Bitcoin today. The Internet was slowly replacing common methods of communication such as snail mail and typewriters at a gradual pace.

These were not immediately replaced, but their relevance is slowly fading. As we pass through the 21st century, mainstream media has joined the Internet Revolution, which has caused media outlets, especially newspapers, to change their landscape and scope. As the Web increased its scope and influence, it was not commonly compared to the relevance of Time Magazine or the New York Times.

In the 1990s, very few people were aware of or even using e-mail, but after only 20 years, millions of people around the world are now using it for personal and business use. In essence, Bitcoin is now following this lead by creating its own technology for blockchain over the Web's current virtual blockchain.

The increasing influence of Bitcoin on currency systems as well as worldwide commerce is set to be in comparison with the depth of the Web's natural ability to evolve the way we all communicate.

Despite being a breakthrough technology, Bitcoin is not reinventing the wheel so much as it is setting the accepted wheel in the Internet world in a thrilling new perspective. However, this may take several years, or even decade before we are able to see how cryptocurrencies can go. Nevertheless, it is moving onward and upward, and a lot of people are now starting to gain interest.

Meanwhile, Bitcoin scared a lot of authorities including governments and the banking industry. This scare was so great that the technology was banned in some areas. . As discussed in Chapter 1, the prohibition of Bitcoin in China caused a crash in the BTC marketplace. It has also gone through the mess at Mt. Gox where bots were allegedly pumping the BTC price, which created a market bubble.

Other crucial factors include the Silk Road shutdown, the licensing controversy in New York, and the IPO of Alibaba. Despite all of these, Bitcoin not only managed to survive these ordeals, but conversely thrived and caught the attention of the largest retailers and companies in the world such as Microsoft, Dish Network, Dell, PayPal, and many more.

To put it simply, snail mail and e-mail are both used as a means of communication. But this is where the comparison ends. Nowadays, probably because of uncertainty, the value of Bitcoin is often compared to the United States Dollar, which is the reserve currency of the world and the most established, most distributed, and most liquid currency today.

People compare Bitcoin to the USD, because they are both regarded as currencies. However, the value of Bitcoin is now beyond that. Currency is just one of the many uses of Bitcoin. Its price is increasing by at least 400% per year. It is possible to send 100 bits of data inside a Bitcoin. You can send a small percentage of a Bitcoin to someone for your business transactions. There is also a market cap in the production of Bitcoin. Bitcoin distribution is completely decentralized, and it is also not restricted by any geographical limitation.

On the other hand, the US Dollar is somewhat similar to the Presidents of the United States—almighty, but they had their time in the world where they once ruled. Now, they are only part of our history.

The value of USD is established at this point solely based on its liquidity and strength as world currency. However, many financial experts believe that it is set for a substantial crash. The Recession in 2009 was only the beginning. The status as a world currency usually lasts only at a maximum of 70 years, and the USD has held this status for more than seven decades now. The influence of the US military force around the world, with more than 100 military bases, is the primary factor that sustains the USD. However, this may not last for long.

An important step in the downfall of the USD as a world currency is the establishment of the BRICS Development Bank, which is composed of Brazil, Russia, India, China, and South Africa. This organization now controls 40% of the currency reserves and population of the world. It was also surprising that the United States was strangely silent when BRICS declared that they are now working with each other without using the USD.

For many years, these countries have been working on bilateral trade agreements without using the world reserve currency. These countries believe that the US dollar has lost its intrinsic value, and it is only a matter of time before it collapses. Meanwhile, the value of Bitcoin rises year after year. Famous financial experts such as Robert Kiyosaki, Ron Paul, Mike Malone, Jeff Berwick, and Peter Schiff believe that the world economy will collapse once the USD falls. Even the legendary George Soros, who made $1 Billion in forex trading, believes that Bitcoin is only a prelude to what will be the ultimate demise of the USD.

But does this mean we will stop using the dollar as our currency? That is unlikely to happen in the next two to three decades. But once it collapses, and falls to its intrinsic value, cryptocurrencies such as Bitcoin will experience an inverse relationship to the market. Its value will significantly rise against the USD as it continues to fade away. The only thing that will stop this from happening is if the Bitcoin ecosystem shuts down.

Hence, comparing the value of Bitcoin to the value of the US dollar is not considered relevant. Even if Bitcoin replaces the USD as the reserve currency of the world, it is irrelevant to measure Bitcoin in dollars because they are thriving in completely different systems. Bitcoin thrives in a decentralized financial system, while USD thrives in a centralized financial system.

Understanding Bitcoin, Cryptocurrency, and the Blockchain Technology

Cryptocurrency refers to a currency in digital or virtual form that uses cryptographic technology to add a layer of security for the transfer process and record keeping. Because of this feature, a digital currency can be difficult to fake.

Being organic is a significant trait of cryptocurrency, and it is also regarded as the best feature. Again, no single body governs cryptocurrency, so the government or the banking industry cannot manipulate it.

Bitcoin is an example of cryptocurrency that uses the blockchain technology.

What is a Blockchain?

A blockchain is a decentralized and distributed digital ledger that is used to record transactions across many computers so that the record cannot be altered retroactively without the alteration of all subsequent blocks and the collusion of the network. More on this later.

By letting virtual information to be distributed but not replicated, blockchain technology has established a backbone on the evolution of the Internet. Originally created for the Bitcoin ecosystem, the technological world is now discovering other possible uses for the technology. In essence, blockchain can also create other forms of digital value.

There is no need to fully understand how the mechanism of blockchain operates in order to use it. But becoming aware of this technology will allow you to understand why this will become a significant part of our future.

Blockchain as a Distributed Ledger

Blockchain refers to the public, decentralized, and virtual record of all transactions of a cryptocurrency such as Bitcoin. The most recent transactions are recorded then added in chronological sequence. It also allows market players to monitor Bitcoin transactions without the need to access a central record. Every computer that is connected to the network will receive a copy of the blockchain that is automatically downloaded.

Imagine a ledger that is replicated several hundreds of times across a computer network. Then picture that this network is created for regular updates, and you now have the essential understanding of the blockchain technology.

The information that is recorded on a blockchain will exist as a public and regularly reconciled database. This is a method of utilizing the network, which has clear advantages. The blockchain ledger is not stored in one location, so the records are public and can be verified by anyone. No central format of this data exists for a thief to steal or a hacker to compromise. The data on the blockchain can be accessed by anyone via the Internet because it is hosted by millions of computers around the world at the same time.

If you are familiar with Google Docs, then it will be easy for you to understand this concept. The conventional method of sharing documents with collaboration is to send a document to another person, and ask them to do some revisions. The issue with this method is that you must wait until that person sends the revised copy again before you can access the changes.

This is the current method in our databases today. Two users cannot mess with the same document at the same time. This is how a majority of the banks now control, transfer, and maintain money balances. They momentarily lock the access while they are making a transfer, then wait for the other side to update the record, then will re-access the record once again for update. If you use Google Docs, both users can have access to the same document in real time. This is similar to a public ledger, but this is a shared record. The distributed part will come into play if sharing involves several people.

Like the Internet, blockchain has its own robustness. By keeping blocks of data which are identical across the network, the blockchain has no single failure point, and it cannot be regulated by a central authority.

Since the creation of Bitcoin in 2008, the blockchain technology has continued running without any major interference. Problems linked with Bitcoin are mainly due to mismanagement or cyber-attacks. To put it simply, these problems are caused by bad faith or human error and not by the underlying framework.

The Transparency of Blockchain

The blockchain network resides in a consensus world of collective wisdom which runs automatic checks and balances every 10 minutes. A self-checking ecosystem of virtual value, the network can reconcile each transaction that occurs in 10-minute intervals. Every group of these transactions is called a block.

There are two significant properties that could result from this:

1. It is not corruptible, because changing any data on the blockchain will require a large amount of computing power in order to override the whole network.
2. Data transparency is embedded inside the network as a whole, and so in essence, it is accessible to the public.

This is theoretically possible, but in practical terms, it is not likely to happen. For instance, taking control of the system in order to catch Bitcoins will also have the same effect of damaging value.

Blocks

Blockchain is composed of blocks which are its basic units. The block is a collection of data containing related information and records about a transaction on the Bitcoin network.

Bitcoin Nodes vs. Miners

Bitcoin nodes constitute the peer-to-peer architecture that keeps the Bitcoin network running. A full bitcoin node fully validates transactions and blocks. It also helps the network to accept transactions and blocks from other full nodes, as well as validate transactions and blocks, and relay them to other nodes.

Most Bitcoin users describe nodes as the miners of Bitcoin, but this is actually not true in the strictest sense of the word. Anyone with a storage device that has enough space and is connected to the internet can run a node. Not all nodes mine Bitcoin. All miners are nodes but not all nodes are miners. Every full node has a complete copy of the blockchain and is able to verify all Bitcoin transactions.

A miner creates blocks in the blockchain which the nodes verify before adding it to the blockchain network. Basically, the miner works on transactions by coming up with the best combination (hash) to store that information. Only the first successful miner of a particular block is rewarded with bitcoin.

The Bitcoin protocol is designed to ensure that new blocks are created and confirmed approximately every ten minutes. The Bitcoin network is unique because it is a distributed network of people and machines working together by using principles of distributed governance.

In summary, Bitcoin nodes help to enforce the rules of the Bitcoin protocol. While Bitcoin miners process transactions and add them into blocks. These blocks are confirmed by Bitcoin nodes.

Decentralized Network

The blockchain network is a decentralized system. Anything that could happen on it is a work of the whole network. Several crucial impacts could result from this. In creating a new method of verifying transactions, some areas of conventional commerce may soon fade away. For example, stock market trading might become simultaneous in the blockchain, or it may make other forms of data recording such as land registry to become completely accessible to the public. Decentralization has been existing for many decades now.

A worldwide network of computers is now using the blockchain technology to simultaneously manage the database, which takes note of the Bitcoin transactions. Therefore, Bitcoin is managed by the system itself and not any single administrative organization. Through decentralization, the network can operate on a P2P basis.

Who can Use the Blockchain Technology?

Take note that there is no need to comprehensively understand blockchain for you to use it and have it become beneficial for your life. At present, the financial world provides the most robust case for the technology. One example of this is global remittances. According to the World Bank, more than $500 Billion worth of transfers occurred around the world in 2015.

Currently, there is also a high demand for developers of the blockchain technology. It is now possible eliminate the need for a third party to process transactions. The general public was able to take advantage of personal computers with the introduction of Graphical User Interface or GUI that was launched through desktop computing. Likewise, the most typical GUIs created for the blockchain are known as the wallet apps that people can use to purchase things using Bitcoin and other digital currencies.

Online transactions are closely linked to the processes of verifying people's identity. And of course, these wallet apps will continue to evolve in the years to come to include other forms of managing our identities.

Cryptotechnology

By keeping data within the platform, blockchain is eliminating the risk, which comes with the data being stored in a central location. The whole platform has no central exposure points, which cyber thieves can easily attack. The World Wide Web has security problems with which we are all familiar. We usually depend on our password security to safeguard our assets and our identity online. On the other hand, the security layer of blockchain revolves around encryption.

This is all based on the concept of private and public keys. The public key refers to a randomly created number strings, which is actually the address of the user on the blockchain. The bitcoins sent across the whole network will be recorded and tagged to this address. On the other hand, the private key is similar to a password, which will provide you access to their Bitcoin or other virtual assets. As a result, the data you store in the blockchain cannot be corrupted. But while this is true, it is still crucial that you safeguard your digital assets by printing it out, which is regarded as a paper wallet.

New Functionality Layer

Through blockchain, the Internet gains a new functionality layer, which allow users to directly transact with each other. In 2016, Bitcoin transactions were worth around $200,000 daily. Through the extra layer of security added by the blockchain technology, emerging online businesses are on track to disrupt the conventional methods in the financial industry.

According to Goldman Sachs, the blockchain technology has the highest potential, specifically in improving the efficiency of settlements and clearing. This can also equate to a worldwide savings of up to $6 Billion every year.

Understanding the Bitcoin Protocol

Like email, Bitcoin is a protocol. Where email is a protocol for sending messages over the internet, Bitcoin is a protocol for sending money over the internet. The Bitcoin protocol defines the rules of a payment network that pays computers around the world for securing the network. The software that implements the Bitcoin protocol uses a special branch of mathematics called cryptography to ensure the security of every Bitcoin transaction.

The rules of the Bitcoin protocol include the requirement that a user cannot send the same bitcoin more than once and a user cannot send bitcoin from an address for which they do not possess the private key. If a user tries to create a transaction that breaks the rules of the Bitcoin protocol, it will automatically be rejected by the rest of the Bitcoin network.

Bitcoin Addresses

Understanding Bitcoin addresses is an important building block because a Bitcoin address is central to sending and receiving bitcoin and making sure that bitcoin is secured properly.

Bitcoin uses public key cryptography in order to create a Bitcoin address. Bitcoin addresses are stored in Bitcoin wallets. There are different kinds of wallets, and safe handling of Bitcoin wallets is really important. That is why it was discussed in this book as a full section.

The thing to understand about public key cryptography is that there is a public key, which is accessible and visible to everyone — in fact you share your public key with people in order for them to send you funds, or someone can use your public key to view transaction details on the public blockchain (like confirm funds in advance prior to engaging in a transaction). But there is also a private key, which only the owner of the Bitcoin wallet should possess and control. Without the private key, any assets stored on the Bitcoin blockchain are inaccessible.

Bitcoin Mining

The Bitcoin network is constantly maintained (and blocks of transactions are confirmed as accurate) by specially designed computer hardware known as mining rigs.

Bitcoin miners have a strong incentive to produce blocks that follow the rules of the Bitcoin protocol. If a Bitcoin miner produces a block that does not follow the rules of the Bitcoin protocol, then Bitcoin nodes will reject the block and the miner will lose out on their chance to win the block reward.

The sheer amount of computer power (known as the hash rate) needed to mine Bitcoin is controversial. For some, the use of electricity to run computer equipment to perform calculations to win the block reward seems like a misallocation of resources, especially given pressing issues such as global climate change.

But Bitcoin's energy consumption creates a cost for running and managing the Bitcoin network. The cost of running the network helps reinforce the underlying value (as the price of bitcoin goes up, the cost of mining goes up, which makes the network more valuable). The energy inputs in a lot of ways mimic the production requirements of other extractive industries that use the investment of capital and energy to produce something that is valuable — such as the process of mining precious metals.

The high level of energy required to perform Bitcoin mining also helps keep the network secure. One threat to Bitcoin and other crypto networks is a 51 percent attack. A 51 percent attack occurs when a bad actor is able to capture more than half of the current mining power and essentially manipulate the underlying blockchain, potentially invalidating previous transactions or otherwise compromising the integrity of the ledger.

So Bitcoin mining, despite the controversy, is enormously valuable.

Consensus Algorithms

The two dominant consensus algorithms currently discussed in the cryptocurrency space are proof-of-work and proof-of-stake. A consensus algorithm is a foundational piece of how these permissionless and distributed systems work. Since there is no centralized gatekeeper or referee, there has to be an orderly standard by which the network can be confirmed and maintained.

Most of the popular cryptocurrencies (but not all, the currency XRP being one exception) currently use proof-of-work as a means of deciding which of the transactions are accurate and how blocks of transactions are bundled and documented on the blockchain, forming an immutable (or censorship-resistant) ledger.

Proof-of-stake, which Ethereum moved to in v2, entails a system of delegated consensus, by which holders of the currency elect to put up some of their coins as collateral and use that collateral to vote as a means of finding consensus (the risk is that if you back bad actors, you will lose your stake or the collateral that you put up). There are other forms of consensus that some crypto projects are trying out too.

Bitcoin Price

Most conversations about Bitcoin eventually find their way to the price of bitcoin. And for good reason. The price movements of bitcoin, since its inception, have been historic. The bitcoin price is characterized by heavy volatility. That means that instead of a steady rise in price over the last decade, bitcoin's price has zig-zagged, reaching all-time highs several times, only to retrace some of its steps, retreating from the highs only to rebound again. One important thing to understand is that on a yearly basis, the price of bitcoin keeps increasing, even if the daily or weekly bitcoin price might see wild fluctuations.

Blockchain and the Evolution of the Internet

Aside from being a platform for cryptocurrency, blockchain can also provide web users with the capacity to build value and verify digital information. Emerging business applications for the blockchain technology includes the following:

The Sharing Industry

With new companies such as AirBnB and Uber becoming global success stories, the sharing industry is now proven as a business model. But at present, customers who like to avail of ride-sharing service have to depend on Uber as a third-party provider. But if payments can be enabled through P2P, the blockchain technology can open the door to direct transaction between the passenger and the driver, which will lead to a genuine sharing industry. One good example is the Open Bazaar, which employs blockchain to build a P2P online platform. Users can download the application on their devices, and they can easily transact with vendors without the need to pay for transaction charges. The protocol implements a no rules policy, which means that personal credibility will be even more significant for these transactions compared to what is currently happening in marketplaces such as eBay.

Smart Contracts

Public ledgers allow the coding of simple contracts that will execute if the pre-set conditions are already established. One example of this is the Ethereum network, which is an open-source blockchain, which was created especially for this purpose. Although it is still in its infancy, Ethereum has gained a lot of traction in the last few years, and cryptocurrency experts believe that it has the potential to leverage the power of blockchain on a genuine global-shaping scale.

At the present level of development of blockchain, smart contracts could be designed to perform basic functions. For example, you can pay one derivative if a financial instrument has already met a specific benchmark through the use of blockchain technology and Bitcoin that enables the automation of the payout.

Government Services

By improving the transparency and accessibility of information, blockchain technology can become a catalyst in the way government administers its basic services as well as the result on polls or elections. Smart contracts can also help to make the process faster and easier. One example is the application Boardroom, which allows organizational decisions to happen within the blockchain. This could disrupt how organizations govern and how they manage digital assets such as data and equities.

Record Keeping

A decentralized method of keeping records online will bring a lot of advantages. Disseminating data throughout the whole platform will safeguard files from getting lost or hacked. For example, the Inter-Planetary File System or IFPS makes it easy to build how a public web could function.

Comparable to how bittorent moves data online, IPFS can eliminate the need for centralized client-server interactions such as the present form of the Internet. A new version of the World Wide Web that is composed of decentralized websites has the potential to expedite the file transfer and streaming. This improvement is not only efficient, but important in upgrading the Internet's presently overloaded systems for delivering content.

Intellectual Property Protection

As you might already know, there is no limit on how you can reproduce and distribute information in the Internet. This has provided many online users around the world a huge reserve of free content. But this is not good news for holders of copyright, because they can lose control over their intellectual property. Through smart contracts, copyright can be protected. It can also automate the sale of creative content via the Web, which eliminates the risk of replication and redistribution.

One good example of this is Mycelia, which employs the blockchain technology to build a P2P music distribution system. Established in the UK by the artist Imogen Heap, the platform allows artists to sell their songs directly to their fan base. It also allows artists to license samples to producers and manage royalties to musicians and songwriters. These functions work through the smart contracts. This use for the blockchain has a robust chance for success because blockchain can be used to release payments in a small percentage of Bitcoin, which are also known as micropayments.

Internet of Things (IoT)

IoT refers to the network-regulated administration of specific forms of electronic devices. One example is the regulation of air temperature within a database facility. Through smart contracts, it is possible to manage the automation of remote systems. This can be done through the integration of network facilities, sensors, and software as well as the exchange of data between systems and objects. The result could improve cost monitoring as well as efficiency of the system.

The most important players in telecommunications, tech, and manufacturing are all looking to dominate the IoT. This includes At&T, IBM, and Samsung. An organic extension of current systems regulated by these companies, IoT apps will be able to be applied in a wide range of purposes from massive management of automated systems, data analytics, and predictive maintenance of mechanized parts.

Management of Online Identity

We have a specific requirement for improved management of our online identity. The capacity to confirm your identity is the cornerstone technology of financial transactions that could occur online. However, the resolution for the risks involved in security that come with online portals are not completely perfect. Public ledgers can provide better ways for proving who you are, alongside the possibility of digitizing personal files. Securing personal identity is also crucial for internet communications in the sharing industry for example. Nevertheless, an outstanding reputation is the most crucial condition for conducting online transactions.

Establishing standards for digital identity can be a highly sophisticated protocol. Aside from the technical challenges, an encompassing web identity solution will require the cooperation between the government as well as private organizations. The problem can be exponentially challenging if we factor in the requirement to navigate the legal systems in various countries. At present, online stores depend on the SSL certificate to ensure that the transactions online are safe.

Information Management

Using social media platforms such as Facebook and Twitter is free, right? This is not completely true. In exchange for using these platforms, you are paying these companies with your personal information. But through blockchain, you can have the capacity to administer and sell the information that their web activities produce. And because this can be easily disseminated in micro currencies, Bitcoin will be used to facilitate this transaction.

For instance, Enigma—a project in MIT—has the capacity to understand that the privacy of the user is key in creating a marketplace for personal information. It uses cryptographic strategies to allow individual information sets to be divided between nodes, and also at the same time process massive calculations over the data group in general. Scalability can be achieved by fragmenting the information, unlike in blockchain technology where information could be replicated on each node.

Stock Trading

Stock trading can also take advantage of the blockchain technology through the improved efficiency of the shared platform. Once implemented, P2P trade confirmation could become more instant against the usual clearance time of three days. However, this could eliminate the need for custodians, auditors, and clearing houses.

Several commodities and stock exchanges are now using early forms of blockchain technology for the services they provide. This includes the Japan Exchange Group (JPX), Frankfurt Stock Exchange (Deutsche Borse), and the Australian Securities Exchange (ASX).

Crowdfunding

Crowdfunding projects such as Gofundme and Kickstarter are now implementing the comprehensive framework for the rising P2P economy. The popularity of these platforms signifies the increasing interest of people who want to have a direct involvement in the development of specific products. The blockchain technology is elevating this interest to the next level by building venture capital funds through crowdfunding.

For example, in 2016, the Decentralized Autonomous Organization (DAO) of Ethereum managed to raise as much as $200 million within 60 days. Crowdfunders bought DAO tokens, which allow them to choose the smart contract project they are interested in. However, the project was hacked and compromised because of poor due diligence. But nonetheless, the test suggests that the technology has the ability to drive new ways for people to cooperate.

Database vs. Blockchain

The difference between a blockchain and a conventional database starts with the structure or how the technology is organized. The database that runs on the World Wide Web usually uses a client-server network structure.

A registered database user who has the right permissions will be able to change the entries that are stored on a central server. In changing the master copy, each time the client is accessing a database through a device such as a computer or a smartphone, they can work on an updated version of the database entry. Database control is still within the circle of administrators, which allows for access and authorizations to be confined by a central entity.

This is not the case with blockchain. For a blockchain database, every participant could maintain, update, and compute new items within. The nodes could work together to make certain that they are all coming from the same sources, which provide built-in security for the system.

The effect of this difference is that the blockchain is well-suited as a way of recording specific functions, while a central server is completely proper for other purposes.

Basically, blockchain permits various parties that don't necessarily trust each other to access the same information without the need for authority from a centralized administration. The transactions could be processed by the users that serve as a mechanism for consensus so that everyone could create the same sharing system of record all at the same time.

The main advantage of decentralized control is that it could eliminate the risks of centralized regulation. In a centralized database, anyone with enough level of access could easily corrupt or even wipe out the data. Hence, the system will highly rely on human administrators.

Many human administrators have earned enough trust that they can have full access to the database. This makes it easy for bank databases to record the money they have in their vaults. There is also a reasonable purpose for a centralized administration, and it is actually more ideal to use in special instances than blockchain technology.

However, this also means that those who need to run centralized administration have to spend substantial amounts of money to make sure that the databases will not be compromised. If the system fails, then the data could be leaked out or even stolen.

Many centralized databases are keeping information that is updated at a certain period of time. But more often than not, these are snapshot of a period that contains outdated information. On the other hand, blockchain systems are capable of keeping relevant information. Blockchain technology could create databases, which can create records of past transactions. They are capable of expanding its previous transactions into an archive while simultaneously offering real-timeimages.

While you can use blockchain systems to act as a records system as well as a platform for facilitating transactions, they are regarded as slow when you compare them to current technologies for digital transactions such as the technologies used by PayPal and Visa. Although it is also certain that the blockchain technology will be further improved in the future, the core structure of the blockchain technology calls for some speed to be left on the wayside.

The system of distributing the networks is used in blockchain so they compound and not share processing speed and power. They each separately provide service to the whole network, and then do some comparison checks with the whole network, until the whole system agrees that the transactions are genuine. On the other hand, centralized databases are used and have been improved significantly ever since their advent in many industries.

Take note that Bitcoin is a read-uncontrolled, write-uncontrolled database. This enables everyone to add a fresh block into the ledger, which everyone could also read. An accessed-granted blockchain, similar to a centralized database could be read-controlled and write-controlled. The protocol or the network can be established so only authorized users could add new entries in the database or read the whole database.

But if trust is not an issue and confidentiality matters most, blockchain databases have no actual advantage over conventional databases with centralized administration.

Adding a concealment system to the blockchain will require complex cryptography, and this calls for more computational power for the network nodes. The best way to do this is to just completely hide the data in a private database, which does not even require connecting with the network.

Challenges Facing Bitcoin

Bitcoin is just a decade-old digital currency, but it has still a long way before it can be accepted by the general public. As a matter of fact, the challenges that this cryptocurrency is facing today are quite the same that it has experienced when it was still in its introductory phase.

When Bitcoin was first released, the primary hindrance was the computer skills and understanding of the blockchain jargon required to scrutinize the platform itself. This revolutionary technology involves solving complex algorithms for verification of transactions, which was quite difficult for a layman to chew.

Since then, the Bitcoin's disruptive features made it enticing for users of the underground market or those who are using the Dark Web. Bitcoin became a popular currency for illegal transactions such as criminal activities like drug deals and money laundering.

As a result, Bitcoin was placed in a bad light, which was worsened by the fact that it can be difficult for government agencies and financial authorities to monitor the transactions in the Bitcoin's blockchain. While some governments such as China have issued an outright ban for Bitcoins, other governments such as Japan and the United States still made their due diligence to understand how this cryptocurrency works.

The price volatility also added another layer of challenge for people to accept Bitcoin as payments. In order for widespread adoption to occur, Bitcoins should be stable, should be usable, and should be easily accessible by the general public.

Some advocates believe that there must be changes in the Bitcoin ecosystem in order to capture the mainstream users. For once, the concept should be simplified to earn the public's trust and interest. At present, around 80% of the global population are still not aware of the existence of the Bitcoin.

Why Hackers Request their Victims to Pay Ransom with Bitcoin

Just recently, the series of attacks on private serves has stirred again a long-time discussion on the vulnerabilities of virtual currencies. Just in case you are still not aware, a dangerous malware has been released and spread over 150 countries around the world. The mechanism of the ransomware attack was quite simple. A personal computer will be infected with a virus, which will encrypt files until the owner pays a certain amount as ransom.

In the recent attacks, the people behind the ransomware are asking victims to pay around $1000 in Bitcoins. And it doesn't end there. If the victim does not pay after three days, the ransom will be doubled, and after seven days and no payment has been received, all the files will be deleted from the computers. Meanwhile, there is no actual guarantee that the files will be restored again and will be safe if the victim pays the ransom.

The involvement of Bitcoin as a mode of paying the ransom again placed this digital currency in bad light. It becomes an easy tool for hackers because of its special features as a virtual currency. In sending money over digital channels, you can either use your credit cards or online banking, which is linked to your personal information such as your name and address.

But this is not the case with Bitcoin. All the dealings you make via this currency can be concealed. Remember, when you choose to trade in BTCs, a private key that is linked to your wallet will be used to create an encrypted code. This code will be publicly linked with the transaction but not with the people behind the dealings.

Hence, each deal is recorded in a public ledger, which anyone could access and check. Security experts believe that among the possible reasons why hackers and cybercriminals are using BTC as a mode of payment is because it is designed to conceal identity.

In the past, hackers preferred PayPal for their unscrupulous transactions, but because of stricter guidelines in using online platform such as PayPal, they now prefer Bitcoins.

Various Ways to use Bitcoin

Send and Receive Money

As a purely digital currency, Bitcoin is borderless. Because it's available nearly everywhere, you can send money around the world just as easily as you send it across the room.

Really all people need to be able to send and receive money internationally using a smartphone and each party to the transaction needs to have a Bitcoin wallet. Sending money is nearly instantaneous — it can take between 10 minutes or up to a couple of hours for the transaction to be processed on the Bitcoin blockchain and then available on the other side of the transactions.

Even with a slight lag, this is still way faster than trying to do a complex international bank transfer or for using an international wire service such as Western Union.

Investment

Similar to buying gold or stocks, some people like to buy bitcoin as an investment in hopes that its value will go up. Historically, the price of bitcoin has been very volatile but overall, as mining has become more difficult and buying has become easier and more popular, the price has gone up over time.

There are a few different investment ideas surrounding the Bitcoin network and the bitcoin currency. Here are a couple of high-level ideas about why people around the world are excited about investing in Bitcoin.

Reserve Currency

A reserve currency is used to settle international trade and is viewed as strong and stable. Right now, the dollar is the world's most dominant reserve currency, followed by the euro. At other times in history, other national currencies — and for a long time gold — have been used to settle international debts, hold as a long term store of value, and are used to denominate values for trade.

Some Bitcoin investors think that because of Bitcoin's digital, open, decentralized, and apolitical nature, it has the necessary attributes to become a global reserve currency. Over time, as adoption and liquidity increases, the price of bitcoin could become less volatile.

Digital Gold

Another potential outcome for Bitcoin is its use as a form of digital gold or a digital store of value. As more and more of everyday life unfolds on the internet, it's only natural that people will start wanting to store value on a digital platform. This allows for easy access, greater liquidity, and the ability to take the value literally anywhere across both the physical and virtual worlds.

Having a single source of digital wealth as an idea is growing in popularity, and even despite its volatility on a month-to-month basis, bitcoin has shown that it is a good store of value over its lifetime.

Protocol Adoption

Bitcoin investors are also bullish on the idea is that the Bitcoin network or protocol will only continue to evolve, mature, and grow. As it does, and as more companies, projects, and people start using the network and building on the protocol, then it will continue to grow in value. A very basic comparison is often made between the growth of the internet and the potential for the Bitcoin to grow.

Bitcoin as a New Asset Class

One way to think about Bitcoin is as a new asset class. In terms of investing, that means Bitcoin and other cryptocurrencies can be useful as a hedge against investments in other asset classes, and also provide a useful diversification function in traditional investment portfolios.

Financial asset classes usually share characteristics among themselves, but they are distinctive from members of other asset classes in the way they behave. This makes them useful in a portfolio context because if one asset class is losing value, other asset classes might be able to withstand the losses, or if they are completely uncorrelated, some asset classes might increase in value as other assets lose value.

Scarcity

There will only ever be 21 million bitcoin ever produced. Now, this doesn't exactly tell the whole story, because as you might remember from reading earlier, each bitcoin can be divided by eight decimal places, but the fact that Bitcoin has a set schedule for creation (the final bitcoin will be mined in 2140) and that there is no entity that can change to underlying Bitcoin network numbers means that it is a deflationary currency and that as time goes on it will become more scarce, and likely more valuable.

Adoption Curve

Studying previous technological shifts shows that there are distinctive phases of tech adoption: Innovators, early adopters, early majority, late majority, and then the laggards. This cycle has happened again and again and is particularly applicable to internet technologies and products.

Depending on where you think Bitcoin is in the technology adoption cycle should help guide potential investment decisions. While identifying the exact phase of Bitcoin's trajectory is difficult — by all accounts, the Bitcoin network and the bitcoin currency are still in the pre-mass adoption phase.

Network Effect

Bitcoin benefits from a network effect. This effect will impact future growth in two ways. The first impact of the network effect is that new growth fuels future growth. Just like the way social networks grow — new users invite other users to interact with — new Bitcoin users help convert other users so that they can share value over the network. Since Bitcoin's total addressable market is the whole world, there is really no limit to the potential spread of the network other than basic infrastructure.

Competition

Bitcoin's network effect also works to keep it competitive in the crypto market place. As mentioned earlier, Bitcoin is the oldest cryptocurrency and enjoys a first-mover advantage, but it also has a very active developer community (not to mention its solid design foundation) which means that Bitcoin continues to be number one cryptocurrency by market capitalization. The longer Bitcoin stays in this position, the more it reinforces its dominance. Ethereum is the second-place cryptocurrency by market cap, but it has completely different economics.

You can read more about Bitcoin at https://academy.binance.com/blockchain/what-is-bitcoin.

WHAT ARE ALTCOINS?

Besides Bitcoin, more than 2,000 altcoins exist. Together they comprise a global cryptocurrency market that is valued at hundreds of billions of dollars. As mentioned earlier, altcoins can exist in several formats. Some altcoin projects are trying to develop completely new kinds of blockchain protocols. These new protocols are often designed for specific traits.

The altcoins Monero and Zcash, for instance, are both new altcoins that were created with greater user privacy and security in mind, but each protocol is built upon different cryptographic principles.

A few altcoins, like Bitcoin Cash and Ethereum, are variants (or what are called forks) of other cryptocurrencies. Bitcoin was forked to create Bitcoin Cash, which enables faster transactions, and Ethereum Classic was forked to create Ethereum after a controversial decision to rewrite some of the transactions recorded on the original Ethereum blockchain. Other altcoins function more like utility tokens (which in this case means they are not necessarily building their own blockchain, but instead they will operate on top of an existing protocol).

In addition to offering digital alternatives to traditional currency, development teams around the world are using distributed and decentralized blockchain technologies to address challenges in computing power, file storage, and other digital bottlenecks with new blockchain-based solutions.

Like with any new technology, no one can be sure which of these cryptocurrencies will succeed, but this guide was created to introduce some foundational cryptocurrency attributes by looking more in-depth at specific projects.

Some Popular Altcoins

Some popular alcoins include:

- Ethereum (ETH)
- 0x (ZRX)
- Augur (REP)
- Basic Attention Token (BAT)
- Bitcoin Cash (BCH)
- Bitcoin Gold (BTG)
- Cardano (ADA)
- OMG Network (OMG)
- ZCash (ZEC)
- Ontology (ONT)
- Ontology Gas (ONG)
- Onchain (NEO)
- Qtum (QTUM)
- Siacoin (SC)
- Status Network Token (SNT)
- Stellar (XLM)
- Stratis (STRAT)
- Tron (TRX)
- Verge (XVG)
- Vertcoin (VTC)

- Ripple (XRP)
- Dash (DASH)
- Digitbyte (DGB)
- Dogecoin (DOGE)
- Eosis (EOS)
- Golem (GNT)
- Lisk (LSK)
- Litecoin (LTC)
- Monero (XMR)
- New Economy Movement (NEM)

There are many other altcoins, but these are the few of them that are worth mentioning. Make sure you carry out your own research before investing on any of these coins.

Buzzer Joseph

ABOUT ETHEREUM

Ethereum (ETH)

Ethereum (ETH) or the Ethereum Virtual Machine is an attempt to build a new version of the internet. Rather than centralized hubs (or private companies) that control massive troves of personal data, Ethereum is designed to create more decentralized information networks enabled by a series of distributed nodes and Ethereum wallets.

The idea of Ethereum was developed in 2013 by Vitalik Buterin, who at the time was a computer programmer and contributor to Bitcoin Magazine. He was advocating for more functionality on the Bitcoin blockchain to make it easier for developers to build applications.

When his plan was met with resistance from the Bitcoin community, he developed the framework for Ethereum, created a team, and published the Ethereum whitepaper. After a pre-sale to raise money to fund the development of the Ethereum Virtual Machine, the network went live on July 30, 2015.

If the internet is like a vast highway, then the current system has few on-ramps and off-ramps. These existing ramps are also controlled by a toll of sorts, which either exists as actual fees or costs that require users to pay in the form of surrendering personal or financial data.

Ethereum helps accomplish the vision of decentralized computing in two ways. The first way is to create a distributed system of nodes, which happens anytime a computer or miner joins the Ethereum blockchain. Anyone with sufficient computing power can become a node, which makes Ethereum a permissionless blockchain.

The second way Ethereum is enabling digital decentralization is through the wide distribution of the network, which makes it possible for developers to build decentralized applications using open-source smart contracts. Remember, a smart contract is basically a computer program that executes a transaction after a series of requirements are met. Most Ethereum apps are written using the Solidity language. There are also other Ethereum-specific languages.

Why is Ethereum Important?

So far, there are three major uses emerging for Ethereum: As a platform for initial coin offerings (ICOs), as a means to create ERC20 tokens, and as a way to create ERC271.

ICOs

As the name implies, an initial coin offering is very similar to when a traditional company launches an initial public offering (IPO) to raise capital in order to grow. In the case of an ICO, a person or group of people get together, create a website or whitepaper explaining a project, and then launch a coin or token sale. While the ICO boom of 2017 helped fuel the meteoric rise of the cryptocurrency market and helped launch a lot of new and interesting projects, the ICO fundraising mechanism was also used to raise money for projects that were not developed enough to ever be successful, and/or were outright frauds.

In a lot of cases, some of the hundreds of ICOs that have been launched in the past two years were launched on Ethereum. It's like the paradox of success, Ethereum developers did such a good job of building a means for people to launch decentralized projects without any kind of oversight or gatekeeper, that the many projects took advantage of the system and general euphoria about raising money in the crypto space.

However, despite the overdone ICO boom, the ability to quickly create and launch a project without having to raise capital through traditional channels has helped many really innovative and interesting projects get off the ground.

ERC20 Tokens

While ERC20 tokens sound like something out of Star Wars, the concept is really pretty straightforward. An ERC20 token is a digital unit of account that is completely exchangeable with another unit of the same system.

In other words, ERC20 tokens are designed to be fungible. This aspect of fungibility allows the tokens to be traded back and forth, much the way dollars can be traded for dollars, or euros can be traded for other euros.

Zooming out, the creation of the ERC20 standard is an important piece of infrastructure because it allows cryptocurrency projects to interoperate in a sense. For example, the 0x Protocol, which was built according to the ERC20 standards, enables the creation of decentralized exchanges, which will allow other ERC20 token projects to exchange tokens and other forms of value.

Besides the infrastructure layer, the ERC20 standard also means that individual token projects can build independent token economies.

In the long-run, well-conceived and well-executed token economies will allow projects to support themselves and drive growth and adoption. Right now, token economies are sprouting up around new ways of sharing digital data, new ways of controlling personal identity, futures markets, and all kinds of interesting ideas that are made possible by ERC20.

ERC721 Tokens

On the opposite end of the spectrum are tokens that fall under the ERC271 standard. Instead of being fungible, or one easily converted for another, ERC271 tokens are non-fungible. Having the ability to create and distribute non-fungible tokens opens the potential to use ERC271 tokens to create collectibles or tokenize (or make a digital representation) of anything that is unique and valuable. This could range from artwork to baseball card collections.

A non-fungible token model is still an emerging field, but interesting projects are developing to explore the possibility of using ERC271 as a means to secure digital property and rights, which could lead to applications that extend way beyond any current cryptocurrency use cases.

Potential applications range from creating digital scarcity to enabling things like genetic algorithms, where one unique digital good could potentially be paired with other unique digital goods, leading to offspring of sorts, with the lineage verifiable and traceable via the Ethereum blockchain.

In the past 18 months, several other open-source permissionless blockchains have launched (NEO, Tezos, Cardano, and EOS are examples), but one of the things that make Ethereum distinctive from its competitors is the size and engagement of its development community, which is working to build various kinds of decentralized apps in the hopes of demonstrating the value of Ethereum.

Why is Ethereum Valuable?

As Ethereum grows to become a massive network, more and more Ethereum wallets are being created to hold ether, which is the Ethereum blockchain's currency.

Ether's main value is that it is the native token to the Ethereum blockchain. Just like on the Bitcoin blockchain, transactions on the Ethereum blockchain come at a cost. The transaction cost on Ethereum, which is known as gas, is paid in ether.

Ethereum currently uses the proof-of-work, which like Bitcoin, relies on a system of validating the blockchain's transactions and creating new coins through difficult computation. As the proof-of-work process becomes more difficult, it will require more resources to contribute to the network.

For Bitcoin this system works, and creates a deflationary effect, because there is a fixed supply of 21 million coins. With Ethereum, there is no fixed supply, so the proof-of-work and intense computation might make less sense. Instead, the Ethereum community will attempt to move to a proof-of-stake system, which is a means of using distributed consensus (rather than mining) to confirm transactions and keep the blockchain moving forward.

You can read more about ethereum at https://academy.binance.com/blockchain/what-is-ethereum.

BITCOIN INVESTMENT STRATEGIES

There are different ways that you can invest in Bitcoin. We will look at the most popular ways here:

Long Term Buying and Holding

This is the Bitcoin investment strategy that we recommend. Here you will buy Bitcoin at a certain price and hold on to it for a period of time in the hope that the value will increase. You may also see this strategy called "hodling". When you decide to buy and hold it is very important that you do not just take anyone's advice on whether Bitcoin will rise or fall. You need to know how Bitcoin works and do your homework using the tools available to come to a decision yourself.

If you are going to adopt a buy and hold Bitcoin investment strategy then we suggest that you do the following:

1. Do not invest more than you can comfortably afford to lose. As we said earlier, Bitcoin is a high risk investment and this should be in your thoughts at all times.
2. When you have purchased Bitcoins don't leave them in an exchange wallet. Get your own wallet and move them there. We will discuss the different types if cryptocurrency wallet and their advantages and disadvantages as a full section.
3. Use a reputable exchange to make your Bitcoin purchases. This may cost you a bit more but it is better to be safe than sorry.
4. Don't purchase all of your Bitcoins in just one trade. Use the principle of Dollar cost averaging (DCA) and commit to purchasing a certain amount every month (or more frequently) throughout the course of the year. When you do this you pay average prices during the year.

Short Term Bitcoin Trading

As we said before this is where you buy Bitcoins at a low price and then sell them at a higher price to realize a profit. The time frame for these investments is short. We do not recommend that you start out with short term Bitcoin trading. As you learn more about Bitcoin you can move to a shorter term trading strategy. It is certainly possible and there are some very large players in the Bitcoin market making profits regularly on short term Bitcoin trades. You need to learn how to trade properly to make this work which takes time and practice.

Bitcoin Mining

In order to make any kind of profit with Bitcoin mining you need to invest in a lot of high end computer equipment and get the cheapest electricity that you can find. And then there are no guarantees! Mining has become a lot harder over the years. There are less and less Bitcoins to find and more and more people mining. It is just not a cost effective way to invest in Bitcoin in our opinion. Use the money you would spend on equipment and electricity to buy and hold Bitcoin instead.

You may have heard of cloud mining for Bitcoin. The idea here is that you pay for a service that will mine on your behalf using the web. In our experience these are either scams or so expensive an investment that you might as well just use the money to purchase your Bitcoins.

Doubling your Bitcoin

Have you seen websites that claim that they can double your Bitcoin holdings? Or maybe you have come across sites that claim they will pay you high levels of interest every day on your Bitcoins? We have one word for these kinds of websites; SCAM!

There are lots of websites that offer high yield investment programs (HYIP) and almost all of these are scams too. What happens here is that these sites take money from people all round the Internet in exchange for high returns. They use the money that they get from new people signing up to pay high returns to the initial investors which creates a buzz.

Then guess what? A few months later the website simply disappears! Most people lose their money and they have no way to get it back. Don't fall for these Ponzi scheme type scams. You cannot double the amount of Bitcoins that you have using these sites. It is more likely that you will lose all of your Bitcoins.

VARIOUS TYPES OF BITCOIN WALLETS

Although the blockchain technology that underpins Bitcoin is very secure, one of the biggest weak points with Bitcoin is storage. Because Bitcoins have risen significantly in value over the years you will not be surprised to know that the number of cyber criminal's intent on stealing Bitcoins has risen too.

And these people are getting smarter and smarter. They are creating bots that will scan online Bitcoin wallets and try and remove the Bitcoins in them. There have been several reports about cyber criminals emptying cryptocurrency exchange wallets over the years and the wallet holders never seeing their Bitcoins again.

We want you to be shocked and concerned by this. If you are going to be a successful Bitcoin investor then you need to hang on to your Bitcoins! It is essential that you keep your Bitcoins safe and fortunately there is a lot you can do to ensure this. The type of Bitcoin wallet that you choose is crucial to the security of your Bitcoins.

It is all about keeping your private key safe. Inside of your wallet your Bitcoins have an associated address which consists of your private key and public key. The public key is the actual address of the Bitcoin and your private key is the password that unlocks those Bitcoins. It is essential that you keep your private key safe.

If a cyber-criminal gets their hands on your private key then they can transfer all of your Bitcoins to other accounts. And you know that once a Bitcoin transaction is verified and confirmed then there is no turning back.

People that are unlucky enough to have Bitcoins stolen from their wallets just have to accept it and get on with their lives. You just cannot do anything to get your Bitcoins back.

Now let's take a look at the different types of wallets and how you can provide the maximum protection for your private key.

Online Bitcoin Wallets

There is no easier way to get started with Bitcoin investing than to setup an online wallet. You can setup a free Bitcoin online wallet even if you have no Bitcoins right now. Cryptocurrency exchanges like Coinbase, Binance, Kucoin, etc. will provide you with an online wallet and you can get one at Blockchain.com as well.

When you are just starting out then an online wallet is a good thing to use. But you would not want to keep a sizeable Bitcoin inventory in an online wallet. Yes it is great that you can access your online wallet from anywhere in the world but so can thieves and cyber criminals!

An online wallet is a "hot" wallet because all you need to access it is an Internet connection. The problem is that most online wallets end up storing your private keys on their servers and if these get hacked you can say goodbye to your Bitcoins.

Another issue is that servers can and do have technical problems and if they suffer a catastrophic issue then your private keys could disappear forever. Some online wallet platforms will limit or suspend accounts for terms of service infractions and you may even have your account shut down permanently and you lose your private keys.

We strongly recommend that if you have a significant amount of Bitcoins that you move them to a cold wallet which is offline. Don't take the chance of not being in control of your Bitcoins.

Online wallets are not all bad. Yes there are security and other risks but if you intend to make frequent Bitcoin transactions then they are useful. You can hold a small amount of Bitcoins in your online wallet for those regular transactions and then move the rest to a more secure wallet.

Mobile Bitcoin Wallets

A mobile wallet is another form of hot online wallet. With a mobile wallet you can access it using your mobile device when you connect to the Internet. If you have a smartphone or tablet that you take around with you wherever you go then this is a very convenient type of Bitcoin wallet.

With a mobile wallet you can make Bitcoin payments to a vendor either online or offline. If you have a Blockchain.com or Coinbase online wallet then there is a mobile counterpart synchronized to your main wallet.

Despite being very convenient, there are issues with mobile wallets. Cyber criminals and hackers can still get hold of your private keys if they are saved on your mobile device or remote servers.

A lot of people lose their mobile phones or have them stolen. Also a lot of mobile phones suffer damage. If you don't make copies of your private keys then you could potentially lose all of your Bitcoins in these scenarios.

To get the best use out of a mobile wallet we recommend that you transfer just what you need to it from a more secure wallet. Then if you lose your phone or it becomes unusable you will still have your private keys safely stored in the secure wallet.

Desktop Computer Bitcoin Wallet

Another choice for you is the desktop wallet. It is a much safer choice than an online or mobile wallet as you download an app for your computer or laptop and you store your private keys in it. One of the most popular desktop wallets is Bitcoin Core. In our opinion this is not the most practical choice. The reason is that Bitcoin Core will actually download the complete blockchain so you will need at least 150 GB of spare disk space to make this work.

The good news is that there are alternative desktop wallets that you can use which do not require you to download the blockchain for Bitcoin. Instead they use simple payment verification (SPV) technology. Some good examples are:

- Electrum
- Armory
- Bither

Desktop wallets are simple to use and so much safer than online or mobile wallets. With a desktop wallet you can disconnect your computer from the Internet to prevent hackers from accessing your private keys. While it is true that a desktop wallet does not have the convenience of an online wallet, you will have control over your private keys. You can also make a backup in case your laptop or computer spoils or is stolen.

Paper Bitcoin Wallet

This may seem a strange thing to try and store your Bitcoins on paper as they do not seem to be a very good match. But paper wallets are another cold storage option as it is impossible for even the most competent cyber criminals to hack a piece of paper!

Of course if you do not take care of a paper wallet in the real world then people can steal it. So if you choose this option then don't leave it lying around. You also need to protect paper wallets from damage as well so use a water resistant container to store them.

A paper wallet definitely does not have the convenience of an online wallet but they are a lot safer. All you need to do is to print off your private and public keys and store the paper somewhere secure such as a safety deposit box. It is recommended you store them in multiple safe locations.

Paper wallets are a good long term option. You can store large amount of Bitcoins in your paper wallet and then have a few available in an online wallet for regular transactions. It is definitely one to consider.

Hardware Bitcoin Wallet

Most Bitcoin experts will tell you that the most secure types of Bitcoin wallets are hardware wallets. We agree and if you are serious about Bitcoin investing then we strongly recommend that you invest in a hardware wallet. They are not cheap but they are worth it.

The majority of hardware wallets will enable you to store other cryptocurrencies as well as Bitcoin. A hardware wallet is usually in the form of a USB stick which you just insert into your computer when you want to make a Bitcoin transaction. Once you are done just remove the hardware wallet and then store it safely.

A really good security feature with hardware wallets is the ability to create private keys offline. You can carry your hardware wallet around with you wherever you go without the worry of having your private keys stolen.

It is really easy to setup and use a hardware wallet. With most hardware wallets you can set a password and PIN code and even add recovery seed words to authenticate access and to recover any stored Bitcoins if you lose your hardware wallet or it stops working.

We recommend that you write down all of your security details for your hardware wallet just in case you forget them. Hide these details in a place that only you know about. If these details fall into the wrong hands then you can lose all of your Bitcoins.

There is no chance of a hardware wallet being hacked so the only thing you have to do is to keep a backup of your security details in a safe place.

Hot Wallets vs. Cold Wallets

You might have seen another classification of cryptocurrency wallets as hot and cold wallets.

Hot wallets are all variants that use the internet. They allow you to use the advanced tools to manage your assets, and also to react fast to changes in value and also to take advantage of them. But they could be attacked by malicious software or hackers. Examples of hot wallets are online wallets and mobile wallet. Desktop wallet can also be considered as a hot wallet if the computer is connected to the internet.

Cold wallets don't use the internet. Because they don't connect to the internet, there are almost no possible means of hack, unless you misplaced the wallet or the device. Good examples of cold wallets are hardware wallet and paper wallet. Also desktop wallet may be considered as a cold wallet if the computer has no internet connection. So if you want a desktop wallet to serve as a cold wallet, never connect the computer where it is installed to the internet.

Non-Custodial vs. Custodial Wallets

Although cryptocurrency wallets can be classified into hot wallets and cold wallets, there is another popular classification of cryptocurrency wallets; non-custodial and custodial wallets.

Non-Custodial Wallets

Hardware wallets (e.g. Ledger) are non-custodial wallets which keep private keys of a wallet offline and only the owner knows it. This is arguably the safest option for storage as the user has full ownership of the coins, but is likely the least convenient as it requires the user to operate additional hardware to spend/use the cryptocurrency.

Non-custodial software wallets (e.g. Trust Wallet, Atomic Wallet, Imtoken Wallet, etc.) is the next option in terms of safety compared to hardware wallets, although they are likely more convenient. The private keys are also owned by the user, but since the wallet is kept on an online device (eg. the phone), there is a higher risk of losing the funds as hackers can access devices which are connected to the internet.

Custodial Wallets

Lastly, arguably the most convenient yet risky storage method would be storing funds on custodial wallets (eg. on a centralized exchange such as Binance, Kucoin, Coinbase, etc.) as users do not own the private keys to the funds.

A hack on the storage location can potentially cause users to lose their funds. An example is what happened during the infamous 2014 Mt. Gox hack which recorded a massive loss of 850,000 BTC, most of which are customers' funds.

In summary, you will probably need to use a combination of different wallets as you become a more serious Bitcoin investor. Hardware and paper wallets, also known as cold wallets are the best choice for long term storage. You can use a desktop wallet for medium term storage and an online wallet for those frequent short term Bitcoin transactions.

LONG TERM BITCOIN INVESTMENT VS. BITCOIN TRADING

Many people confuse the words, investing and trading, one for the other. It's understandable considering both are activities by which you can make your money earn more money and as such, both are actually investments! But they're different and you'll need to know whether it's trading you want or investing, particularly for the long term.

Trading is basically short-term investment. You buy a financial asset like Bitcoin and the moment its price is up to a certain percentage, (say 10%, 20%, 30%, 40% or even 50%), you sell it immediately, even if it's just within a few hours. Trading is a very quick way to make profits and during times when markets are moving sideways, no clear trend if bullish or bearish, you can still make a killing with your return on investments. This's because during sideways movements, prices will still move up and down many times. If you're able to generate at least a 10% profit for every time the market moves up before plunging down, it's possible for you to double your money in just a week or two.

On the other hand, investment or more specifically long-term investment, is a strategy where you just buy a financial asset, such as a cryptocurrency, hold on to it for several months or years before selling at a much higher price. Because of its buy and hold nature, this investment strategy's also referred to as a "buy it and forget it" strategy. Long term investors can also be called Hodlers.

Both trading and investing have their pros and cons. Trading requires you to closely monitor your investments so you can quickly catch its price as it hits your minimum rate of return. But that requires that you practically do it full time, which is one of the reasons why many people don't invest in cryptocurrencies or even stocks. They need to monitor their investments hour in and hour out to make sure they earn big time and don't lose money. Most people don't have the luxury of time to do that because they've jobs or businesses to run. But those who do it, are able to earn more income from their investments in a shorter amount of time.

Most investors find long-term investment appealing because they don't have to be on top of their investments day in and day out. They just buy and forget about it. They can, just for information's sake, check out the market price of their market-driven investments once every month. But most other long-term investors simply wait for a year or more before checking in on their investments.

Why's that so? Particularly if they invest in lower risk investments like blue chip stocks, their prices generally go up through the years regardless if they monitor them or not. But the profit opportunities may be generally much lower compared to trading strategies.

So what did you notice between the two? The higher the expected returns, the higher the risk or in this case, the workload. So if you're willing to put in much more time and effort to earn bigger and quicker profits, trade. But remember that you need to have a good knowledge of cryptocurrencies in order to make fortunes from trading them, unlike long term investing. If you want to just sit back, relax, and reap your rewards after several years, go for long-term investing instead.

Investing in Cryptocurrencies for the First Time

The first thing you'll need to do to start is to choose a particular cryptocurrency to invest in. Even if cryptocurrencies sound like a generic group of investments, each of them still has their own unique characteristics that in effect, differentiate them from one another. As such, it would be foolish to assume that if you've studied one, you've studied them all. Therefore, you must exert good effort in researching on at least the major cryptocurrencies before choosing which to invest in.

After you've chosen the cryptocurrency of your investment choice, it's time to decide on which platform to buy them. In other words, it's time to decide on which cryptocurrency exchange to sign up with and buy your first cryptocurrency investment.

What are exchanges? Exchanges refer to institutions or businesses where buying and selling of specific financial assets are allowed. If you're looking to buy or sell shares of stock, then you'll need to do so through a stock exchange such as the NASDAQ or the New York Stock Exchange (NYSE). If you are looking to trade futures and options contracts, then the Chicago Mercantile Exchange is one of the best exchanges to go to. For investing in cryptocurrencies, you'll need to do it through a cryptocurrency exchange.

One of the main reasons why you'll need to sign up for an account with a cryptocurrency exchange is this: it's the only place where you can buy sell cryptocurrencies. Unlike shares of stock, currencies, or bonds that have physical versions and regulated markets, cryptocurrencies are purely digital in nature and thus, have no active markets outside the digital or online markets that cryptocurrency exchanges offer.

After deciding on which platform to buy your cryptocurrencies, go on and create an account with that exchange. Generally speaking, the account opening and the verification process can be a bit tedious because most of these exchanges, being unregulated by any government financial institution are very careful to make sure that they'll be transacting with the person who you claim to be. The more they're able to do that, the more they'll be able to ensure your accounts' privacy and safety. So while it may be a bit tedious, you can be more patient knowing that at the end of the day, it'll all be for your own benefit.

After opening an account online, most exchanges will probably ask you for a scanned copy of any valid government issued ID from your country, such as a driver's license or passport. On average, cryptocurrency exchange accounts are validated and processed within 3 working days but in some cases, more than a week. Some of them require that you verify your account before you can start trading on the platform. Others will give you a daily transaction limit, say 2 BTC. This means that you cannot withdraw or deposit more than 2 BTC daily without verifying your account.

One last thing before buying cryptocurrencies: consider getting a cold storage hardware wallet to ensure the safety of your cryptocurrency investments. As mentioned earlier in it's highly recommended that you get a cold storage hardware wallet to ensure the safety of your cryptocurrency investments' private keys and consequently, your cryptocurrency investments. But if you're on a tight budget or simply don't want to spend extra, you can always use hot storage wallets, but at relatively higher risk for hacking and losing your hard earned cryptocurrency investments.

After you've gotten your wallet regardless if it's hot or cold storage, it's time to buy your cryptocurrency on your chosen exchange. After you've successfully bought your cryptocurrencies in that exchange, transfer your private keys immediately to your cold storage wallet - if you've chosen to use one, or to your hot storage wallet of choice.

One thing you'll simply need to know about buying your cryptocurrencies on exchanges is that they don't come for free as exchanges will charge you a transaction fee for their services. Please don't worry - transaction fees aren't excessive. Exchanges, after all, are businesses that also need to make money to continue operating successfully and consistently. Cryptocurrency exchanges would be hard pressed to continue providing you with great service if they don't make enough money to sustain their operating expenses and upgrade their systems regularly. Transaction fees are normally a fixed percentage of your transaction so that it only goes up when the value of your transactions go up. Most exchanges charge around 0.5% to 5% as transaction fee.

So to summarize the steps on how to start investing in cryptocurrencies:

- First, choose your cryptocurrency or currencies.

- Choose a cryptocurrency exchange on which you can buy your chosen cryptocurrency, and open an account with that exchange.
- Now after your account with your chosen cryptocurrency exchange has been validated, choose the type of wallet in which you'll store your private keys and cryptocurrencies, preferably a cold storage hardware wallet.
- Buy your cryptocurrency through your validated account with your exchange.

Some Secured Centralized and Decentralized Exchanges

Some of the biggest and most popular cryptocurrency centralized exchanges include: Coinbase Pro, Binance, Kucoin, Kraken, Bitfinex, Gemini, etc.

Some of the biggest and most popular decentralized cryptocurrency exchanges include: Uniswap, Tokenlon, Aave, Curve Finance, Compound Finance, Balancer, etc

You can check out some of the trusted cryptocurrency exchanges and things to consider when choosing an exchange for trading at https://www.buzzingpoint.com/2020/09/secured-cryptocurrency-exchanges.html.

Strategies for Successful Bitcoin Trading

If you are really interested in Bitcoin trading then the first thing that you need to realize is that you need to use common sense and maintain self-control. Don't go into it thinking that you are going to make a ton of money in a day. If you get too greedy then you are very likely to fail.

Learn and Practise with a Demo Account

You need to learn everything that you can about Bitcoin trading before you start to do it for real. Knowledge is great but there is nothing like experiencing how Bitcoin trading works in the real world. To give yourself a good start with Bitcoin trading sign up with a cryptocurrency exchange that will allow you to use a demo account to experience how things work in the real world. You will see real time prices for Bitcoin and it will help you to get used to the Bitcoin trading interface.

Have a Trading Plan

Successful Bitcoin trading relies on having a good strategy in place. Sure you might get lucky with your first few trades, but sooner or later your luck will run out and this can be very expensive.

One of the biggest mistakes that newcomers to Bitcoin trading make is that they follow the news, see that a lot of other people are making Bitcoin trades and this compels them to do the same thing. Experienced traders like this because it will force the Bitcoin price up and they can profit from previous purchases.

Don't follow trends blindly. Create a plan that defines the price that you should purchase Bitcoins for and the price that you should sell them at to realize the profit that you want. If you stick to a plan like this then you will significantly reduce the risk of panicking if you suddenly see price fall.

Start with Small Capital

When you are starting out with Bitcoin trading only invest small amounts with trades. This is all part of your learning curve and early training. No matter how good an opportunity seems resist the temptation to go "all in".

Use your demo account to perform a lot of trades before you start spending real money. If you clean out your demo account then this is not a big deal but losing all of your real money is completely devastating.

Keep your Emotions in Check

The thought of losing money can be really alarming to you. Like I said earlier, Bitcoin is volatile and in one day the price can go down by a significant amount. The good thing is that the price can rise significantly in no time at all as well.

You must keep your emotions in check if you want to be successful with Bitcoin trading. Thinking logically will always be the best strategy. Never let your emotions determine which Bitcoin trades you should or shouldn't make.

It is understandable that you will be excited about the opportunities that Bitcoin trading offers. But we strongly recommend that you take this a step at a time and learn everything that you can about trading.

Use a few demo accounts to practice with before you start investing real money. The more accustomed you are with the trading environment, the better. If you make mistakes with your demo account, work out what went wrong and avoid making the same mistake in the future.

Real Life Bitcoin Investment Strategies

Now let's look at some of the real life Bitcoin investment strategies that are working well for some savvy investors. I have made no secret of the fact that Bitcoin is a volatile digital currency and it goes up and down in value on a regular basis. That is why we recommend that you adopt a long term approach to your Bitcoin investing so that if the price does drop you give it time to recover.

So here we will take a more in depth look at some of the "real life" methods that successful Bitcoin investors use to make a profit.

Cost Averaging Investment Strategy

This really is the best Bitcoin investment method for beginners because it removes the need to enter the Bitcoin market when the timing is right. A lot of novice Bitcoin investors spend a lot of time and really stress out waiting for the price of Bitcoin to fall to the right level.

When you use the cost averaging strategy for your Bitcoin investing, you will spread your risk over a time period. All you need to do is make purchases at regular intervals and then hold them in your secure wallet.

Cost averaging refers to the strategy of continuously buying a specific financial asset (e.g., stocks, bonds, currencies, and cryptocurrencies) at smaller increments regardless if the market price for that asset is going down or up. It's also quite obvious to say that this's a good strategy when the price of a particular financial asset has been going up but even when prices are going down?

Seriously? Yes! Doing that when prices are going down helps you bring down your average cost on that financial asset, which means you can recoup your losses much easier than if you simply bought once and waited for the price to go back up to your buying price.

To help you understand better, here's a real life instance of cost averaging strategy.

Assuming you bought 1 Bitcoin at $20,000 and its price tanked to just $15,000. In order to recoup your losses, you'll need to wait for its price to go all the way back up to $20,000, right? Right!

But if you just bought another Bitcoin when it tanked to $15,000; that gives you 2 Bitcoins at an average buying price or cost of $17,500 only. Therefore, you simply don't have to wait for Bitcoin prices to climb back up to $20,000 to break even. You will break even when the price rises to $17,500. In fact, by the time the price rises back to $20,000, you would've made a $2,500 profit already because of the cost averaging strategy.

Considering you can't just perfectly predict if the price will go down or up, it's best to spread out your total investment money for cryptocurrencies in 5 installments so you can apply cost averaging. So if you're actually planning to invest a total of $1,000, then spread it into 5 monthly investments of $200 per. That can eventually help you average your cost down if the prices go down within the next 5 months.

Investing a Lump Sum into Bitcoin at a Time

This method is definitely not one for the faint of heart but we want to cover all bases here. When you invest a lump sum in Bitcoins you will purchase them at a specific price point. There is an element of risk when you do this.

Let's assume that you have $50,000 to invest. Naturally you want to get as many Bitcoins as possible for your investment. In order to have the best chance of doing this you have no choice but to wait until the Bitcoin price goes down.

There is no other alternative here. You must wait and time your entry into the Bitcoin market as well as you can. The problem is that in practice the price of Bitcoin fluctuates very often so predicting the next price dip is really tough to do.

If you have a lump sum to invest right now we wouldn't advise that you start with this. It takes experience to make a good judgment of the right price dip. Even the experts get this wrong sometimes.

When you are new to Bitcoin investing and want to invest a lump sum you may see a price dip and then think to yourself "if I just hang on for a while it may go down even more" or "what if the price never reaches my low point?"

The same scenario applies to selling your lump sum investment. How do you know the best price to sell your Bitcoins for? It may be very difficult to sell at the price that you need to make the profit you planned for.

If you sell too soon and the price goes up even more then you will criticize yourself heavily. Think what you could have done with all of that extra profit! Obviously a lump sum investment will provide you with a much higher profit than the dollar cost averaging method if you get the timing just right.

Bitcoin Investing Hedge Fund

You may not be aware of this but there are actually cryptocurrency hedge funds available that include Bitcoin. This could be a good alternative for you if you do not want to learn about Bitcoin investing that you will need to do if you want to use other investment strategies. The biggest drawback with any hedge fund is the expensive performance and management fees.

Cryptocurrency hedge funds will insist that you pay the management fee upfront. Usually these fees are in the region of 2% of your investment so if you want to invest $100,000 then you are going to have to pay around $2,000 as a management fee which leaves you with $98,000 for investing in cryptocurrencies.

You will be appointed a hedge fund manager and they work on a profits percentage basis. This can be as high as 20% so if you were able to secure a $40,000 profit from your investment then you will have to pay $8,000 to your hedge fund manager.

These figures may startle you and cryptocurrency hedge funds are not going to be everyone's idea of a good thing. But when you think about it you will have totally hands off investing here which can make big profits for you.

Best Practices with Bitcoin Investment

Although nothing is ever guaranteed when investing in cryptocurrencies there are certain practices that you can follow that will maximize your chances of success.

Understand how Bitcoin Works

We have given you all the information that you need in this guide to understand how Bitcoin really works. You need to know the principles of blockchain and how Bitcoin trades are made. Don't get caught up in the technicalities but make sure that you have a firm understanding of Bitcoin before you make any trades.

Go for Long Term Investment

You may have heard a lot of stories about traders who make money from Bitcoin trades every day. Some of these may be true but these people have a lot of experience and know what they are doing! Go for a long term investment strategy (buy and hold) instead to battle against the volatility of Bitcoin.

Always Choose a Secure Wallet

A full section of this book was used to explain the different types of wallets for Bitcoin and their security issues. Online wallets are the least secure and hardware wallets are the most secure. For convenience it works the other way around with online or "hot" wallets being the most convenient and offline or "cold" wallets being the least convenient.

Bitcoins are very valuable so you need to have the right wallets to protect them. If you are going to trade regularly, then just keep enough Bitcoins in an online wallet for this and then move the rest to your cold wallet. If thieves get hold of your private keys, then you can say goodbye to your Bitcoins.

Use Reputable Exchanges to Buy and Sell Bitcoin

Due to the high value of Bitcoins there are plenty of thieves and scammers out there who want to steal yours from you. Only use a reputable cryptocurrency exchanges such as Coinbase, Kraken, Binance, Kucoin, etc. to buy and sell your Bitcoins.

Always check out a cryptocurrency exchange thoroughly. Do they have a track record? Are there user reviews? If you can't find these things then look for another exchange. If an exchange is making promises of Bitcoin deals that seem too good to be true, then run away from such exchange.

Watch Bitcoin Trends

It is always a good idea to keep an eye on the price fluctuations of Bitcoin. Use tools like Bitcoin Wisdom and Cryptowatch to stay in the loop. This is especially important if you are thinking about investing a lump sum into Bitcoin. You want to buy at the lowest price and sell at the highest price.

Don't Start with Bitcoin Trading

Start as a Bitcoin investor. Once you get more experience as a Bitcoin investor then you can try your hand at Bitcoin trading. We do not recommend that you start trading straight away. You need to learn a great deal about Bitcoin pricing and be able to effectively control your emotions to trade successfully. There are demo accounts available that you can use to practice Bitcoin trading. Use these to the full and learn from any mistakes that you make before you start using real money to trade Bitcoins.

Don't Start with Bitcoin Mining

Do not get involved in Bitcoin mining when you are starting out. You will need to make a significant investment in high end computer equipment to have any chance of success and it just makes more sense to use this money to purchase Bitcoins instead.

Always remember that Bitcoin is Volatile and High Risk

Bitcoin is a highly volatile digital currency. This means that there are opportunities to make significant gains and the risk of losing a lot of money too. You need to accept this and always bear it in mind to be a successful Bitcoin investor.

Trade with the Amount you can afford to Lose

Bitcoin trading is very risky. That is why you should always trade with the amount you can afford to lose, so that you will not lose all your funds if any negative unusual event happens.

Avoid Scams

Unfortunately there are many cryptocurrency scams. Bitcoins are very valuable and thieves will do everything that they can to steal them from you. Watch out for fake exchanges, phishing in emails and too good to be true Ponzi schemes.

CRYPTOCURRENCY SECURITY TIPS

Technologies have arrived as a hurricane and have imposed a new game board. This economic revolution is unstoppable. It is so powerful that it can be very helpful if you are in favor of its current, but it is precisely that complexity that makes it necessary to have absolute control over it, so as not to drown within its tides.

Many people distrust cryptocurrencies, without really knowing what they are afraid of. Possibly because they were told there are a lot of risks and threats involved. But they also forgot that no system is risk-free. It has also been discovered that most people fall victim to attackers simply because they cannot recognize a cybersecurity threat. Therefore they become victims. But once you know the various forms these cyber threats take, you are likely not to fall victim.

This section is dedicated to giving you the keys to protect yourself and your crypto assets, how to recognize a crypto threat and possible ways to avoid them. These tips will also help you know what to do in case you mistakenly fall victim to these heartless cyber criminals who work tirelessly to snatch you your hard earned crptocurrencies.

Strategies Used by Cyber Criminals to Steal your Cryptocurrencies

As a cryptocurrency trader or investor, you need to understand the tools and means that cyber criminals use to compromise the security of your cryptocurrencies.

Malware

All computer programs with malicious intentions that are undesirably entered into the computer of the person to be attacked are classified as malware. It can be of several types. The most common are:

Computer Virus: They are small programs that are introduced in the code of our own system, causing it to stop working in the worst case or causing some kind of discomfort if they are milder. In the case of your desktop or mobile wallets, if they access the internet at some time, they can be attacked by a virus that would stop them being useful.

Computer Worms: They are viruses with the dangerous ability to self-replicate. In the case of the virus, it must be activated more or less consciously by the user, and affects only the part for which it was programmed. However, worms can multiply and affect foreign parts, even transmitted through networks. That is, if you are infected by a worm or worm that in principle is not designed to affect your wallet, it could reach them.

Trojans: These are programs that allow outside access to your computer. They receive this name from the famous *Trojan Horse* that opened the doors of the wall of the legendary city to the Greeks, and in fact does the same with your computer. It allows that, through the connection, a third party can access and control all the content of your computer. Within this type of malware, there are several subtypes, depending on their purpose: allow third-party access to the system (backdoors), theft of bank data (bank worms), theft of passwords (password stealers), keyboard logging (keyloggers), etc.

Spyware: It is a software programmed to investigate the victim, allowing access to their records, and temporary files. Its main function is to find your passwords to be able to use them later. Keep in mind that if you opt for the option of more privacy to preserve your cryptocurrencies, the one in which only you know the access data, this type of malware directly affects your greatest advantage.

Adware: They are programs whose purpose is only to show advertising at discretion, being able to delay and saturate the system, but that does not pose an imminent danger in relation to the security of your assets.

Ramsomware: This type of software is based on stealing your data and then request an economic rescue for them, rather than using them at will. Keep in mind that depending on the wallet or platform you use, on many occasions you will be the only one who will have access to that data, with no one behind who can return it to you in case of forgetfulness, so in the cryptoeconomic world, this type of malware can have a big impact.

Exploits: They are small programs whose function is to facilitate vulnerabilities. Its task is to destroy defensive elements so that other malware can act more easily.

Rootkit: This is a program that allows third-party access to your computer, but also focuses on eliminating the evidence of it so that it is not detected. It is responsible for deleting the traces of the cybercriminal's passage so that, if not detected, no measures are taken to eliminate this malware, thus prolonging its actions over time.

Phising

They are all those resources that cybercriminals use to obtain the data with which you operate. The most common way to proceed is to supplant the identity of reliable entities or to be shown as secure platforms, so that you enter your data to interact with them, so that, instead of obtaining the desired access or benefit, you end up sending them all your credentials.

The way in which each cybercriminal uses this technique can be personal, and its effectiveness lies in ingenuity, since it is nothing more than a hoax. The more information they have about the victim, the more effective it will be, because they will know what platforms they use to impersonate them.

A booming variant of this type of attack is pharming. In this case, you enter your data in a real page of habitual use with complete peace of mind, but at some point in that exchange of information, by attacking the official URL of the page you are using, derive the sending of data to another page of your interest to get hold of them. Often, the submission is usually made to a page identical to that expected so that the victim does not suspect this interference.

Something similar is the phising car. In this case, the data is entered when making a purchase and a payment is made on a similar page but that is not the one in which we believe we are operating, so that the payment is made in favor of the cybercriminal without a real purchase, and product shipping is never done. Instead of losing data, in this case only the purchase money is lost.

Since purchases with cryptocurrencies are not as widespread as with traditional money, this type of strategy may be less effective, but it should be taken into account because these criminals might implement these strategy in the cryptosphere in future.

These are just some of the popular tools and strategies that cyber criminals use to rob the real owners of their valuable assets, including cryptocurrencies.

Tips to help you Protect your Cryptocurrencies from Getting Hacked

You have now seen some of the tools and strategies that cyber criminals use to rob you your valuable assets. The next step is to know the various ways to protect your cryptocurrencies, so as not to fall victim to these criminals.

Never use your Exchange Wallets to Store your Long Term Crypto Assets

Only keep the funds you will for regular trading in your exchange wallets and then move the rest to a more secure location, preferably a cold wallet or a wallet where you have access to the private key or recovery phrase.

If you are using a Mobile Wallet, make sure you Activate all the Mobile Phone Security Features

While it is very difficult for a desktop computer to be stolen due to its size and its fixed and secure location, a mobile phone can be stolen more easily. Its small size and lightness makes it easily stolen and transported, and even taking it everywhere can cause us to accidentally lose it. The consequence is that if someone is steals your device, they could have access to the data you have in it, and even the wallet where you store your cryptocurrencies that you have stored if we are using it as a purse. Therefore, do not forget to have activated, all the anti-theft security options which include:

- **Inbuilt Security Features:** PIN code, Automatic lock, screensaver pattern, fingerprint identification, etc.
- **User-Added Security Features:** Installing a phone encryption app, remote eraser app (explained below), etc.

Be Careful when Downloading any App from Google Play Store

What most cyber criminals do is to create an app that resembles the original app of a website. They usually include malicious scripts that steal information from your device without your permission. When most users search the original app on Google Play store, these clone apps appear. A user who has no prior knowledge of this trick might mistake the clone app for the original app. When the user launches the clone app and inputs the login details of the original account, the malicious scripts send the login details to these hackers, who now use it to login to your original account and rob the user.

For example, when you search for **Trust wallet app** on Google play store, you will discover two apps with the name; one developed by **DApps Platform Inc** and the other developed by **Sam**. Obviously, the latter is a malicious clone of the former.

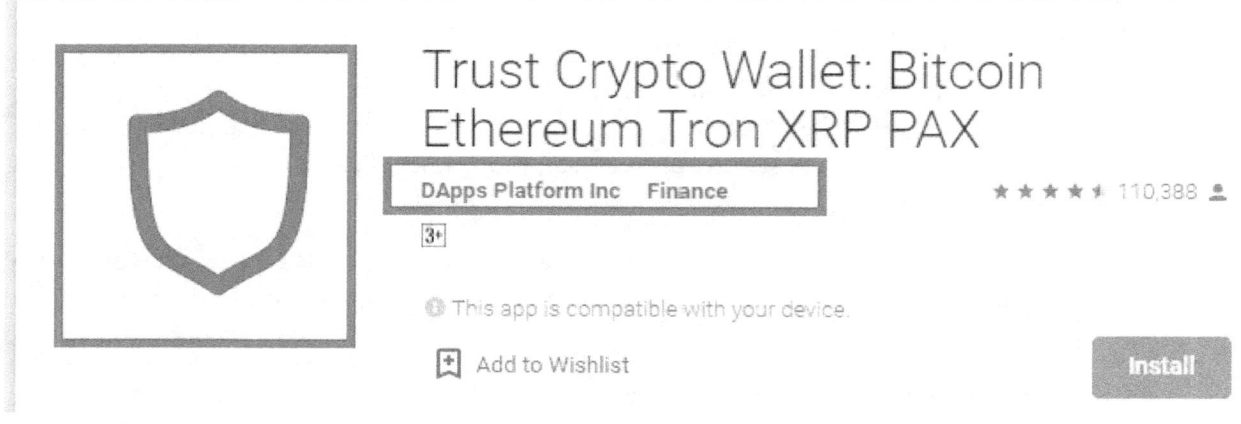

Original Trust Wallet app

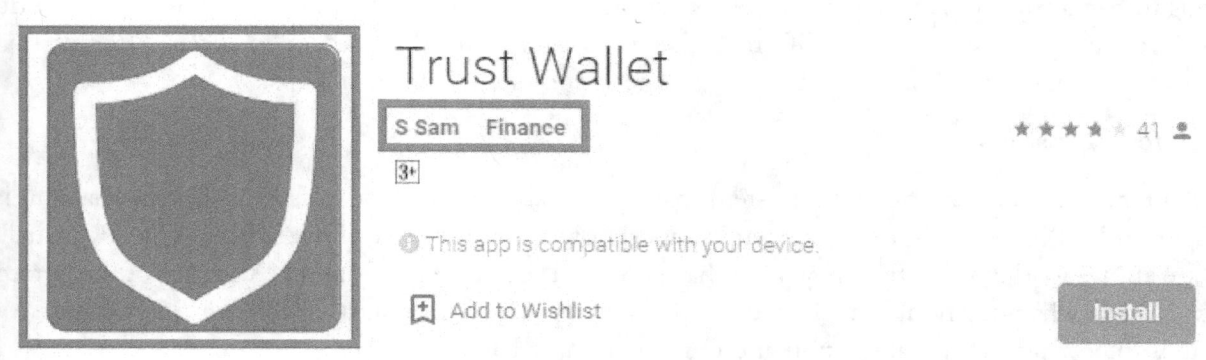

Fake Trust Wallet app

To avoid falling prey to these hackers, always visit the website of the app developers. You will see their app download link, which will take you to play store. This way, you are rest assured that you are downloading and installing the original app.

Another way to distinguish an original app from a malicious clone app on Google play store is to check their reviews and ratings. Most times, the original app always has a more positive ratings, than the fake app.

Make sure you Activate Two Factor Authentication (2FA)

Always activate 2FA or multi-signature authentication feature for all your exchange apps and even the emails you use for signing up with those exchange platforms.

Victims of hacking are most often Android smartphone users who don't activate 2FA for all their mobile apps. Google Android's open operating system makes it more open to viruses, and therefore less safe than iOS. As a result, most hackers add applications on behalf of certain cryptocurrency resources to the Google Play Store. When the application is launched, the user enters sensitive data to access their accounts and thereby gives hackers access to it.

To be on the safest side, activate 2FA for any mobile app that has 2FA feature. This is because a successful hack on any of your mobile apps can give the hacker full access to other apps on your phone, including your cryptocurrency exchange apps.

Avoid Using SMS Authentication

Positive Technologies, a cyber-security company confirmed that it is very easy to intercept an SMS with a password confirmation, transmitted practically worldwide by the Signaling System 7 (SS7) protocol.

Also, turn off call forwarding to make a hacker's access to your data impossible. Use 2FA software solution in place of SMS authentication.

Avoid Public Wi-Fi

If you a cryptocurrency investor or trader, avoid public Wi-Fi at all cost. There are many hackers that attack their victims through public Wi-Fi, so you must pay a lot of attention whenever you connect to the web using your phone, laptop or tablet. Better, don't connect if you're not sure. Also, never lend your phone to unknown people, especially if the phone contains your cryptocurrency wallet or data.

Never Backup your Cryptocurrency Details Online

There is virtually no place on the internet that is 100% hack-free. No matter how secure the place seems to be, don't store your login details or recovery phrases online.

The best option is to backup your cryptocurrency details offline in multiple locations. For example, you can write down your wallet recovery phrases in three different sheets of papers and keep them in three different save locations. Just make sure that at any point in time, you have access to one of those backups.

Regularly Check for Intrusions

When you install a new version of an operating system, you will be able to note the default programs that run in your Task Manager under Processes. Note down that list and know the number of processes that your PC usually opens. Hackers are always working silently. They might have infected your PC already and be waiting for the perfect moment to strike. That's why you should regularly check for new processes that start when your PC starts. If you find something unwanted, you should take action and remove it immediately.

Block Invisible Trackers

Crypto hackers use spy ads or set 'invisible' trackers to monitor your online activity without your permission. To stay safe from such sneaky hackers, download Privacy Badger extension in your browser; Chrome, Firefox, Opera, etc. It blocks ads and tracking cookies that do not respect the 'Do Not Track' setting in a user's web browser. Now, when you visit any site, in case it finds a tracker on the website, it will give a warning and block the tracker.

Always use a Password that is Hard to Guess

Make sure your password is not a common word or your phone number that can be guessed easily. Miss it up with small letter, capital letters, numbers and special characters. You can add the special character in between. For example, **#Iam@ACrypto@Investor#**. Notice how the letters are mixed up. If possible dedicate a unique password for different crypto apps. If that is going to confuse you, then dedicate a particular password only to your crypto assets. Never use that password in any other platform outside the cryptosphere.

Secure Browsing with Trusted Security Extensions

To protect yourself from phishing attacks, do not click on websites that has HTTP instead of HTTPS in the address bar and if the website looks weird, just don't click on it. Also, download these extensions in your browser to help secure your browser and data:

- **HTTPS Everywhere:** https://www.eff.org/https-everywhere
- **Cookie AutoDelete:** https://addons.mozilla.org/en-US/firefox/addon/cookie-autodelete/
- **Netcraft Extension:** https://www.netcraft.com/apps/browser/

Activate a Remote Eraser for your Mobile Device

When a cryptocurrency exchange you are using is hacked, the hackers can log into your crypto exchange and gain access over your cryptocurrency. A simple solution is to activate a 'kill switch', which is a remote eraser. It can save your crypto if you mobile gets stolen. Once activated, 'kill switch' can wipe all of your data and lock your phone remotely. As a result, the thief no longer has access to your exchange wallet or any data on your mobile. You can setup 'kill switch' function on both iOS and Android.

For iOS:

Go to **Settings > iCloud > Sign in with your Apple ID > Turn on Find My iPhone**.

If your phone is lost or stolen, to activate the kill switch:

1. Visit https://www.icloud.com/find
2. Log in with your Apple ID and set your phone to "lost mode."
3. You will have the option to remotely wipe all your data and it will be locked.

For Android:

1. Go to https://www.google.com/android/find and sign in to your Google Account.
2. If you have more than one device, click the lost device at the top of the screen.
3. If your lost device has more than one user profile, sign in with a Google Account that's on the main profile. On the map, you'll get info about where the device is.
4. Select Erase. This will permanently delete all data on your device (but might not delete SD cards).

These are some of the tips to help you protect your cryptocurrencies. Do not depend only on these tips. Check for other latest security tips online. You can also check out this article for more tips, https://distill.io/kb/guides/protect-your-cryptocurrency-from-hacks/.

How to Recover your Lost Cryptocurrencies

In the crypto world, you are the maximum and only responsible for your assets. You are your own bank. The decision to delegate more or less to platforms such as exchange houses or wallets, to invest in one or another type of currency or to make free transactions is yours. You are completely alone.

No one can manipulate your money if you do not want, or deny access to it, or invest it without your consent, and only you decide the value it has and the movements you want to make. The utopia of a free financial system is at your fingertips. But on the other hand, you officially have no one behind who responds to the losses or helps you with the dangers.

There are, in principle, no official entities or bodies that respond legally for your cryptocurrencies. In the future there may be, as in the cases of Japan or Korea, countries that are already more friendly with crypto economics and that feel certain bases of regularization, but today a somewhat complicated paradigm is presented. It is the governments that have to promote these initiatives and are not very excited to favor a free system that "harms" the current economic system, very controlled by its mechanisms.

So, you should be aware of your own responsibilities and, where appropriate, know what external forces can act in your favor in this poorly regulated environment.

Fund Recovery in Hot Wallets and Exchange Platforms

When you deposit your cryptocurrencies in a hot wallet or keep your assets in an exchange house you are ceasing, in a way, to be your own bank. Your assets no longer depend exclusively on you. You already know that in case of theft, closing of the company or scam, you could lose them.

Some exchange houses, wallets and web platforms, in their own internal policies choose their ability to secure currencies and return policies, but this is no more than good intentions as there is no legal framework that obliges them to do so. The only obligation they have to keep their word is to maintain their honesty and reputation for attracting customers, but as we have seen before, if they had not had the real capacity to materialize these good words, they would not have the legal obligation to do so.

Even so, before interacting with any of these platforms, you would be interested to inform yourself if they have any type of insurance or policy to compensate for losses in case of an incident. Better than nothing. It also looks for past information on cases in which they have made use of that policy to verify that this is more than words. Although, remember that being able to compensate for a first attack does not ensure that you can do it again with a second.

But, above all, what you should value is that the purse or the exchange house offers you the private keys of access to your stored cryptocurrencies. This will allow you to access them at any time. In case the company disappears, or decides to freeze the funds for some reason, you would always have access to your stored assets. As long as you have the permissions to act directly on the blockchain, you will still own your money.

You should also inform yourself of the means that the platform in question puts at your disposal to recover the access passwords in case you lose them. If you could not access the wallet (and also did not have the private keys of your cryptocurrencies), you would lose the funds deposited in it that would remain in possession of the platform and, technically, it would not be a robbery.

Fund Recovery in Cold Wallets

Cold wallets are the only ones that allow you to be the exclusive and sole owner of your assets. At least, as long as you keep the private keys in desktop purses, hardware type or paper and derivatives.

But what would happen if you lost these accesses? Indeed, you would lose your money. Therefore, even in this very restrictive method, you should have certain supports, come from yourself or from companies that work with this storage method.

Regarding becoming your own support, you should keep some copy of the private keys. It is true that the more you multiply them, the more exposure and capacity they are captured. But printing at least a couple of times your keys on paper and keeping them in secret places would give you the opportunity to recover them if you lose one of them. Similarly, sporadically copying the contents of your hardware wallet or installing a desktop wallet on several devices would give you the option of being your best help in case of loss by having another recovery point.

As for some cold storage systems, they have methods to recover lost passwords that you should rely on. Many cold storage platforms originate a random sequence of about twelve words called seeds with which you can recover lost data. Or, for example, Ledger devices allow you to use other compatible devices to recover passwords. Find out about these media well, as they can become your only allies in the cold storage system.

Trusted Detective

If we do not find an efficient response in public services, we can always go to a private service. In the same way as in the physical world, there are detectives of the virtual world that track potential criminals until they find them and the foreign cryptocurrencies they took away.

It is not a standardized trade and it is difficult to find a good detective, but there are experts who offer themselves as such and whom you can turn to in case of theft.

CRYPTOCURRENCY MARKET ANALYSIS & TOOLS

As a cryptocurrency trader or investor, you need to understand the market of any coin before you buy or invest in it. There are factors that affect the prices of all crypto coins generally. Also there are internal factors that affect individual cryptocurrencies. That is why it is always advisable to study and analyze the market of a particular coin before you invest in it.

A proper market analysis will help you know the best time to buy the coin and the best time to sell it off. Although there is no way to predict with 100% accuracy, the price of any cryptocurrency, but proper market analysis will help you know the signs that indicate the approaching of loss or profit.

There are two main types of market analysis in stock market:

- Fundamental Analysis (FA)
- Technical Analysis (TA)

The knowledge of both types of analysis will help you predict with a higher level of accuracy, the market condition or price of a particular coin at a particular time. This section of this book will teach you the basics of each of these types of market analysis and how you can combine both for a more realistic result.

Cryptocurrency Fundamental Analysis

Fundamental Analysis (FA) is a market analysis approach used by investors to estimate the intrinsic value of an asset. By looking at a number of internal and external factors, their main goal is to determine whether the said asset is overvalued or undervalued. This will help them whether it is worth investing in the asset. It is good to note that FA alone cannot help you to properly analyze any asset. It will only help you know the value of the asset and probably the growth rate if some factors act favorably, which might not always be the case. Once you have discovered a good asset with the help of FA, you also need to carry out Technical Analysis (TA) to know the best price to buy the asset and the best price to sell off the asset in order to maximize your profit.

The first step in FA is to discover the strong metrics that will help you estimate the true worth of the coin. Also note that there are many FA metrics, but most of them can be easily manipulated by the team behind the project. For example, numbers of Twitter followers or Telegram/Reddit users are probably not good FA metrics because it is easy to create fake accounts or buy engagement on social media.

We will classify these strong metrics into 3 categories: on-chain metrics, project metrics, and financial metrics.

On-Chain Metrics

On-chain metrics are those that can be observed by looking at data provided by the blockchain. The simplest way to study these metrics is to pull the information from websites or APIs specifically designed for the purpose of informing investment decisions. For example, websites like ConMarketCap and CoinMetrics have on-chain analysis for most of the popular coins like Bitcoin, Ethereum, etc.

Below are some of the key indicators under this category.

- **Transaction count:** The number of transactions within a period of time. This is a good measure of activity taking place on a network.
- **Transaction value:** Tells you the amount that has been transacted within a period of time.

- **Active addresses:** The blockchain addresses that are active in a given period.
- **Fees paid:** This can tell you about the demand for block space. If the fee increase with time, it means that users are competing with each other to have their transactions confirmed faster.
- **Hash rate and the Amount staked:** In Proof of Work cryptocurrencies, hash rate is often used as a measure of network health. An increase in hash rate over time can also implies that there is a growing interest in mining. More miners are online to secure the network. Also, if the amount staked is increasing with time, it implies that more investors are interested in the cryptocurrency project.

Project Metrics

Project metrics involve a qualitative approach which involves studying and evaluating the quality of the essential aspects of the project. This will help you know if the project has a promising future or not.

Some of the key indicators in this category include:

- **The whitepaper of the project:** Whitepaper is a technical document that gives us an overview of the cryptocurrency project. A good whitepaper should reveal the code technology used, use cases it aims to cater to, roadmap for upgrades and new features, supply and distribution scheme for the cryptocurrency.
- The project team: You also need to check it there is any team behind the project. Has the team previously handled any successful cryptocurrency project? If there is not team, check to make sure the develpopers are working consistently to improve the project. If the project has a public GitHub, check to see how many contributors it has, and how many future activities they have.
- **The main competitors of the project:** Check their whitepaper to see if they revealed their main competitors. If they did, research about these competitors to know what they are up to. If the competitors have stronger teams, then there are possibilities that they may overshadow the cryptocurrency projects that have weak teams.
- **Tokenomics and initial distribution:** If the project will create a token, check to know if the token has real utility. Will the wider market will recognize and value the token? Also, focusing on the distribution might give you an idea of any existing risks. For instance, if the vast majority of the supply was owned by only a few parties, then you might conclude that it is a risky investment, because those parties could eventually manipulate the market.

Financial Metrics

Finance is the key aspect of any project. Here, you analyze the various metrics that directly or indirectly determines the financial state of the project at any given time. These metrics will help you know whether the rate at which your investment in the asset will add value. Other interesting metrics that might fall under this category are those that concern the economics and incentives of the crypto asset's protocol.

Below are some of the key indicators under this category.

- **Market capitalization (network value):** This reveals the hypothetical cost of buying every single available unit of the crypto asset (assuming no slippage). It is the product of the circulating supply of the crypto coin and the price at any point in time. Market capitalization can be misleading because it's impossible to truly determine how many units are in circulation for a given cryptocurrency. Coins can be burned, keys can be lost, and funds can simply be forgotten about. What we see instead are approximations that attempt to filter out coins that are no longer in circulation.
  Market capitalization is used extensively to estimate the growth potential of cryptocurrency networks. Some crypto investors say that small-cap coins have more growth potentials than "large-cap" coins.

Others say that large-cap coins have stronger network effects. Therefore, they have greater growth potentials than unestablished small-cap coins.

- **Liquidity and Trading Volume:** A liquid market is a competitive market flooded with asks and bids, leading to a tighter bid-ask spread. Liquidity is a measure of how easily an asset can be bought or sold. Being familiar with liquidity can help you carry out effective fundamental analysis, because it acts as an indicator of the market's interest in a prospective investment.

    Trading volume is an indicator that can help us determine liquidity. It is usually displayed in the exchange chart of any cryptocurrency.

- **Supply mechanisms:** Maximum supply, circulating supply, and rate of inflation can affect the investment decisions of some investors. Some cryptocurrency project teams reduce the number of new units they produce over time, making them attractive to investors that believe the demand for new units will outstrip their availability.

    Some investors see a rigidly-enforced cap as damaging in the long run. Their reason is that it disproportionately rewards early investors, whereas a steady inflationary policy would be fairer for newcomers.

Also know that some of these indicators mentioned above can be manipulated. For example, in the case of market cap of a coin. That is why you should not only use FA to analyze the market value of a coin.

Real Life Application of Cryptocurrency Fundamental Analysis

The metrics to be considered in carrying out fundamental analysis of any coin have been discussed. Now, you also need to know how FA can be applied in real life.

Assuming you join a group where trade signals are released at random, in order to make sure that the coin you chose to trade has a high growth potential, you carry out FA. You can choose two to three coins and carry out FA on them individually, then compare their results to know the one that has the best real value and promising future.

In summary, FA can provide invaluable insights into cryptocurrencies in a way that technical analysis cannot. Being able to separate the market price from the "true" value of a network is an excellent skill to have when trading. Of course, there are things that TA can tell us, which you can't predict with FA. That's why many traders use a combination of both FA and TA these days. You can learn more about Crypto Fundamental analysis at https://academy.binance.com/en/articles/a-guide-to-cryptocurrency-fundamental-analysis.

Cryptocurrency Technical Analysis

Technical analysis is the study of statistical trends, collected from historical price and volume data, to identify opportunities for trade. Technical analysts observe patterns of price movements, trading signal and other analytical tools to evaluate the strength and weakness of an asset. Technical analysis attempts to understand the market sentiment behind price trends by looking for patterns and trends to determine future price movements.

Traders use technical indicators to gain additional insight into the price action of an asset. These indicators make it easier to identify patterns and spot buy or sell signals in the current market environment. There are many different types of indicators, and they are widely used by day traders, swing traders, and sometimes even longer-term investors.

Important Technical Analysis Terms

When carrying out technical analysis, there are some inevitable terms. You need to understand these terms.

Market Trends

Market trends are the major market movement of an asset that determines its price and trading volume at any time. It is simply the perceived direction of price movements over a particular period. Market trends apply to all assets and all markets where there's movement on prices or volumes bought and sold. Market trends are analyzed by comparing historical price movements against a current price.

The key tool in technical analysis for trend identification and confirmation is a *trend line*. A trend line is simply a straight line connecting two or more price points and extending into the future. There are two major types of trend lines: *Uptrend lines* and *Downtrend lines*.

An uptrend line has a positive slope and is formed by connecting two or more low points. At least three points must be connected before the line is considered a valid trend line. In order for a trend line to have a positive slope, the second point must be higher than the first. Uptrend lines indicate that net demand is increasing even as the price rises. A rising price combined with increasing demand is very bullish, and shows strong determination on the part of buyers.

Uptrend line

A downtrend line has a negative slope and is formed by connecting two or more high points. At least three points must be connected before the line is considered a valid trend line. In order for a trend line to have a negative slope, the second point must be lower than the first. Downtrend lines indicate that net supply is increasing even as the price falls. A declining price combined with increasing supply is very bearish, and shows the strong resolve of sellers.

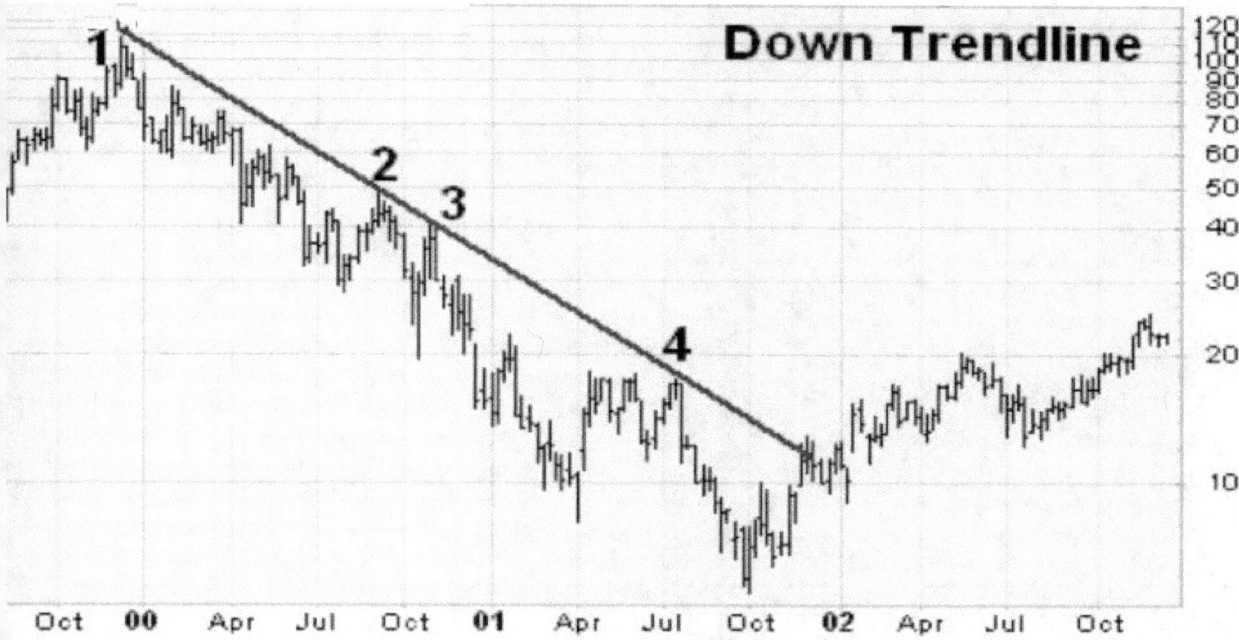

Downtrend line

According to the second tenets of Dow Theory, there are three phases of market trends:

- **Accumulation Phase:** This is the period when 'intelligent' investors start buying or selling the asset against the general market opinion. During this phase of the market, the price of the asset doesn't change much because these knowledgeable investors are in the minority.
- **Absorption (Public Participation) Phase:** After some time, the market catches on to these 'intelligent' investors. And a result, they will no longer be in minority. A rapid price change takes place when trend followers and other technically oriented investors follow the trend. This continues until rampant speculation begins.
- **Distribution Phase:** After huge speculation, because of the limited supply of the asset, the price begins to retrace as these 'intelligent' investors begin to distribute their holdings to the market. As a result of the bag dump, the price of the asset starts falling, alongside the volume. This is the final phase of Dow Theory.

Phases of a major market trend

Resistance and Support

Assets' price movements are not linear; the price will face *resistance* as it goes up or *support* as it goes down. In technical analysis, support and resistance are predetermined levels of the price of an asset at which it tends to reverse its trend. These levels are denoted by multiple touches of price without a breakthrough of the level. Traders often buy at support and sell at resistance.

Resistance is a level where an uptrend can be expected to pause or rebound that indicates a concentration of sellers. When the resistance level is broken, it most time becomes a support level.

To illustrate how resistance works, let's assume that buyers kept buying a crypto coin at a particular price range until the price of the coin goes above that price range. However, once it reaches, say $4,250, the sellers started dumping their bags. However, if the buyers have enough momentum to increase the price of the coin above $4,250, then the price will continue to rise until it reaches another resistance level. Upon the breach, the $4,250 resistance level now becomes support.

Support is a level where a downtrend can be expected to pause or rebound due to a concentration of buyers. When the support level is broken, it most time becomes a resistance level.

To illustrate how support works, the sellers (bears) started selling off their bags of a particular coin. As a result of the bag dump, the price of the coin went down. The moment the price comes down to a certain level, say $3,800 and buyers (bulls) start buying back the coin. This will of course bounce up the price of the off this level. If the sellers are carrying enough momentum and actually manage to drop the price of the coin below $3,800, the price will continue falling until it reaches another support level.

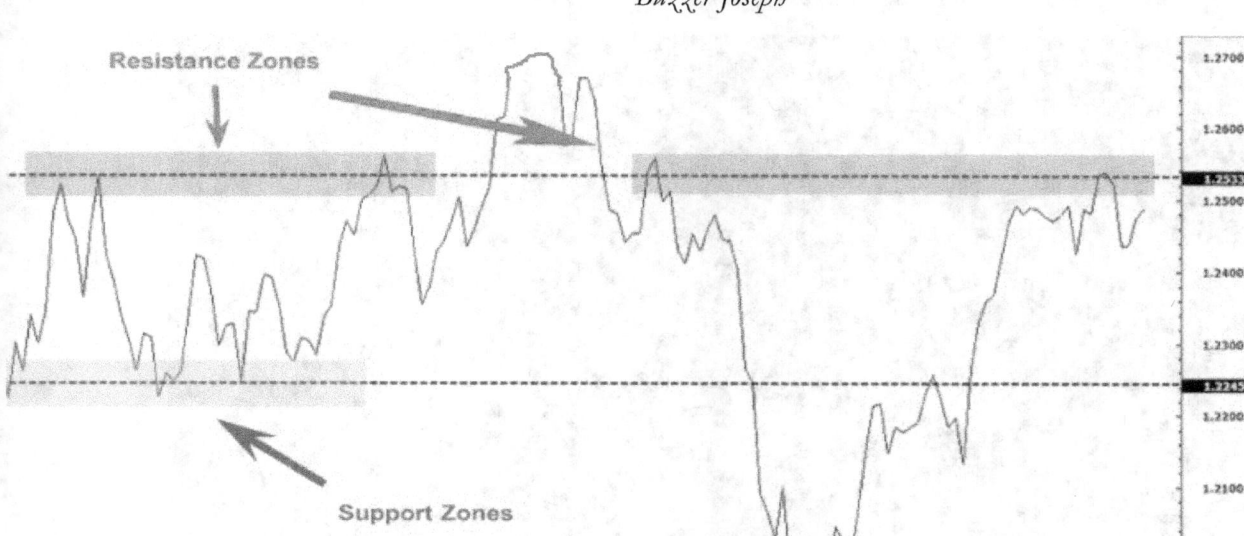

Resistance and Support

NOTE: In technical analysis, support is often used as an *entry* point and resistance as an *exit* point. In the case of strong trends, the price can go through support/resistance without stopping.

Essential Technical Analysis Tools/Indicators

Indicators are the tools of choice for battle-tested technical analysts. Each technical analyst will choose tools that best fit their unique play style, to help them make realistic price predictions. Some like to look at market momentum, while others want to filter out market noise or measure volatility. It will be difficult to say that a particular indicator is the most important because what one analyst will swear to be the ultimate indicator another will dismiss completely. We will explain some of the popular and effective tools for TA.

These tools include:

- Japanese Candlestick Charts
- Moving Average Convergence Divergence (MACD)
- Bollinger Bands (BB)

Japanese Candlestick Charts

Candlestick charting is based on a technique developed in Japan in the 1700s for tracking the price of rice. It has now become a suitable technique for trading any liquid financial asset, including cryptocurrencies. Candlestick can be studied individually (simple patterns) but more often used in groups (complex patterns). The purpose of Candlestick charting is to determine the market trend.

If you have even visited an exchange's website, then there is a possibility that you have seen these charts.

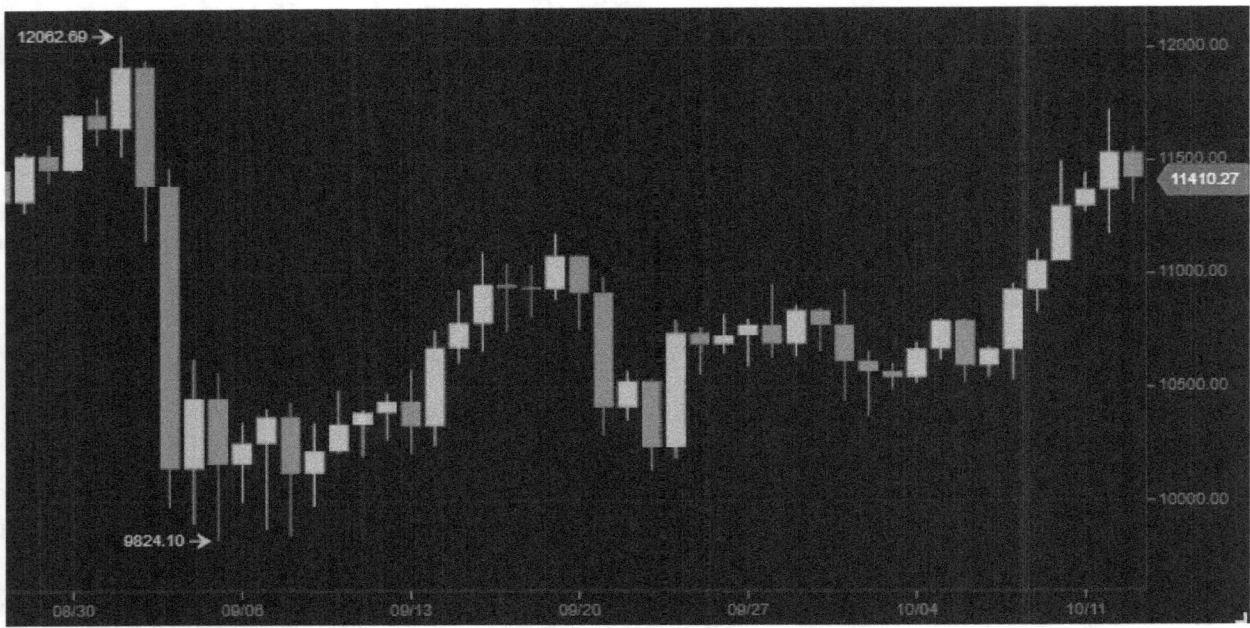

Japanese candlestick charts

The first thing you will notice is the red and green candlesticks lying one after another. Each candle shows you the price movement of the asset during a specific time interval. Along with the closing price, each candle shows the opening price, the lowest, and highest price of the given time-period as well as the closing price.

There are two types of candlesticks:

- **Green (or White) Candle:** It is also called the *Bullish candle*. The close is above the opening.
- **Red (or Black) Candle:** It is also called the *Eearish candle*. The close is below the opening.

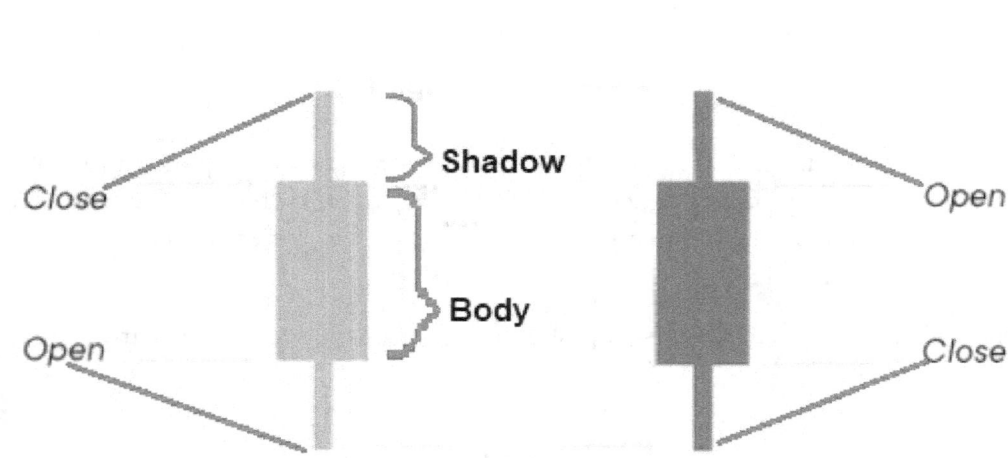

Japanese candlesticks

Every candle has a body and a couple of shadows that are sticking out of it. The body shows you the difference between the opening and closing price. The shadows show you how high or how low these opening and closing prices have gone respectively.

In a green candle, the upper shadow is the close price, while the lower shadow in the open price and vice-versa for red candlesticks.

These candlesticks clearly show you exactly where the market turned and help you identify different patterns which may help you predict how the market will act.

There are two reversal patterns on candlestick graphs:

- **Bullish Reversal Patterns:** Here, the buyers or bulls close the market. This means that a green candle closes the market.
- **Bearish Reversal Patterns:** Here, the sellers or bears close the market. This means that a red candle closes the market.

NOTE

When a technical analyst examines the price chart, along with the technical tools, they also need to be mindful of the time frames that they are considering. Popular time frames that traders most frequently study include: 15-minute chart, Hourly chart, 4-hour chart, daily chart (1-Day), etc.

The time-frame that a trader chooses is directly dependent on their personal trading-style. Short term traders study the hourly or the 15-minutes chart. While long term traders study the 4-hour, daily, or even weekly charts.

You can study more about how to read crypto charts at https://blockgeeks.com/guides/learn-how-to-read-crypto-charts/.

Moving Average Convergence Divergence (MACD)

Moving Average Convergence Divergence (MACD) is a trend following indicator. The MACD is used to determine the momentum of an asset by showing the relationship between two moving averages. It is made up of two lines: the MACD line and the signal line.

The MACD lines displayed below can be interpreted as follows:

- If the blue or purple line (MACD line) is above the orange or red line (Signal line), the momentum is bullish.
- On the contrary, if the blue line is below the orange line, the momentum is bearish.
- When the lines diverge, it denotes a strengthening of the current trend while a convergence shows a trend reversal.
- When the lines cross, it is likely that the change in momentum is confirmed.

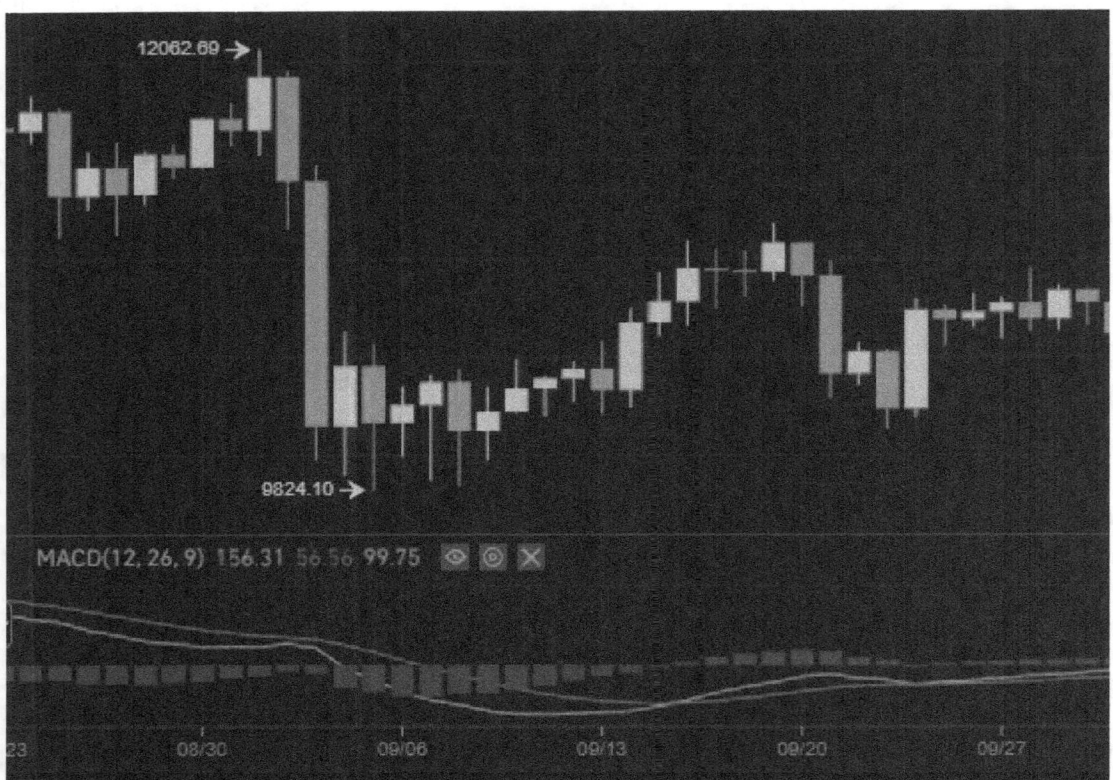

MACD indicator

By looking for divergences between the MACD and the price action, you might gain insight into the strength of the current trend. For example, if the price is making a higher high, while the MACD is making a lower high, the market may be reversing soon. What does this mean? It means that price is increasing while momentum is decreasing, so there is a higher probability of a pullback or reversal occurring.

Bollinger Bands (BB or BOLL)

Bollinger Bands display a graphical band (the envelope) with a simple moving average in the middle. The width of the envelope expresses the volatility.

Volatility refers to the rate at which the price of an asset can increase or decrease. As volatility increases and decreases, the distance between the bands increases and decreases as well.

Another important concept of Bollinger Bands is *Squeeze*, which refers to a period of low volatility, where all bands come very close to each other. This may be used as an indication of potential future volatility. On the other hand, if the bands are very far from each other, a period of decreased volatility may follow.

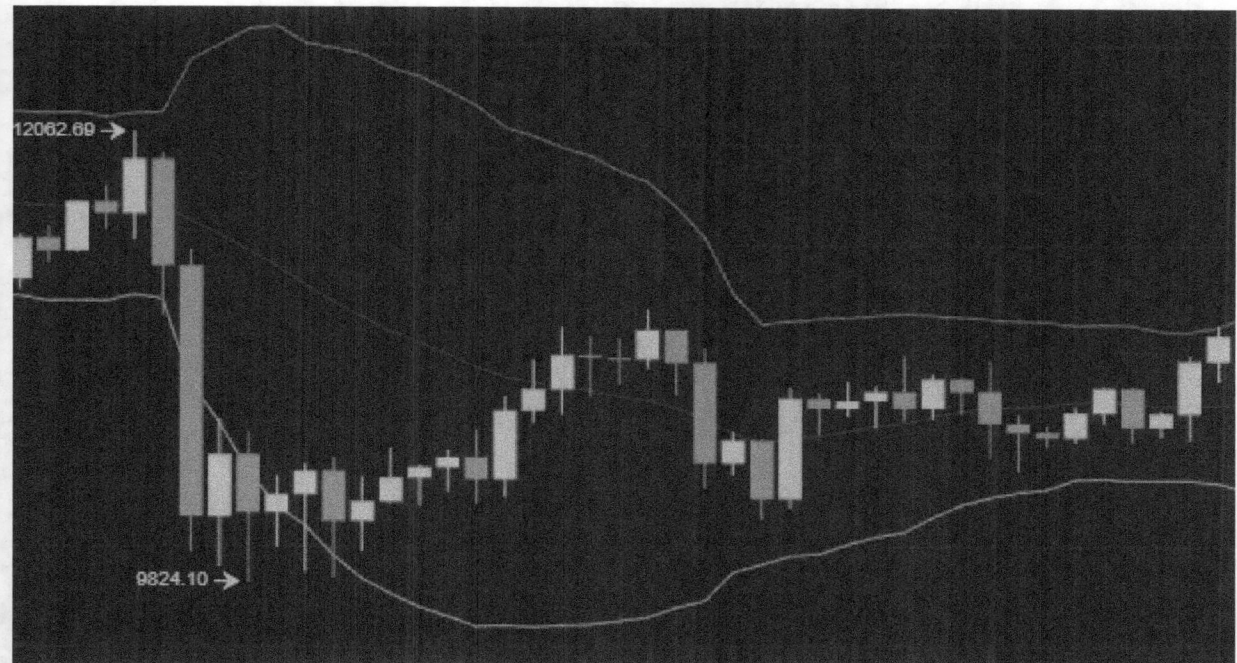

Bollinger Bands indicator

There are other important TA indicators such as Relative Strength Index (RSI), Moving Average (MA), Stochastic RSI (StochRSI), etc.

You can read more about these essential TA indicators at https://academy.binance.com/en/articles/5-essential-indicators-used-in-technical-analysis.

How News affect the Prices of Assets

Media is one of the most effective means of influencing the public.

The third tenet of Dow Theory says that:

"The stock market incorporates new information as soon as it becomes available. Once this news is released, the price of the asset changes to reflect this new information. The price reflects the sum of all the hopes, fears, and expectations of all the market participants. Factors such as interest rate movements, earning expectations, revenue projections, major elections, product initiatives, etc. are all integrated into the market price."

For example, if a news update was released that a popular asset or coin will be listed in one of the major exchanges like Binance, Coinbase, Kucoin, the price of that asset will skyrocket because many investors who have not heard of the asset will like to buy it. Also, some other investors who have already bought the coin will like to add more to their portfolio. As a result, the price will go up. Short term traders also utilize such news update to make more profit. As soon as the price sky rockets, they dump their bags make more profits. This means that the price of the asset may fall after some time, probably few hours or days after the coin has been listed on the exchange platform.

My advice is that once you have invested in a particular crypto coin, follow the social media channels of that project, especially on Twitter, so that as soon as any news update is dropped you will be notified.

Best Websites/Tools for Crypto Coins Analysis and News

If you must succeed in the cryptosphere, then you must stay updated and also carry out researches. To do these, you need to know the recommended cryptocurrency websites and tools that will help you in market analysis. You also need to know good crypto news sites to stay updated.

Some of the recommended Sites/Tools for Crypto Market Analysis include:

- CoinGecko: https://www.coingecko.com/
- CoinMarketCap: https://coinmarketcap.com/
- CryptoCoinCharts: https://cryptocoincharts.info/
- BitInfoCharts: https://bitinfocharts.com/

Some of the recommended Crypto News Sites include:

- CoinDesk: https://www.coindesk.com/
- CoinTelegraph: https://cointelegraph.com/
- TodayOnChain: https://www.todayonchain.com/
- News BTC: https://www.newsbtc.com/
- Bitcoin Magazine: https://bitcoinmagazine.com/
- Bitcoinist: https://bitcoinist.com/
- CryptoSlate: https://cryptoslate.com/
- Bitcoin News: https://news.bitcoin.com/

CRYPTOCURRENCY TRADING BASICS

In this section, we will discuss some of the basic things you need to know before you start trading or investing in any cryptocurrency.

Day Trading Guide

Day trading is a special type of short term trading done by active traders who execute intraday strategies to profit off of price changes for a given asset, like cryptocurrencies. Day trading can be a very lucrative venture as long as you do it properly, but it can also be very challenging for novices, especially for those who don't have a well-planned strategy. The main feature of day trading is that the traders buy the asset and sell it off the same day for profit, or some times for loss.

To be successful in day trading, you must be well grounded in technical analysis and also possess a high degree of self-discipline and objectivity.

Below are some of the strategies used by day traders:

- **Scalping:** With this strategy, they attempt to make numerous small profits on small prices changes throughout the day.
- **Range trading:** With this strategy, they discover favorable support and resistance levels to determine buy and sell decisions.
- **News-based trading:** News generally affect the prices of assets. So with this strategy, day traders typically seize trading opportunities from the heightened volatility around news events.
- **High-frequency trading (HFT):** This strategy involves the use sophisticated algorithms to exploit small or short-term market inefficiencies.

Day Trading Advice

- **Do not day-trade large-cap coins:** The prices coins with of large market capitalization like BTC, ETH, etc. are the less volatile. They need huge capital investment to move the price up. They yield best in long term investment.
- **Day-trade low-cap coins with high growth potentials:** Coins with low market capitalization are the most volatile. Their prices can easily go very high and also come down very low within a short period of time. Note that not all low-cap coins will yield high ROI in day trading. Look for low-cap coins with very high growth potential, especially on short term basis.
- **Trade with the amount you can afford to lose:** Always remember that day-trading is riskier than long term trading. So in order to make sure you don't get wrecked financially, trade with the amount you can afford to lose because crypto market is generally volatile and can go south any moment. If you are not willing to take the risk involved in day trading, then consider investing for long term in cryptocurrencies.
- **Always Start with Small Capital:** Focus on a few coins rather than going into the market head-first and wearing yourself thin. Going all out will only complicate your trading strategy and can mean big losses.
- **Be ready to devote your Time to the Trade:** Day trading is a business that requires a lot of time. If you want to perfect your strategies, after you've practiced, you'll have to devote a lot of time to it. This isn't something you can do part-time or whenever you get the urge. You have to be fully invested in it because the prices of crypto coins are generally volatile. If you don't have much time to devote to day-trading, then focus on long term trading.

- **Know and apply the necessary Strategies:** There are several different strategies day traders use including swing trading, arbitrage, and trading news. These strategies are refined until they produce consistent profits and effectively limit losses. The risk and reward levels of these strategies vary. Swing trading strategy is the riskiest and also has the highest reward level.

In summary, the main differences between day trading and long term trading is that day traders take more risk and use capitals they can afford to lose. But this capital must be tangible if you must make a fortune from day trading. Long term traders are investors who are willing to hold the asset for a very long time, no matter the level of fluctuation in the market. They only sell when they have made huge profit, most times, not less than 100%. While day traders are willing to sell their bags off the same for profit or loss, say plus or minus 5% or 10%.

For more tips on Day trading, check out this beginners guide on day trading at https://academy.binance.com/en/articles/a-beginners-guide-to-day-trading-cryptocurrency.

Bitcoin vs. Stocks

Many investors ask, "Between Bitcoin and Stocks, which one is more profitable?"

The answer cannot be complete without a proper comparison between the two. Check the comparison chart.

Question	Bitcoin	Stocks
Scarcity Is the asset scarce? Is the supply limited?	Yes (21 million BTC maximum guaranteed.)	Depends (Companies can always issue more stock.)
Counterfeit Resistance Is the asset hard or impossible to fake?	Yes (It is independently verifiable via blockchain.)	Yes, but... (Stocks are verified by companies, but may require auditing.)
Portability Can you use or transfer the asset anywhere?	Yes (Can be used to pay or to transfer value anywhere in the world.)	Not quite (Generally can't use stocks outside of the stock market.)
Decentralization Is this asset independent in a way that no central authority controls it?	Yes (Creating and governing it involves a network of decentralized nodes or computers.)	No (All stocks come from just one company, and are usually held by a few controlling shareholders.)

Divisibility Can one unit of this asset be divided into smaller quantities?	Yes (There are 100,000,000 satoshis in one bitcoin.)	Sometimes (Generally not divisible, unless a company engages in a stock split.)
Durability Is this asset protected in the long-term?	Yes (As a digital asset, Bitcoin won't deteriorate.)	Depends (Stocks are reliant on a company's longevity.)
Fungibility Can this asset be traded for other goods or assets?	Yes (You can use Bitcoin to pay for other asset classes, as well as a wide array of goods.)	Yes to a limited extent (You can cash in or cash out, or you may enter certain deals, but you don't usually use stocks to pay for goods on a whim.)
User-friendliness and Awareness Is the asset easy to use? Is it known to more people?	Not quite yet (Though awareness is increasing, Bitcoin has a long way to go in terms of general knowledge. Given its 10-year history, this is understandable.)	Not quite (Just a tiny fraction of the world's population deal with stocks, despite its centuries-old existence as an asset class.)

Bitcoin vs stock [Source: Binance.com]

These are the key things you should note:

- Bitcoin is more volatile than stocks, this means that the price of Bitcoin can increase or fall to the extreme. In fact, the value of Bitcoin can make or break a millionaire.
- Because of the uncertainty in the price of Bitcoin, it is advisable to limit the amount of Bitcoin in an investment portfolio.

The summary is *don't put all your eggs in one basket*.

Coin vs. Token

Most users use the word "Coin" and "Token" interchangeably. Though they have similarities, but in the real sense, there is a difference. The similarity is that both are cryptocurrencies.

A digital *Coin* is a cryptocurrency that is native to its own blockchain. Example of crypto coins are BTC, ETH, NEO, ADA, LTC, XRP, ADA, XLM, etc. Each of these coins exist on their own independent blockchain. Altcoins are considered as coins, but they are not Bitcoin.

Tokens are cryptocurrencies that are created on existing blockchains. The most common blockchain token platform is Ethereum. Tokens that are built on the Ethereum platform are known as *ERC-20 tokens*. Example is the Binance coin; an ethereum-based (ERC-20) token that can be used to trade cryptocurrencies and pay for fees on the Binance exchange. Other examples of ERC-20 tokens are EOS, TRX, VET, ICX, OMG, ZIL, AE, etc. Tokens that are built on the NEO platform are known as *NEP-5 tokens*. Examples of NEP-5 tokens are ONT, NEX, ZPT, TKY, DBC, etc.

The Basic Unit of Bitcoin

One of the special attributes of cryptocurrencies is their divisibility. Bitcoin is not excluded. It can be split into smaller units to ease and facilitate smaller transactions.

The basic unit of a bitcoin is **Satoshi**, (called Sat. for simplicity); gotten from *Satoshi Nakamoto* - the name of the man who created the protocol used in blockchains and the bitcoin cryptocurrency.

- 100,000,000 Satoshi = 1 BTC (Bitcoin)
- Therefore 1 Satoshi = 1/100,000,000 BTC = 0.00000001 BTC
- Thus a Satoshi is equivalent to 100 millionth of a bitcoin.

NOTE:

For simplicity, bitcoin fractions are measured in Satoshi. For example:

- 0.00000001 BTC = 1 Satoshi
- 0.00002000 BTC = 2000 Satoshi
- 0.99999999 BTC = 99999999 Satoshi, etc.

How to Convert any USD Amount to BTC or Satoshi

Once you have known the basic unit of bitcoin and its value, you can convert any amount in USD to BTC or Satoshi.

This becomes very useful when you want to sell your BTC for USD. You need to know the amount of satoshi that is equivalent to any amount in USD.

For this, you need to know the current equivalent of 1 BTC in USD.

The formula for convert any USD amount to BTC is:

$$= \frac{\text{USD amount you wish to convert to BTC}}{\text{Current value of 1 BTC in USD}}$$

For example, assuming you have 2.5 BTC in your wallet and a client wants to buy 2000 USD worth of BTC. Assuming the current value of 1 BTC is 12,000 USD.

Then the current equivalence of 2000 USD in BTC

$$= \frac{2{,}000}{12{,}000} \text{ BTC} = \mathbf{0.16666667\ BTC}$$

NOTE: Always approximate to 8 decimal places.

It can also be said that 2000 USD is equal to **16666667 Sat.**

The Basic Unit of Ethereum

The basic unit of Ethereum (ETH) is called *Wei*, just as the basic unit of Dollar is *Cent* and that of Bitcoin is *Satoshi*.

NOTE: *Gwei* (Giga Wei) is the most commonly used unit of ether because "gas" prices are easily specified in Gwei.

1 ETH = 1,000,000,000 Gwei

But 1 Gwei = 10^9 Wei = 1,000,000,000 Wei

There are new digital currency denominations that are used to denote the smaller ETH transactions correctly. The table below shows the various typical units of ethereum, including Gwei. Notice in the table that the denominations each have their own slang (in parentheses)—which are their nicknames based on influential figures in the world of cryptography.

Denominations of Ether

Unit Name	Wei Value	Number of Wei
Wei (wei)	1 wei	1
Kwei (babbage)	1e3 wei	1,000
Mwei (lovelace)	1e6 wei	1,000,000
Gwei (shannon)	1e9 wei	1,000,000,000
Twei (szabo)	1e12 wei	1,000,000,000,000
Pwei (finney)	1e15 wei	1,000,000,000,000,000
Ether (buterin)	1e18 wei	1,000,000,000,000,000,000

Typical units of ethereum [Source: Investopedia.com]

How to Convert any USD Amount to ETH or Gwei

Just as we did for BTC, you can convert any USD amount to ETH or Gwei.

This becomes very useful when you want to sell your ETH for USD. You need to know the amount of ETH that is equivalent to any amount in USD.

For this, you need to know the current equivalent of 1 ETH in USD.

The formula for convert any USD amount to ETH is:

$$= \frac{\text{USD amount you wish to convert to ETH}}{\text{Current value of 1 ETH in USD}}$$

For example, assuming you have 2 ETH in your wallet and a client wants to buy 150 USD worth of ETH. Assuming the current value of 1 BTC is 450 USD.

Then the current equivalence of 150 USD in ETH

$$= \frac{150}{450} = 0.333333333 \text{ ETH}$$

NOTE: Always approximate to 9 decimal places.

It can also be said that 150 USD is equal to **333333333 Gwei**.

The Best Time to Buy Bitcoin

As a cryptocurrency trader or investor, your main aim is to make profit. You can only be in profit when your selling price is higher than the cost price.

So when buying Bitcoin, your target should be to buy when the price is low. But most times, it is very difficult the price of Bitcoin at any point in time. The best way to ensure that you bought at a fairly low price is to do cost averaging, which has been explained in this book. You keep buying at different price ranges.

The secret to making more profits in Bitcoin trading is to buy when the majority of traders are afraid to buy and sell when the majority of traders are willing to buy.

Always remember that the prices of cryptocurrencies are highly volatile, so make your own research before you invest. Always utilize Technical Ananlysis.

The Best Time to Sell Bitcoin

Once you have gotten enough Bitcoin bag, your next target is to maximize profit. Most times, selling all your bags at a particular price is not the best decision. You might sell at a particular price and Bitcoin price goes higher.

The best solution is to target different percentage profits. For example, depending on the nature of market for that period, you might target, say 30%, 50%, 100% or more. Once you reach any of these percentage profits, you dump a certain percentage of your total Bitcoin bag.

You also need to be smart while doing this. Study the market trends. Adjust your decisions according to market trends. For example, you might want to sell half of your bag when you reach 30% profit and the other half when you reach 50% profit. Assuming your first target has been met and you sold half of your bag. Then Bitcoin price continued to increase and you reached 45% in profit. Suddenly market trend changed and price began to drop, say back to 35% profit. What a smart short term trader will do is to sell off all his bag if he predicts that the price will fall further. Then buy back when the price has fallen below 30% profit.

The above strategy becomes very useful in a bearish market where the prices of cryptocurrencies fluctuate. In a bullish market, you may target a particular percentage profit. Once you sell off your bag, you wait until the price falls again to buy back at a lower price.

Note that there are some trading decisions that will favour only short term traders. It takes a lot or experiments to understand the Bitcoin market. Analyze the market before you take any step.

How to Track Bitcoin Transactions and Know its Status

There are times you will might need to track your Bitcoin transactions. For example, assuming you bought Bitcoin from a trusted thirdparty, and you were informed that the Bitcoin has been sent to your wallet address. Remember that the coin will reflect in your wallet after the transaction has been confirmed by at least one network. This might take up to 30 minutes or more. To know the current status of the transaction, you need to track it. You can you blockchain.com explorer.

To Track any Bitcoin Transaction:

Copy the recipient's Bitcoin wallet address or the transaction hash/ID to your clipboard. A transaction hash/ID is a unique string of characters that is given to every transaction that is verified and added to the blockchain. If you are buying Bitcoin from a thirdparty, the transaction hash will be sent to you.

Go to https://www.blockchain.com/explorer. Paste your Bitcoin wallet address or the transaction hash in the search bar and click press the Enter key.

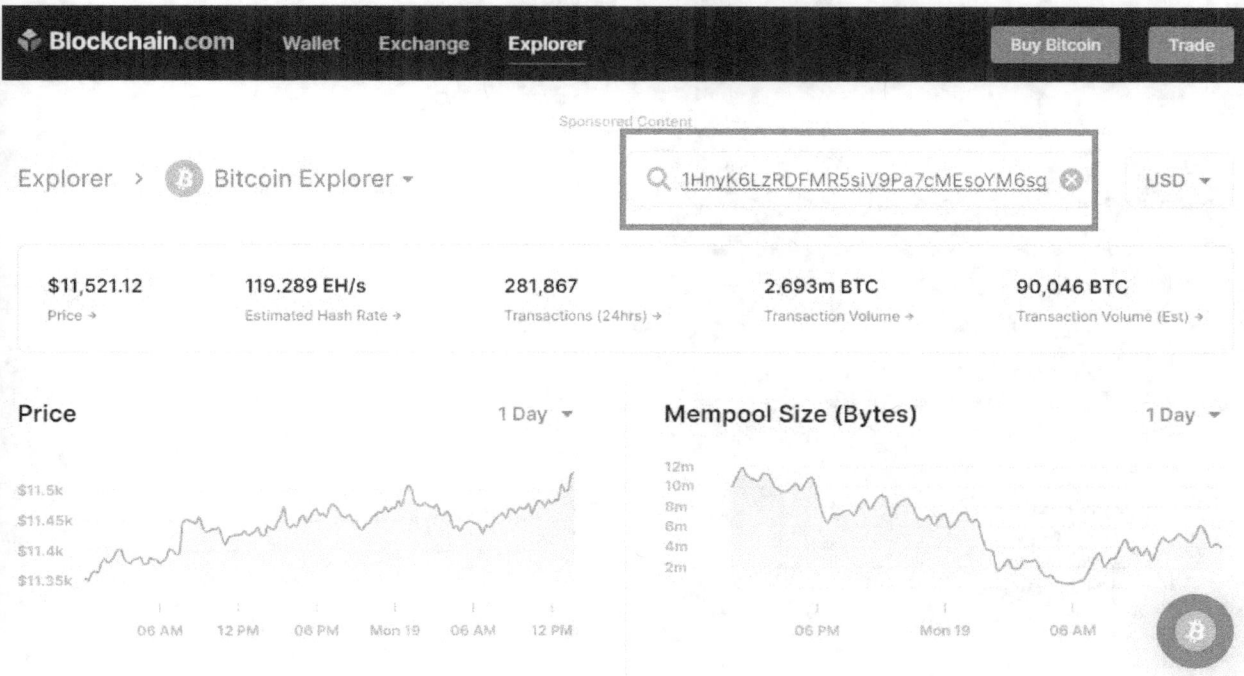

Paste your Bitcoin wallet address or your transaction hash

If you pasted a Bitcoin wallet address, you will be notified that there are 2 blockchains with result(s) to your search. Select **BTC Address**.

Select BTC address

Under the **Transactions** section, you will see the status of the last transaction of the wallet address. You can click the hash to see more details about the transaction.

Status of the last transaction

NOTE: You can also use blockchain.com explorer to track Ethereum (ETH) and BitcoinCash (BCH) transactions. Just click the drop down arrow near Bitcoin explorer and then select Ethereum Explorer or BitcoinCash explorer.

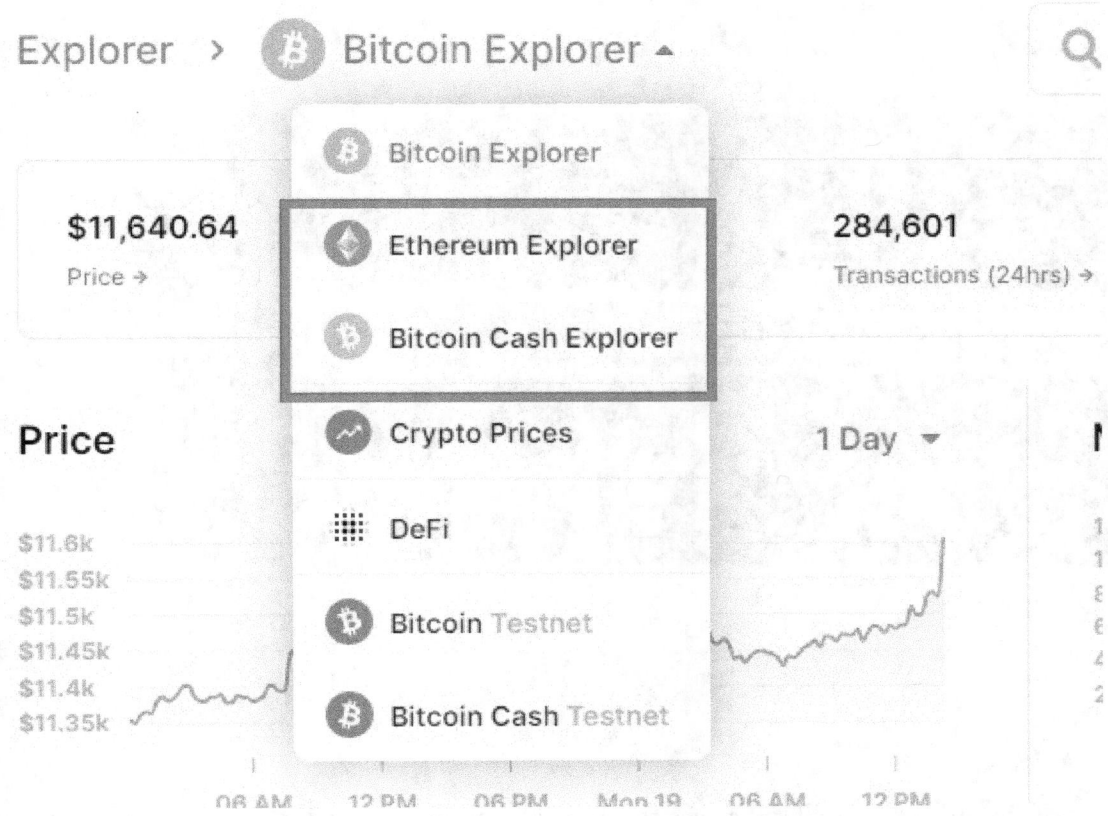

Select another explorer

How to Track Ethereum Transaction and Know its Status

Ethereum also has a special explorer you can use to track any ethereum transaction. **Etherscan.io** allows you to explore and search the Ethereum blockchain for transactions, addresses, tokens, prices and other activities taking place on Ethereum network.

To Track any Ethereum Transaction:

Copy the recipient's Ethereum wallet address or the transaction hash/ID to your clipboard.

Go to https://etherscan.io/. Paste your Ethereum wallet address or the transaction hash in the search bar and click on **Search**.

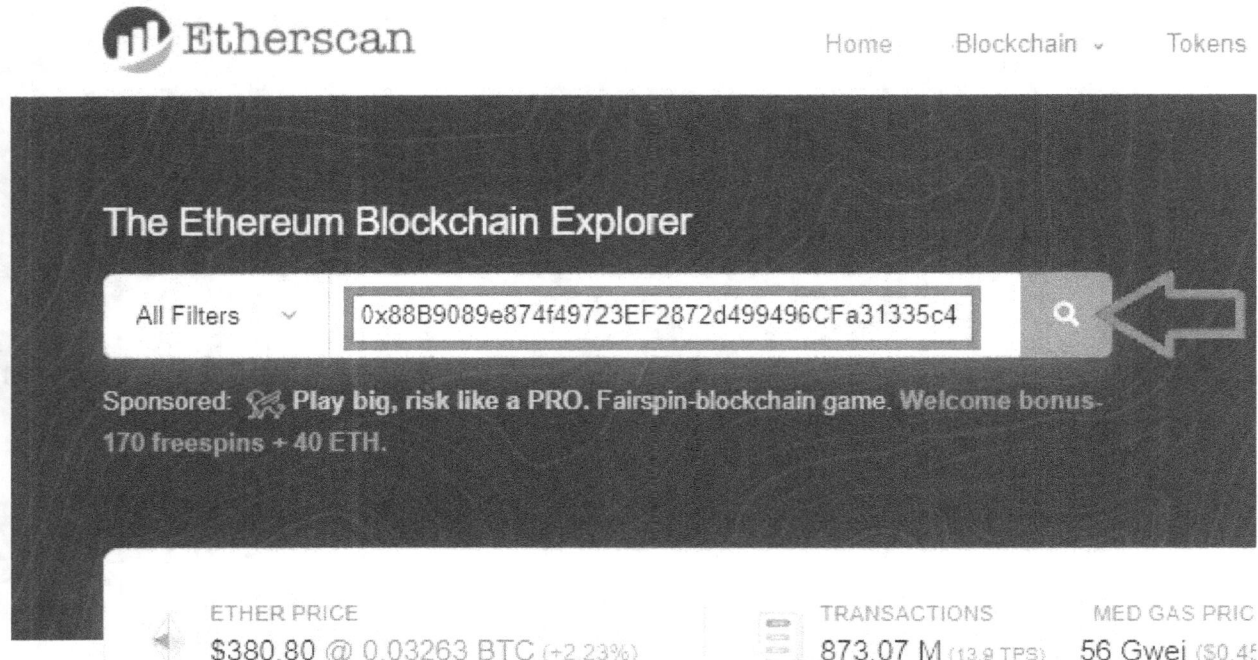

Paste your ethereum wallet and address and press search

You will see an overview of the Ethereum wallet that has the address. In the Transaction section, you will see the details of each transaction, with the latest transaction being at the top. You can click the **Transaction hash** (Txn Hash) to see more about the transaction.

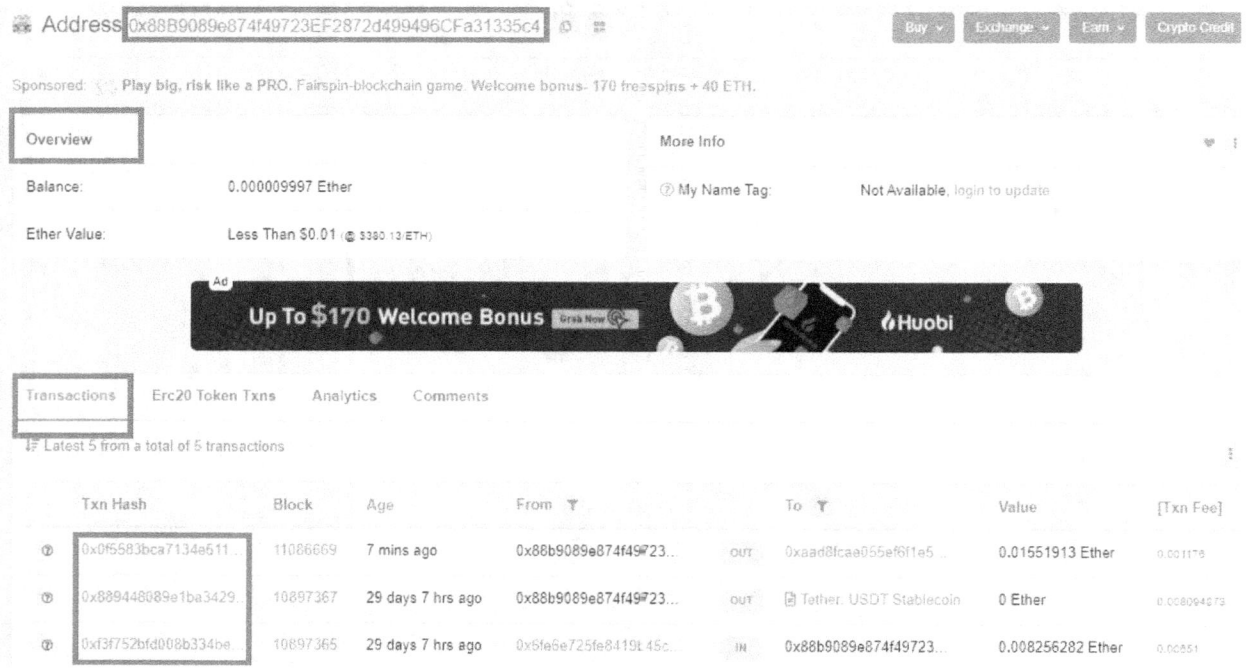

The ethereum wallet details

How to Choose a Secure Crypto Exchange Platform

Exchanges platforms provide you with the necessary tools you will need to trade between cryptocurrencies or fiat-to-cryptocurrencies. There are a lot of centralized and decentralized exchanges out there, but there are many things you also need to consider before choosing and signing up with an exchange. Some of the things you should consider include:

- **The supported Trading Pairs:** Check if it supports all the trading pairs you may need like: fiat-to-crypto pairs, crypto-cross pairs. If you are a seasoned trader, you should look out for exchanges that support leverage and margin trading.
- **User-friendly Trading App:** Almost all exchanges have trading apps. If you are a beginner, you will need an exchange whose trading apps are user-friendly.
- **Trading Fees:** Exchanges charge you a small percentage as trading fee. Some exchanges charge a higher rate than others. Kucoin and Binance charge little trading fee.
- **Available Coin Pairs:** Make sure that the exchange you chose has the coin pairs you want to trade. For example, ONG/BTC, NEO/ETH, etc.
- **Insurance:** Always check if the exchange is insured so that if the exchange is hacked, you don't lose your funds.
- **Reputation:** This is also very important. If the exchange is associated with a lot of theft and scams in the past, stay away from such exchanges. Customers' reviews and ratings can help you out.
- **Trading Volume/Liquidity:** Check the 24 hours trading volume of the exchange to ensure it is liquid enough to provide high trading volume, especially if you are an investor.
- **Supported Locations:** Does the exchange platform legally support your location or country? Some exchanges are not available for some countries.

Recommended Centralized Exchange Platforms

Centralized exchange platforms allow you trade crypto-to-crypto, fiat-to-crypto and vice versa. If you want to be a short term trader, you will be needing these platforms a lot.

Below are some of the recommended centralized exchanges:

- *Binance
- *KuCoin
- Coinbase Pro
- Kraken
- *Crypto.com
- Bittrex
- Gemini
- eToro

NOTE: Some exchanges offer discounts and bonuses to new users who registered with a referral code. The links that started with asterisk (*) are referral links. Binance and KuCoin offer discounts up to 20% for new users while Crypto.com offer $50 bonus.

Recommended Decentralized Exchange Platforms

Unlike in a centralized exchange where a middle man sets the price bids, decentralized exchanges cut off the middle man to provide a "trustless" trading environment. They are also called peer-to-peer exchanges, where the transactions based on smart contracts and atomic swaps. Also note that decentralized exchanges only support crypto-to-crypto trades. It does not support fiat-to-cryptocurrency trades.

Below are some recommended decentralized exchanges:

- Uniswap
- *Tokenlon
- Aave
- Curve Finance
- Compound Finance
- 0x Protocol
- SushiSwap
- Balancer

Each of these exchanges has its pros and cons. You can read more about them at https://www.buzzingpoint.com/2020/09/secured-cryptocurrency-exchanges.html. There are many other trusted centralized and decentralized exchanges you will discover in the article.

How to Calculate your Percentage Profit in Short Term Cryptocurrency Trading

In order to succeed in short term trades, you should target small percentage profits from 10% and above. Immediately you buy a crypto coin at a low price, calculate your exit percentage level. Once the price reaches that level, you sell off your bag and take profit.

To know the Satoshi value that will give you 10% profit, multiply your entry price by 1.1

For example if you bought a coin at 100 satoshi and want to know the Satoshi value that will give you 10% profit,

Do this: 1.1 * 100 = 110 satoshi or 0.00000110 BTC

The same applies for any other percentage profit.

- **For 20% Profit:** Multiply your entry price by 1.2
- **For 30% Profit:** Multiply your entry price by 1.3
- **For 50% Profit:** Multiply your entry price by 1.5
- **For 100% Profit:** Multiply your entry price by 2
- **For 200% Profit:** Multiply your entry price by 3
- **For 900% Profit:** Multiply your entry price by 10
- **For 1000% Profit:** Multiply your entry price by 11

And so on…

How to Calculate your Percentage Profit in Long Term Cryptocurrency Trading

For long term altcoin trades, you are expected to extract your capital and probably with a little profit (convert it to BTC or any other stable coin) once you are up to 100% in profit. Once you do this, it now implies that whatever that is left is your profit. The reason for this advice is because nobody can predict the exact nature of cryptocurrency market with certainty. So if the price crashes after you have removed your capital with a little profit, your will not disappear.

NOTE:

- In this section, I assume that you are trading BTC pairs in your centralized exchange platform. For example, ETH/BTC, NEO/BTC, XRP/BTC, etc.
- Whenever you buy an altcoin with BTC, always take note of your total investment capital and the unit cost price in satoshi. You can write it down in a notebook. Also take note of the number of units of the coin you bought. These two values will help you when calculating your percentage profit. You can see the latter when you go to the exchange app order history.

We will do a little derivation to get the formula for calculating the number of units of the coin to sell in order to extract your investment capital with some profits.

Let's start...

Total investment capital (in satoshi) = Unit cost price in satoshi * Total number of units of the coin bought 1

Assuming you wish to extract your investment capital after the unit price of the coin has gone up by a certain amount, say X%;

Then the number of units to sell in order to extract your investment capital

$$= \frac{\text{Total investment capital in satoshi}}{\text{Current unit price at X\% price up movement in satoshi}} \quad \text{...........2}$$

At X% price up movement, while extracting your investment capital, you should also take some profit, say Y% of your total investment capital.

So at X% price up movement, the number of units of the coin to sell in order to extract your investment capital plus Y% profit

$$= \frac{(Y\% * \text{Total Investment Capital in satoshi}) + \text{Total Investment Capital in satoshi}}{\text{Current unit price at X\% price up movement in satoshi}}$$

$$= \frac{(1 + Y\%) * \text{Total Investment Capital in satoshi}}{\text{Current unit price at X\% price up movement in satoshi}} \quad \text{...........3}$$

Current unit price at X% price up movement in satoshi

= Unit cost price in satoshi + (X% * Unit cost price in satoshi)

= (1 + X%) * (Unit cost price in satoshi) 4

Substitute equation 4 into equation 3;

At X% price up movement, the number of units of the coin to sell in order to extract your investment capital plus Y% profit

$$= \frac{(1 + Y\%) * \text{Total Investment Capital in satoshi}}{(1 + X\%) * (\text{Unit cost price in satoshi})} \quad \text{...........5}$$

The number of units of the coin that will remain after you have extracted your investment capital with Y% profit

= (Total number of units of the coin purchased) - (Equation 5) 6

Where;

X% is the percentage by which the coin's unit price has gone up. It is at this price that you wish to extract your investment capital plus Y% profit.

Y% is the extra percentage profit you wish to extract alongside your investment capital.

Note that equation 4 is the unit selling price of the coin in order to extract your investment capital, plus Y% profit.

This derivation might seem a bit cumbersome for you if you are not good at mathematics. But let's take a practical example to help you understand it better.

NOTE:

Once you have used equations 5 to calculate the number of units of the coin to sell in order to extract your investment capital plus Y% profit and equation 4 to calculate the selling price, go to your exchange app and setup a sell limit order using these two parameters you calculated.

Also note that the trading fee was assumed to be 0%. But in most cases, it is not zero percent. Binance and KuCoin charge 0.1% as trading fee.

Example: If you bought 2000 units of a coin at 100 satoshi, how do you know the number of units of this coin to sell in order to extract your capital plus 10% profit after the price of the coin has doubled?

Solution

From the above question,

Total number of units of the coin bought = 2000 units

Unit cost price of the coin = 100 satoshi = 0.00000100 BTC

The price of the coin will double at 100% increase in price.

This implies that X% = 100%

The extra percentage profit to extract alongside the investment capital = Y% = 10%

Recall from equation 1 that;

Total investment capital (in satoshi) = Unit cost price in satoshi * Total number of units of the coin bought

= 100 * 2000 = 200,000 satoshi = 0.00200000 BTC

Substituting these values in equation 5;

The number of units of the coin that will remain after you have extracted your investment capital with 10% profit

$$= \frac{(1 + 10\%) * 200{,}000}{(1 + 100\%) * 100}$$

$$= \frac{(1 + 0.1) * 200{,}000}{(1 + 1) * 100}$$

$$= \frac{1.1 * 200{,}000}{2 * 100}$$

$$= \frac{220{,}000}{200} = 1{,}100 \text{ units of the coin}$$

From equation 4, the selling price of the coin after the price of the coin has doubled

= (1 + 100%) * 100

= (1 + 1) * 100 = 2 * 100

= **200 satoshi** = 0.00000200 BTC

Therefore, the number of units of this coin to sell in order to extract your capital plus 10% profit after the price of the coin has doubled is **1,100 units**.

After you have sold 1,100 units of the coin, from equation 6, the number of units of the coin left

= 2,000 − 1,100 = **900 units**

So you now go to the exchange app, for example, KuCoin or Binance.

Set 0.00000200 BTC as the selling price and 1100 as the number of units to sell and click the **Sell** button.

You can allow the remaining 900 units of the coin to ride until you are satisfied with the profit level or sense a bearish market coming.

Any money you make from the 900 units is purely profit.

Considering Cost Averaging

Most times long term traders or investors buy a particular coin at different price ranges so as to average out their unit cost. In such a case, you need to sum the various investment capital for each "Buy" period to get your total investment capital.

Also, you need to use the cumulative average formula to get the average unit price of the coin. Once you get these two parameters, you can use the above derived formulas.

Here is what I mean.

Assuming you first bought 100 units of a coin, say Akropolis (AKRO) at 150 satoshi. Then the price came down further to 120 satoshi, you bought another 100 units. Also the price tanked further to 100 satoshi, you bought another 100 units.

The total investment capital is

= Investment capital of first buy + Investment capital of second buy + Investment capital of third buy + ...+ Investment capital of the last buy ……………………………………………………………………………………………………..7

Investment capital for each buy period

= *Unit price of the coin * Number of units of the coin bought* …………………………………..8

Unit price of the coin

$$= \frac{Total\ investment\ capital}{Total\ units\ of\ the\ coin\ bought}$$

$$= \frac{Investment\ capital\ of\ (First\ buy + Second\ buy + Third\ buy + \cdots + last\ buy)}{Number\ of\ units\ of\ the\ coin\ on\ (First\ buy + Second\ buy + Third\ buy + \cdots + Last\ buy)} \ \ldots\ldots\ldots\ldots\ldots.9$$

In the case of the above example, there was 3 buy periods.

Therefore;

Investment capital of the first buy

= 150 * 100 = 15,000 satoshi = 0.00015000 BTC

Investment capital of the second buy

= 120 * 100 = 12,000 satoshi = 0.00012000 BTC

Investment capital of the third buy

= 100 * 100 = 10,000 satoshi = 0.00010000 BTC

Therefore, the total investment capital of AKRO

= 15,000 + 12,000 + 10,000 = **37,000** satoshi = **0.00037000** BTC

The unit price of AKRO

$= \frac{15,000+12,000+10,000}{100+100+100} = \frac{37,000}{300} =$ **123.33** satoshi = **0.0000012333** BTC

So, these are the two parameters you will use in equation 5.

How to Calculate your Cryptocurrency Profit in Excel

If you still find it difficult to understand the calculations above, there is another easier alternative, which you will love so much. I have built a simple calculator to help you know the number of units of a coin you bought that you should sell at a particular price level in order to pull out your investment capital and a little extra percentage profit.

The calculator assumes you bought at only one price level. If you bought at more than one price level, you can use equations 7 to 9 to calculate the average unit price and the total number of units of the coin bought before using the calculator.

The calculator works only for BTC trade pairs. For example, ETH/BTC, XRP/BTC, NEO/BTC, ZEC/BTC, etc. If you don't trade BTC pairs, then use the formulas in this book. They will do the job for you.

BTC TRADING PAIR PROFIT CALCULATOR	
Type the Coin Name (eg. BTC, ETH)	AKRO
Type the Unit Price you Bought the Coin (in Satoshi)	100.00
Type the Number of Units of the Coin you Bought	2000
This is your Investment Capital (in Satoshi)	200000.00
Type the Capital Pull Out Percentage (eg type 50 for 50%)	100%
Type the Extra Percentage Profit you also Wish to Pull Out	10%
This is the Number of Units to Sell to Recover your Capital (plus the specified profit)	1100.00
This is the Number of Units of the Coin that will Remain (Your Pure Profit)	900.00

NOTE:
This is a simple calculator to help you know the number of units of a coin you bought that you should sell at a particular price level in order to pull out your investment capital plus a little extra percentage profit.
This calculator assumes you bought at only one price level. If you bought at more than one price level, then you need to calculate the average unit price and the total number of units of the coin bought before using this calculator.
This calculator also works only for BTC trade pairs. For example, ETH/BTC, XRP/BTC, NEO/BTC, ZEC/BTC, etc.
Here is a simple challenge you can solve with this calculator: If you bought 2000 units of a coin, Akropolis (AKRO) at 100 satoshi, how do you know the number of units of this coin to sell in order to extract your capital plus 10% profit after the price of the coin has doubled?
The parameters you need to enter are: coin name (AKRO), unit price of the coin (100 satoshi), capital pull out percentage (100%), extra percentage profit to pull out alongside your investment capital (10%).
The calculator will calculate the number of units to sell in order to recover your capital plus the specified extra capital. It will also show you the number of units that will remain after you have pulled out your capital plus some profits. If you are a long term bitcoin trader, you will appreciate this calculator.
NOTE: To learn more about cryptocurrency trading, check out this book on Amazon - **How to Make Money with Bitcoin Trading & Investment for Beginners:** Complete Guide on How to Buy & Sell Bitcoin for Huge Profits, DeFi Yield Farming & Other Cryptocurrency Investments Tips.

BTC trading pair profit calculator

You can download this calculator from my Google drive at http://bit.ly/btcprofitexcelcalculator. For free Microsoft excel and Goggle sheets tutorials, visit microsofttut.com.

LEGIT WAYS TO MAKE MONEY WITH CRYPTOCURRENCIES

The crypto world now has many avenues to make money. Bitcoin is not the only cryptocurrency that can make you rich. There are many other opportunities you will discover in this section. Always note that crptocurrency businesses are associated with high risk and high rewards. So never invest all your money in cryptocurrency and blockchain businesses.

DeFi Yield Farming and Staking

In DeFi yield farming, you deposit one or two stable coin and a token through smart contract to earn a reward in return. DeFi stands for Decentralized Finance. In yield farming, the two key players are the liquidity providers and the liquidity pools. When you deposit your stable coins, you become a liquidity provider. Liquidity pool is what powers the marketplace where users can lend, borrow or even exchange tokens.

When liquidity providers deposit stable coins into a liquidity pool, some crypto users borrow from this pool, and as a result, they pay extra fee. A percentage of these fees are shared between the liquidity providers according to their contribution in the liquidity pool. This form of yield farming is called **DeFi Liquidity Staking**. Here, you are rewarded with the token you staked with the stable coin.

Pamp liquidity staking is an example. Here, you will stake your Pamp token with an equivalent stable coin. There are many staking pairs:

- PAMP/ETH
- PAMP/USDT
- PAMP/LINK
- PAMP/BONK
- PAMP/UNI

For any of the pairs you staked, you earn pamp token as rewards.

In the first form of DeFi yield farming, a liquidity pool is created with the sole aim of minting a new token, in which a percentage of it is distributed among the liquidity providers. More yield farming strategies will emerge in future.

Some popular liquidity pool providers include:

- Uniswap
- Curve Finance
- Bancor
- Kyber Network
- KeeperDAO
- Balancer
- Compound Finance
- Yearn.finance

NOTE: There are also high risks involved in yield farming. Always invest the amount you can afford to lose. Some of the risks are loss of funds due to smart contract bugs and flash loan attacks.

Cryptocurrency Trading

You can make cool money by trading Bitcoin and some other altcoins. You buy these coins at a low price and sell them off when their prices go up. You can trade fiat-to-crypto pairs or crypto-to-crypto pairs.

To make much profit with Bitcoin trading, invest it in long term. You can also make more money by trading some altcoins that have short term potentials. To successfully trade cryptocurrencies, you need to have a good knowledge of cryptocurrency market analysis (Fundamental Analysis and Technical Analysis). You will also need a good exchange platform.

Crypto Coins Investment

Here, you buy some coins that have good future potential at a low price, hodl them in your wallet for some months or even years. When the prices have gone up, you sell them off to make more money. It is very similar to crypto trading, but may take more time to yield high profit, unlike short term trades. In fact cryptocurrency investment is long term trading.

Instead of locking up your spare money in your local bank account for years without making much profit, invest it in bitcoin or any altcoin that has growth potential (like ethereum) and make huge profit, up 500%.

Cryptocurrency Affiliate Marketing

Most cryptocurrency exchange platforms have affiliate programs. Once you sign up with the exchange, you will be given a unique affiliate link. When you refer a crypto trader to sign up through your affiliate link, you will be rewarded with some native token of the exchange which you can convert to bitcoin or any other altcoin. For example, KuCoin rewards its affiliates with KCS.

You can share your affiliate link in social media groups and pages or share it directly to a friend. If you have a blog, you can write a review about these exchanges and add your affiliate links in the article.

Some of the popular cryptocurrency affiliate programs that pay well are:

- Coinbase: https://www.coinbase.com/affiliates
- eToro: https://www.etoropartners.com/
- Binance: https://www.binance.com/invite.html
- Kucoin: https://news.kucoin.com/en/referral-bonus-program/

NOTE: Always check the affiliate terms and conditions of these exchanges before participating.

Bitcoin and Altcoin Mining

Bitcoin mining is no longer as lucrative as it used to be some years back. Apart from Bitcoin mining, you can also mine some other alt coins to make money.

By helping to verify transactions on these crypto networks, you as a miner help to prevent the issue of double spending, a user tries to spend the same token twice. The first miner to come up with a target hash (usually a 64 digit hexadecimal number) is rewarded. To learn more about Bitcoin mining, check out this article at https://www.investopedia.com/tech/how-does-bitcoin-mining-work/.

Generally cryptocurrency mining is not as lucrative as some other money making opportunities like trading and yield farming.

Freelance Sites that Pay with Cryptocurrencies

There are many freelance sites where you can work and get paid in bitcoin and other altcoins. But note that you will need a bitcoin or other altcoin wallet where your earnings will be deposited.

Some of these freelance sites that pay with cryptocurrency include:

- Cryptogrind.com
- Read.cash
- Bitgigs.com
- Crypto.jobs
- Blocklancer.net

Micro Job Sites that Pay with Cryptocurrencies

You can also earn bitcoin or any other altcoins by just doing a micro job like viewing ads, completing surveys or doing any other mini task.

Some of these micro job sites that pay with cryptocurrency include:

- App.Paid.co
- Kriptode.com
- Timebucks.com
- Stakwork.com
- Earnsats.co

There are other ways to make money in the cryptosphere. You can check out this article at https://medium.com/lucrative-business-ideas/how-to-make-money-with-bitcoin-f8e03b5c9ed0.

Buzzer Joseph

CLASSIFICATIONS OF CRYPTOCURRENCIES BASED ON THEIR MARKET CAPITALIZATION

One of the most useful metrics for estimating the real worth of a cryptocurrency is *Market Capitalization*. It is simply the amount needed to buy all the available supply of a crypto coin at any point in time. Market capitalization of a cryptocurrency is the product of the *total circulating supply of the coin* and the *price of each unit of the coin*. We discussed market capitalization in detail under the *Cryptocurrency Market Analysis and Tools* section of this book. In this section, you will learn the various classifications of cryptocurrencies based on their market cap. This will help you take a smart cryptocurrency investment decision, especially in the long run.

Generally, all cryptocurrencies can be classified based on their market caps into the following groups:

- Large-Cap Cryptocurrencies
- Mid-Cap Cryptocurrencies
- Low or Small-Cap Cryptocurrencies

Coinmarketcap.com lists cryptocurrencies in ascending order of their market cap.

Today's Cryptocurrency Prices by Market Cap

The global crypto market cap is $392.15B, a ▼ -0.02% decrease over the last day. Read more

#	Name	Price	24h	7d	Market Cap	Volume	Circulating Supply
1	Bitcoin BTC	$13,520.66	0.36%	1.84%	$250,573,677,590	$30,545,122,107 / 2,259,144 BTC	18,532,650 BTC
2	Ethereum ETH	$379.84	-1.41%	-4.12%	$43,026,058,593	$13,410,097,014 / 35,304,334 ETH	113,273,331 ETH
3	Tether USDT	$1.00	-0.00%	-0.06%	$16,700,249,838	$46,306,236,827 / 46,300,281,702 USDT	16,698,102,134 USDT
4	XRP XRP	$0.235756	-0.17%	-6.22%	$10,676,140,836	$2,835,538,619 / 12,027,418,757 XRP	45,284,665,028 XRP
5	Bitcoin Cash BCH	$240.82	-7.40%	-7.76%	$4,470,029,883	$2,844,764,252 / 11,813,011 BCH	18,562,000 BCH

Coinmarketcap cryptocurrency list

Large-Cap Cryptocurrencies

These are cryptocurrencies with more than 10 billion USD market cap. Companies with more than 10 billion USD market cap are classified *large-cap companies*. The price of cryptocurrencies that fall under this category does not fluctuate much, hence they have the least volatility.

According to Coinmarketcap data, *Bitcoin* (BTC) has the highest market cap. In fact it is the safest coin to invest in. But this does not mean it will yield the best Return on Investment (ROI). Other coins under this category are: Ethereum (ETH), Tether (USDT), Ripple (XRP).

Mid-Cap Cryptocurrencies

These are coins with market caps between 1 billion USD and 10 billion USD. Their market cap is lesser than those of large-caps. This also means they have more volatility than those of large caps. Mid-cap coins usually have more ROI than large-cap coins during bull market season. Also, they experience more severe price dump than large-cap coins during bear market seasons.

Some of the popular coins under this category are: Bitcoin Cash (BCH), Chainlink (LINK), Binance COin (BNB), Litecoin (LTC), Polkadot (DOT), USD Coin (USDC), Cardarno (ADA), Bitcoin SV (BSV), EOSIO (EOS), TRON (TRX), Crypto.com Coin (CRO), Wrapped Bitcoin (WBTC), Stellar (XLM), Tezos (XTZ), UNU SED LEO (LEO), Neo (NEO), etc.

Low or Small-Cap Cryptocurrencies

These are coins with market caps below 1 billion USD. They have the highest volatility. This means they can make you very rich during bull market seasons and can also wreck you during bear market seasons.

Some of the popular coins under this category are: Dai (DAI), Cosmos (ATOM), NEM (XEM), Filecoin (FIL), Huobi Token (HT), Binance USD (BUSD), IOTA (MIOTA), VeChain (VET), Dash (DASH), THETA (THETA), Ethereum Classic (ETC), Zcash (ZEC), Maker (MKR), Uniswap (UNI), OMG Network (OMG), UMA (UMA), Compound (COMP), Celsius (CEL), Ontology (ONT), FTX Token (FTT), Waves (WAVES), Aave (AAVE), Dogecoin (DOGE), yearn.finance (YFI), BitTorrent (BTT), HUSD (HUSD), Basic Attention Token (BAT), Synthetix Network Token (SNX), DigiByte (DGB), etc.

NOTE:

These are the coins under the various categories as of the time this book was written. Some low-cap coins may upgrade to mid-cap with time. Also, some mid-cap coins may downgrade to low-cap with time. To see the most updated list of cryptocurrencies according to their market cap, visit *coinmarketcap.com*.

Which Category of Cryptocurrencies are the Best to Invest In?

There is no direct answer to this question. Just know that each category or class of coins has its advantages and disadvantages. For example, large-cap coins have the most stable prices, but most times, has the lowest ROI, especially on short term investment.

Generally, *the larger the market cap of a coin, the more capital needed to change move the price, either up or down.*

For example, assuming you invested on a coin with a 10 billion USD market cap, the coin needs an extra investment of 10 billion USD to yield 100% profit. So the price of the coin cannot be easily changed. Now compare it with an investment on a low-cap coin, say 50,000 USD. A whale can easily move the price by 100% by investing 50,000 USD in the coin. But once the whale takes back his capital, the price of the coin will crash. This brings about the high price volatility of low-cap coins.

So what most smart investors do is this: *during bull market seasons, they investment more in low-cap coins with high growth potentials and enjoy high ROI. Then during bear market seasons, they save their capitals by investing more in large-cap coins, especially Bitcoin and Ethereum.*

NOTE:

This is not a financial advice. Make your own research before you invest in any cryptocurrency because crypto coins investment are high-risks high-rewards investments.

But do not for any reason invest all your capital in one cryptocurrency, no matter how promising it looks.

You can read more about cryptocurrency market capitalization from this article at https://blockgeeks.com/guides/cryptocurrency-market-cap/.

CENTRALIZED CRYPTO EXCHANGE TRADING GUIDE

In this section, you will learn the basic things to help you trade successfully and securely on centralized exchange apps. KuCoin and Binance apps were used for illustration because a good knowledge of the two apps can help to easily master any other exchange apps. The two apps have many common features and also some unique features. So study this section carefully!

How to Sign Up with Any Exchange Platform

Before you can use any centralized exchange platform, you need to first register with the platform and then login to the account. The sign up form for any decentralized exchange is very simple.

Here are some of the things you need to put in place before sign up with an exchange platform:

- **A Valid Email Address:** It is recommended that you create a separate email account specially dedicated to crypto trading. Use Gmail account. Whenever you withdraw or deposit funds into your account or login from another device, you will be notified via email.
- **A Strong Password:** Always create a very strong password that will be hard to guess. Don't use your phone number or date of birth. Ensure that your password contain alphabets; both lower and upper cases, numbers (0 to 9), and special characters.
- **Phone Number:** Most exchange platforms require that you bind a phone number to your account. This is for security purpose. You can dedicate a phone number for this purpose. But make sure that the phone number is always active.
- **A Two Factor Authentication (2FA) App:** 2FA adds an extra security layer to your account. This means that even if a hacker gets your phone number, username and password, the hacker cannot still login to your exchange account unless he provides a 6-digit time based passcode generated by the 2FA app. The most recommended 2FA apps are *Google Authenticator* and *Authy*. You can get them for free from Google or apple play store. We explained how to setup your 2FA app in another section of this book. **NOTE:** 2FA is not required during sign up, but will be required when you wish to add an extra security layer to your apps. Meanwhile, download and install the 2FA app on your mobile device.

Once you have put all these in place, go to the exchange website to sign up with them. Follow the screen to screen instruction. It is simple. You can sign up directly from the website and then download and login through the mobile app, or you sign up through the mobile app and then login.

Some of the 3 most recommended decentralized exchange platforms include:

- **Binance:** https://www.binance.com/en/register?ref=FZMGZJNX
- **KuCoin:** https://www.kucoin.com/ucenter/signup?rcode=2Qe8gbd&lang=en_US
- **Coinbase Pro:** https://pro.coinbase.com/

Spot Trading vs. Futures and Margin Trading

Crypto spot trading, futures trading and margin trading are not the same. They have similarities and differences which you need to know in order to know the one to dive into.

Spot Trading

When it comes to cryptocurrencies trading, spot trading is the most basic type of investment you can make. This essentially entails purchasing crypto such as Bitcoin and holding it until the value increases or using it to buy other altcoins that you believe may rise in value. At any point, you can decide to buy or sell any of these currencies against USDT, BTC or any other base coin (such as KCS in the case of KuCoin or BNB in the case of Binance), depending on the trends you see or the strategies that you have. Spot trades occur in the spot market and are characterized by the immediate or near-immediate delivery of the commodity, in this case cryptocurrencies.

For example, if you want to exchange your ETH to BTC, you'd go to the ETH/BTC spot market. Once your orders are filled, your coins will be swapped instantly. Spot trading is one of the easiest ways of trading cryptocurrencies, with the least level of risk.

Note that whenever we mention cryptocurrency trading in this book, we mean crptocurrency spot trading.

Margin Trading

In margin trading, you borrow money from an investment broker (third-party), and then use the borrowed money to buy more asset than you can normally buy on the same spot exchange, while paying daily interest fee to the lender. In effect, trading on margin amplifies results; both to the upside and the downside. You also make huge loss if the price of the asset goes south because the lender does not bear the loss with you. You still have to pay back the money you borrowed completely, plus the daily interest fee.

An exchange with margin is where you can trade with leverage, but you will pay a daily interest rate and bleed paying fees.

Margin refers to the amount of capital you commit from your own pocket. *Leverage* means the amount that you amplify your margin with. So, if you use 2x leverage, it means that you open a position that's double the amount of your margin. If you use 3x leverage, you open a position that's three times the value of your margin, etc.

Futures Contract Trading

A futures contract is a type of derivatives product that allows traders to speculate on the future price of an asset. It involves an agreement between parties to settle the transaction at a later date called the expiry date. The underlying asset for a contract like this can be any asset like cryptocurrency, commodities, stocks, and bonds. Future contracts trading is the most "advanced" type of trading.

In the Bitcoin derivatives market, Investors enter into an agreement/contract to buy Bitcoin at a predetermined price and a specified time in the future. If your guess is okay, you earn profit when the contract expires. Also, in futures trading, investors don't own actual bitcoins, rather they trade on the speculations of the market prices of Bitcoin. Bitcoin contracts which can either be futures, perpetual contracts, swaps, or options obtain their value from the value of Bitcoin.

In futures contract trading, there's no daily cost of interest (except in perpetual futures contracts). The futures contract will either trade at a premium or discount. When you place a trade on a futures contract, you will know exactly how much interest you will be paying over the life of the contract.

Which one should you go for?

As a new trader with little experience, I will recommend spot trading because it is less risky. In the case of loss, you only lose part of your capital.

Of all the three types of trades, margin trading is the most risky because in the event of loss, you will lose multiples of what a spot trader will lose, plus the daily interest fee you have to pay.

In the case of future trading, a small percentage drop in price can make you lose your entire capital if you chose a very high leverage. Also, you have to wait for the contract to expire before you can take your profit if your price guess is correct.

In summary, margin trading involves significantly more risk than spot trading. The same applies to future trading. Only experienced investors with a high tolerance for risk should consider margin and future trading.

You can check out this Complete Guide to Cryptocurrency Trading for Beginners article at https://academy.binance.com/en/articles/a-complete-guide-to-cryptocurrency-trading-for-beginners.

How to Set Two Factor Authentication (2FA) for your Exchange Apps

Two factor authentication is a extra security feature that is used to secure apps. After setting 2FA for any account, you will be required to provide a 6 digit code alongside your username and password. This 6 digit code is randomly generated by another app. The most popular 2FA app is *Google Authenticator* app. This means that even a hacker got your username and password, without access to this randomly generated code, the hacker cannot login to your account from any device.

NOTE: It is always recommended to activate 2FA for all your exchange app. Also activate 2FA for the emails you use in signing up with the exchange platform.

To Set Up Two Factor Authentication (2FA):

1. You need to download and install a 2FA app on your mobile device. The two most popular 2FA apps are *Google Authenticator* and *Authy*. You can get them for free from Google or apple play store.
2. Now open the exchange app or any other app you wish to secure. Go to **Settings** > **Google Verification** or **2 Factor authentication**.
3. Copy the setup key from the app you wish to secure. A setup key is usually a 12 or 16 digit code that will be required by the 2FA app in order to generate the random 6 digits passcode. Write down your setup key in a safe place so that if you lose your phone, you can easily setup a new 2FA app with it. Alternatively you can chose to scan the QR code with your 2FA app.
4. Now launch your 2FA app and tap the **+** sign to add a new account. Specify if you wish to scan a QR code or enter a setup key.
5. Enter any name as the account name. You can use any name of your choice that is associated with the account you wish to secure. For example, if it is your Binance app, you can type **Binance** as the account name. Paste the setup key you copied from the app you wish to secure. Then click on **Add**.
6. The 2FA app will generate a 6 digit code that is time based. Once the time elapses, a new code will be generated.
7. Copy the code and go back to the app you wish to secure to confirm that everything is working fine. Paste the 6 digit code. If you got everything fine, you will get a success notification.
8. So anytime you wish to login to the secured app, you must provide a 6 digit passcode from your 2FA app.

Different Ways to Buy and Sell Cryptocurrencies

To Buy a Cryptocurrency, you have 3 main options:

1. You can buy with a credit card from an exchange app. Most times, you need to complete your KYC (Know Your Customer) with the exchange platform before you can buy a crypto coin with your credit card.

2. You can exchange some of the crypto coins you bought earlier for the new one you wish to buy in your exchange platform.
3. You can also pay your trusted friends who are willing to sell their coin to you in your local currency. There are some other third-party sites that offer this service. But you need to be very careful. Make sure you trust the source before you make payment, else you will be scammed. If possible, look for apps that implement escrow feature so that the seller only receives your money once you have acknowledged that you have gotten the coin. You simply give them your wallet address of the coin you wish to buy.

To Sell a Cryptocurrency, you also have 3 main options:

1. You can sell it through an exchange platform. If you sold it for fiat money, you can cash out the funds into your bank account. If you sold it for another cryptocurrency, you can send the coins to your personal wallet. But make sure your wallet accepts those coins before sending the coin there.
2. You can sell to a friend who wants to buy the coin you wish to sell. Make sure you sell only to people you trust to avoid being scammed.
3. Also, there are third-party sites that buy cryptocurrencies, especially BTC at a fixed rate.

How to Use KuCoin Exchange App

You need to know how to use KuCoin app. It is easy, but there are some important features and tips you need to know in the app in order to trade successfully and securely with the app.

Mastering KuCoin App Home Interface

When you first login to your KuCoin exchange app, you will see the home page. Here, you will see the current prices of some popular cryptocurrencies like BTC, ETH and KCS in USDT. You will also see the top gainer and top loser lists.

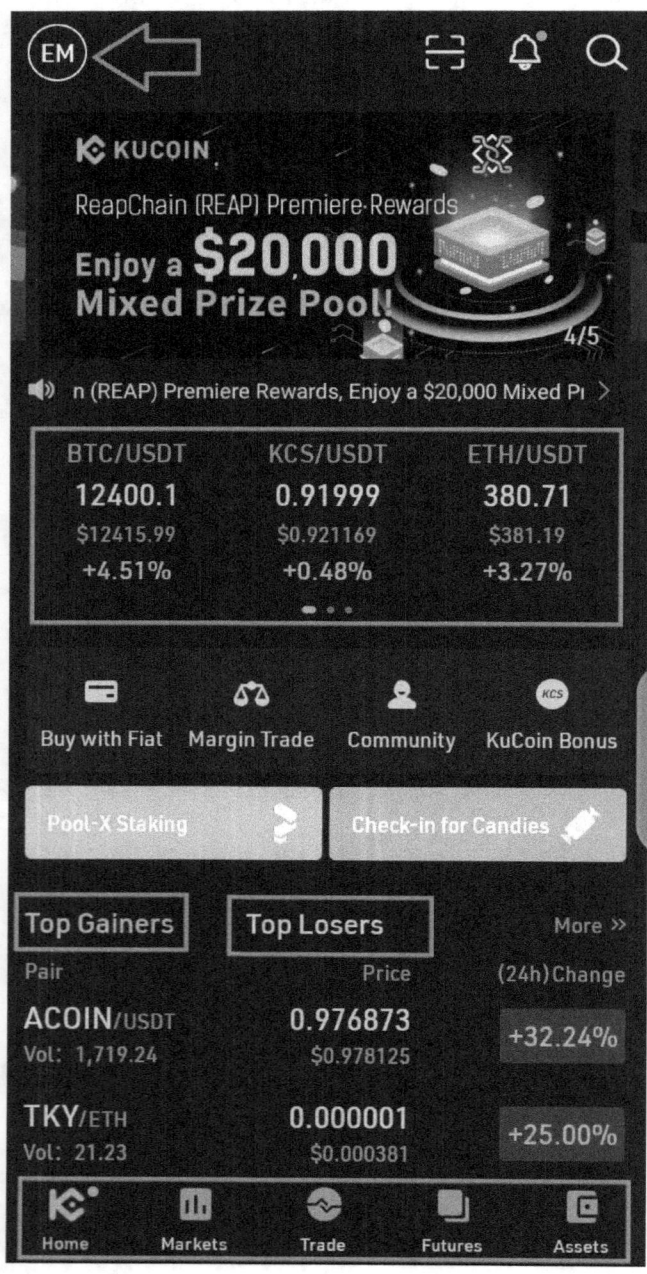

KuCoin home page

KuCoin App User Profile

At the top left corner of the KuCoin app home page, you will see the user profile link. When you click on the link, you will see some other important features like Settings, Security, KYC, History, Red Envelope, Invite friends (referral), My Bonus, KCS pay fees (80%) and Support.

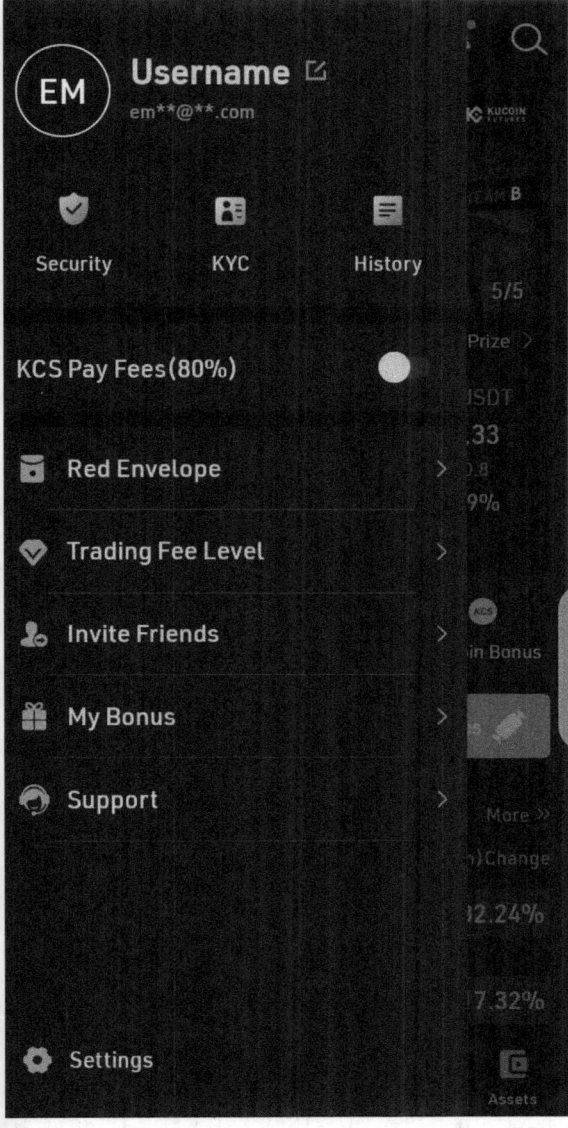

KuCoin user profile

KuCoin App Security Set Up Guide

Before you start trading with your KuCoin app, there are some security settings you need to setup. You can access KuCoin security settings from the home page, then click on the **user profile link > Security**. Below are some of the important security settings you need to put in place.

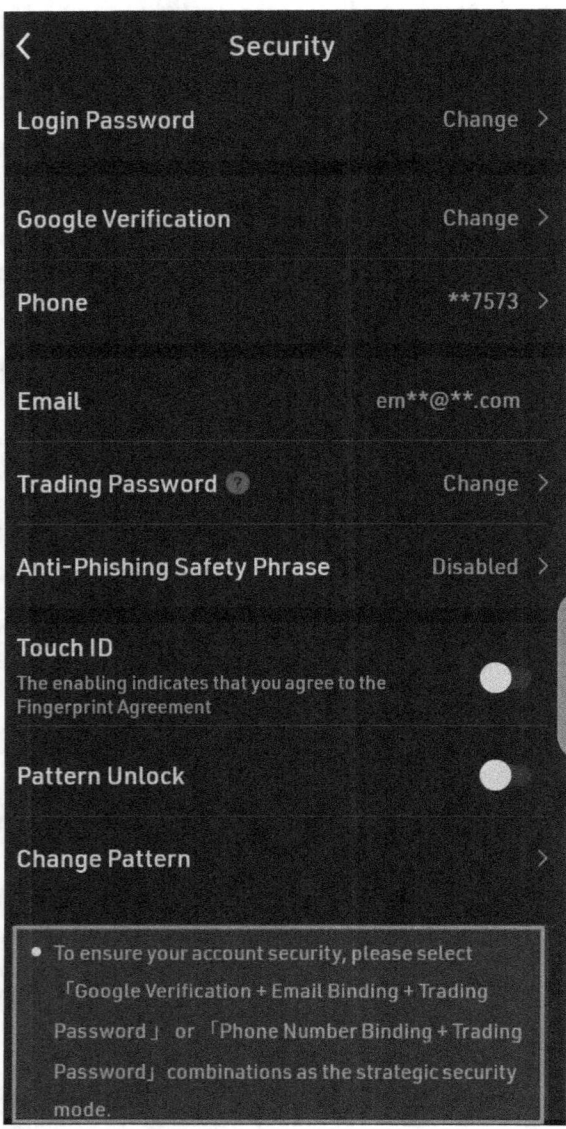

KuCoin security setup

- **Trading Password:** Before you can buy, sell or even withdraw any coin from your KuCoin app, you need to type your trading password.
- **Google Verification:** This is also known as two factor authentication. You need to set it up for your account so that if hackers hack your email address and your account password, they can't still be able to access your account from a new device or move out your funds without providing the time-based 6 digits passcode from your 2FA app. I have already explained how to setup 2FA for any app in this book.

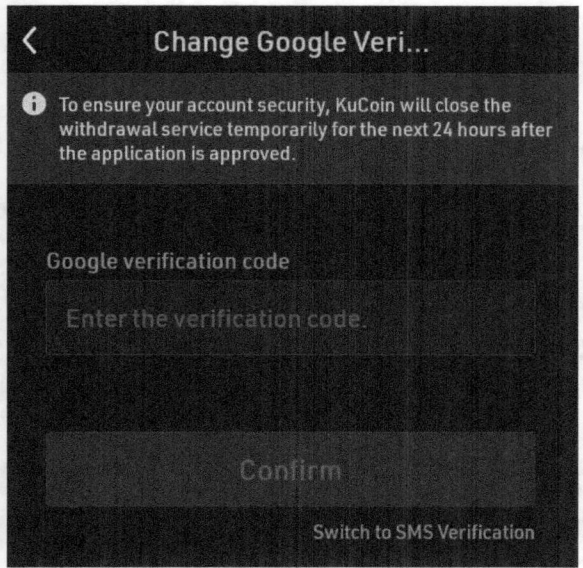

KuCoin google verification (2FA)

- **Phone Number Binding:** This is another important security feature. You also need to verify the phone number linked to your KuCoin account.
- **Email Binding:** You need to verify the email address you used for signing up with KuCoin. Before you can withdraw funds from your account, a verification link will be sent to that email address. Also other notifications will be sent to the email address.
- **Pattern Unlock:** When you activate this feature, any time you launch the KuCoin app from your phone, you must first draw your phone pattern before you can access your account. You can also create a unique pattern unlock for your KuCoin app. Only the person who knows your pattern can have access to your account.
- **Anti-Phishing Seed Phrase:** In order to prevent phishing emails and phishing websites, set your security anti-phishing safety phrase (for example a motto, etc.). When you log into the website or receive an email, it will be displayed in the email from KuCoin or login window. If it is not displayed or the safety phrase is incorrect, it means that you may have logged into a phishing site or received a phishing-email. In such cases, please do not proceed any further. Contact KuCoin support immediately for help.
- **Touch ID:** You can also use your phone fingerprint for extra security. It is an alternative to pattern unlock.

To activate any of these security features, click on the **user profile link** from the app **home** page > **Security** and then click on the desired security feature you wish to setup. Follow the screen to screen instruction.

NOTE:

There are some security combinations that KuCoin suggests that work best. For example:

- Google verification + Email Binding + Trading Password
- Phone Number Binding + Trading Password

The first option gives you the strongest app security. For each of the combinations, you can add Pattern Unlock or Touch ID.

You can learn more KuCoin security tips at https://support.kucoin.plus/hc/en-us/articles/360015207473-KuCoin-Security-Notice.

How to Use the KCS Pay 80% Fee Feature

When you click on the user profile link at the top left corner of the home page, you will see the "**KCS Pay Fee (80%)**" function. It is toggled OFF by default. Once you toggle it ON, the trading fee of any coin you purchase on KuCoin will be charged from your KCS token balance. For any crypto coin traded on the KuCoin platform, if you choose to use KCS to pay the trading fees, you will enjoy a 20% discount on the trading charges. This means that you need to have enough KCS token in your trading account to enjoy this discount.

NOTE:

- To calculate the trading fees, convert the coins into the equally valued amount KCS based on the conversion ratio of the quote currency and KCS exchange rate.
- The platform will provide a 20% trading fee discount for KuCoin VIP users based on their current VIP discount.
- Sub-accounts are provided the same "KCS Pay Fees" privileges as the Master account.

How to Change KuCoin App Default Currency

When you launch your KUCoin app for the first time, you will notice that the default currency is Yen (¥). When you deposit funds to your KuCoin account, your account balance will be shown in this default currency. You might want to change your app default currency to a currency that is more universal like USD.

To achieve that:

1. From the app home page, click the **user profile link** at the top left corner of the page. Then click on **Setting** located at the bottom.
2. Now click on **Currency** to change the app default currency to any currency of your choice.

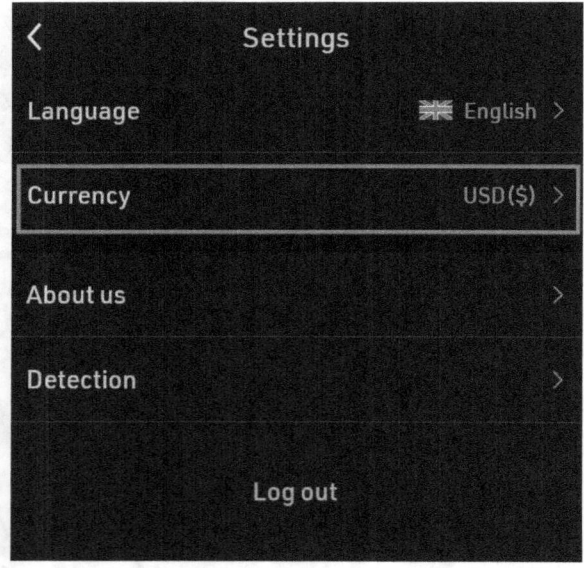

Change KuCoin app default currency settings

Important KuCoin Pages

At the bottom section of KuCoin home page, you will see 5 important tabs: **Home**, **Markets**, **Trade**, **Futures** and **Assets**.

Markets

KuCoin markets

The second tab is the KuCoin "Markets". This is where you see all the tokens and coins that are featured on KuCoin with their available trading pairs like BTC pairs, ETH pairs, KCS pairs, etc. You will also see the list of all the trading pairs you marked as "favorites" here.

By default, the app displays the **Spot** market. But if you are a margin trader, you can click on the **Futures** tab.

Trade

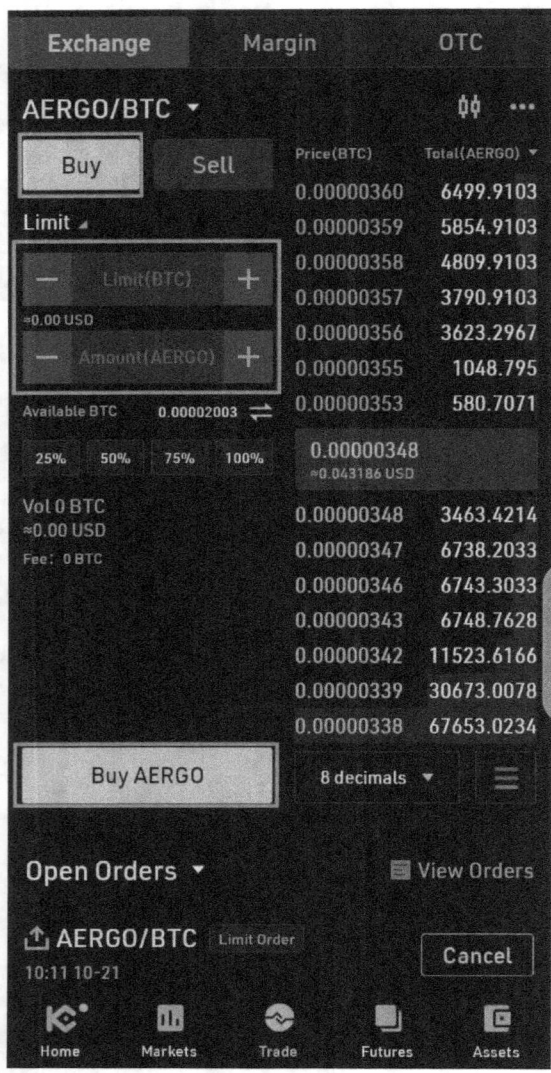

KuCoin trade page

This is where you buy and sell your coins. Now, you will see the order book for the crypto pair to guide you. On the right side pane, both **Buy** and **Sell** orders are visible. The orders in **Red** are the Sell orders while the ones on Green are the **Buy** orders.

To buy a coin, you activate the green **Buy** tab. Next, you input your choice unit buying (cost) price in the **Limit** box and the number of units of the coin you wish to buy in the **Amount** box and then click the green **Buy** button.

To sell a coin, you activate the red **Sell** tab. Next, you input the unit price you wish to sell in the **Limit** box and the number of units of the coin you wish to sell in the **Amount** box and then click the red **Sell** button.

KuCoin sell

To access KuCoin technical analysis tools, click on the **chart** icon at the top right corner. This will show you the price charts. You can select any chart you wish to study, such as 8 hours, 1 day, 1 week. To see more chart options click on **More**.

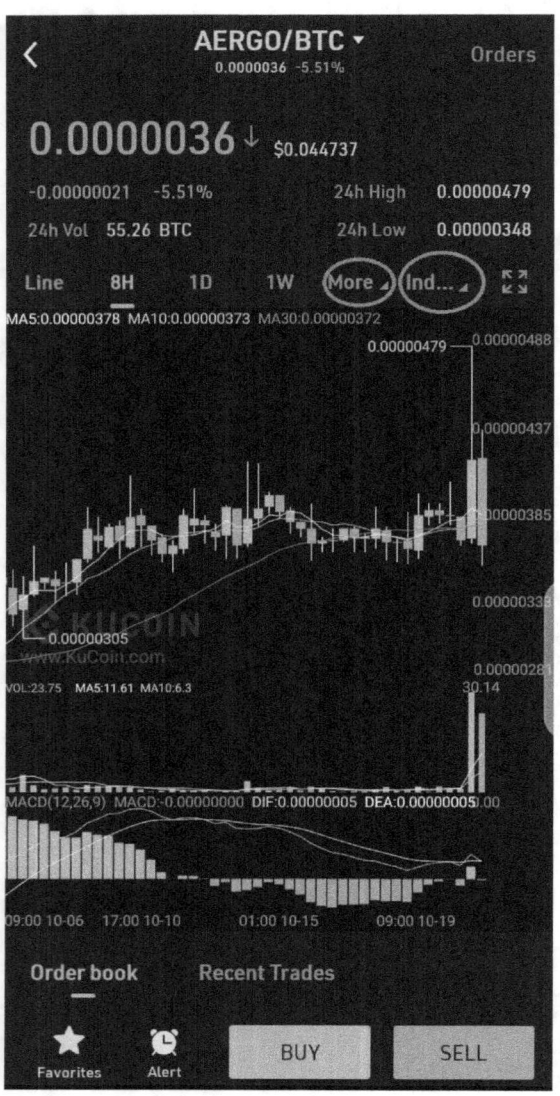

KuCoin price chart

To see all KuCoin available indicators, click on **Indicator** and then select the main and sub indicators you wish to use for Technical Analysis.

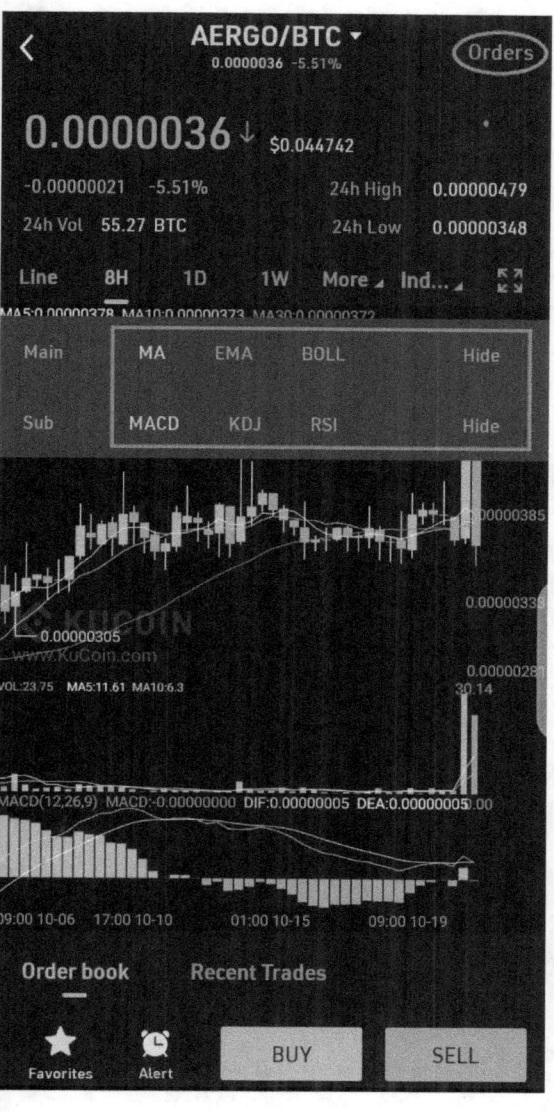

KuCoin indicators - TA tools

You can also access your order history by clicking on **Orders**. If you are a margin trader, you can click on the **Margin** tab.

In the **Open Order** tab, you will see all your buy and sell orders that have not been filled. You can cancel open orders individually or all at a time by clicking on **Cancel All**.

Any stop order you set will be seen in the **Stop Order** tab.

The **Order History** tab shows you all the filled orders you have made.

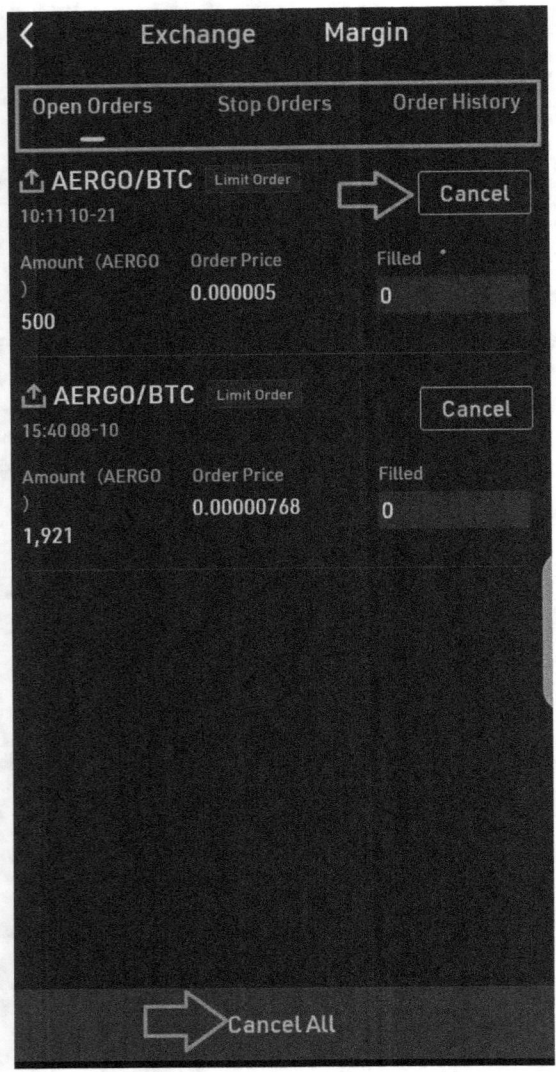

KuCoin orders

KuCoin Futures

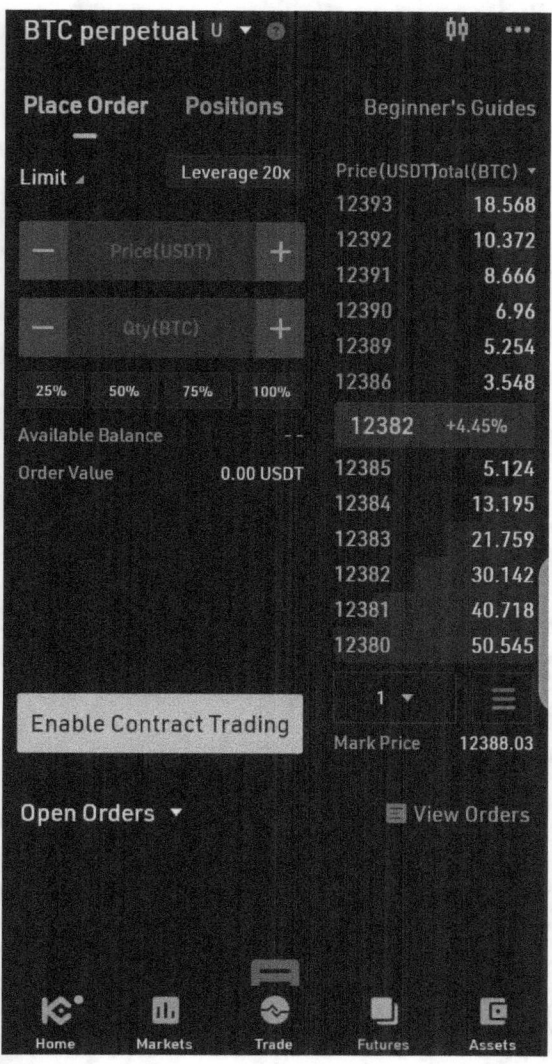

KuCoin Futures

The fourth tab is "Futures". Kucoin futures is also called *KuCoin Mercantile Exchange*. It is an advanced cryptocurrency trading platform which offers various leveraged futures that are bought and sold in BTC/USDT. Instead of fiat currencies or other cryptocurrencies, KuCoin Futures handles BTC/ETH only, and all the profit and loss are in Bitcoin/USDT.

A Futures in KuCoin Futures is an agreement to buy or sell a particular crypto asset at a predetermined price and a specified time in the future. In Futures market, you trade financial Futures with others at KuCoin Futures instead.

You can check out this beginner's guide to KuCoin Futures Trading at https://support.kucoin.plus/hc/en-us/articles/360039172094-Beginner-s-Guide-of-KuCoin-Futures.

Assets

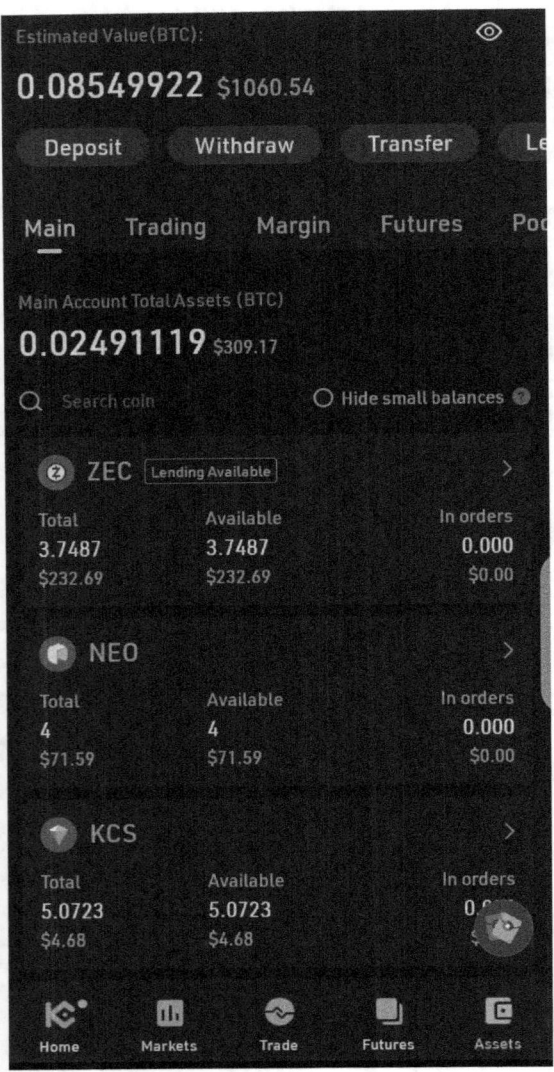

KuCoin assets page

This is where you see all your kuCoin assets; the coins you bought and the current value of the amount invested in each coin. For spot trading, you should only concentrate on the **Main** account and **Trading** account tabs.

When you fund your account, it appears on your Main account. But if you wish to trade with the fund, then you need to first transfer the fund to your trading account.

You can only withdraw funds in the **Main** account. So if the fund you wish to withdraw is in the **Trading** account, you need to first transfer it to the Main account.

When you click on any coin in the Main account tab, you will see the transaction history of that coin.

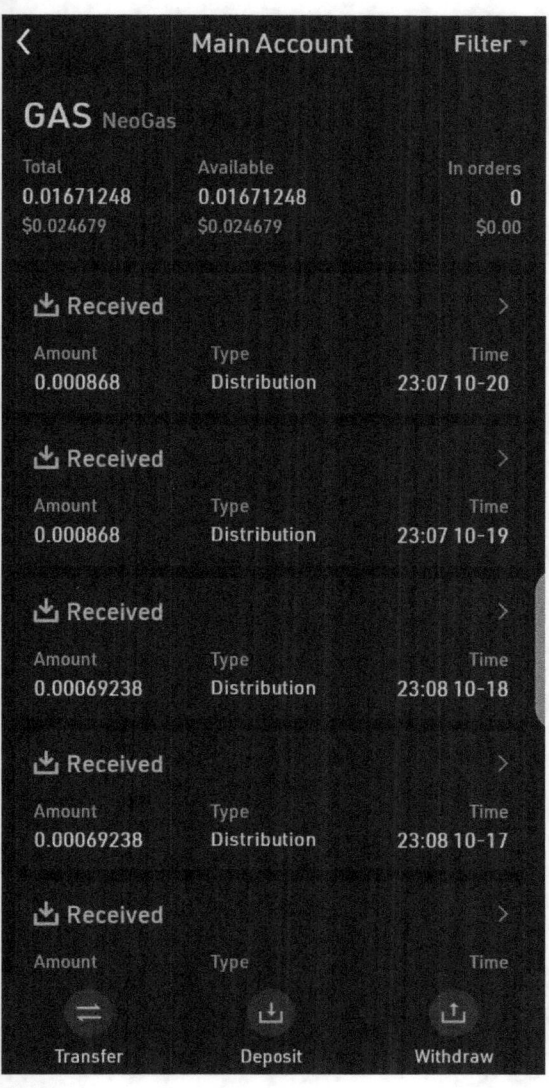

Transaction history

How to Transfer Funds between your KuCoin Main Account and Trading Account

1. From the **Main** account tab in the **Assets** page, click on **Transfer**.
2. Now select the coin you wish to transfer from your Main account to Trading account. If you wish to do it the other way round, click the double face arrow.
3. Specify the amount you wish to transfer. You can click on **All** to transfer everything.
4. Then click on **Confirm**.

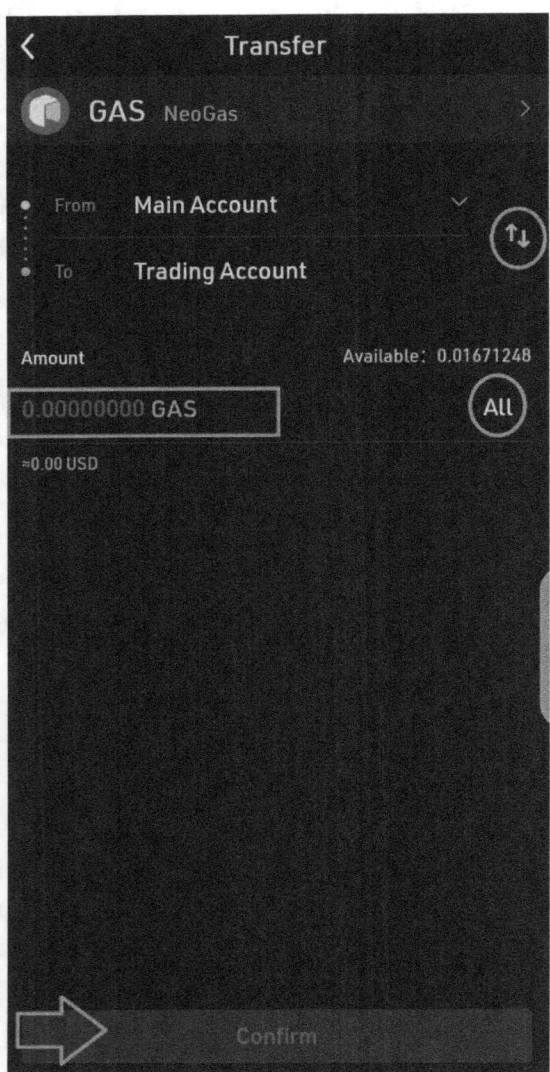

Transfer funds within your KuCoin accounts

How to Deposit Funds into your KuCoin Main Account

To deposit a coin into your KuCoin **Main** account, you need to copy the wallet address of that coin.

1. From the **Main** account tab in the **Assets** page, click on **Deposit**.
2. Select the coin you wish to deposit. You can simply search the coin.
3. KuCoin will display the wallet address of the coin. Copy the wallet address to your clipboard and then send it to the person who will send you the coin.

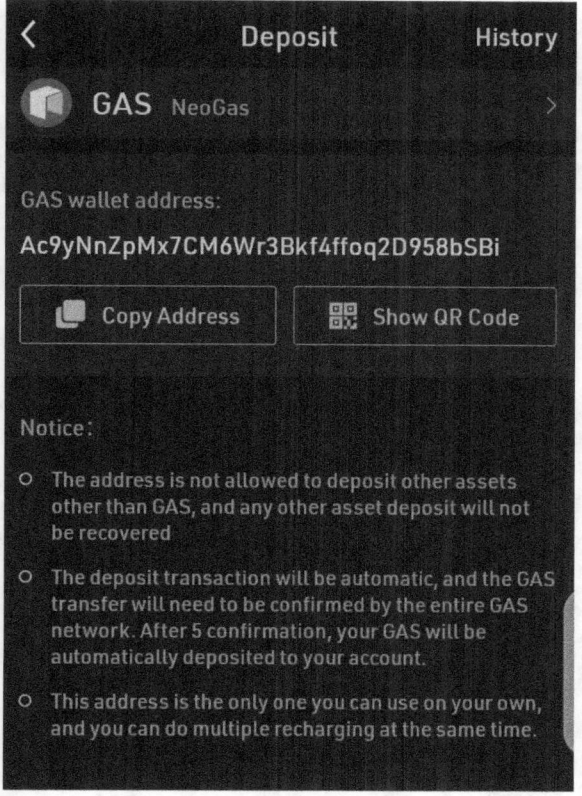

Deposit funds into your KuCoin account

NOTE: If you send the wrong wallet address to the fund sender, you will never recover the fund. So make sure you are copying the right wallet address. For example, if it is BTC, copy your BTC wallet address.

How to Withdraw Funds from your KuCoin Main Account

1. From the **Main** account tab in the **Assets** page, click on **Withdraw**.
2. This will take you to the withdraw page. Now select the coin you wish to withdraw.
3. Paste the recipient's wallet address. Make sure it is the wallet address of the same coin, else your coin will not reach the destination address and will be lost forever once you withdraw it.
4. Specify the amount you wish to withdraw.
5. Optionally, you make a remark.
6. Then click on **Confirm**.

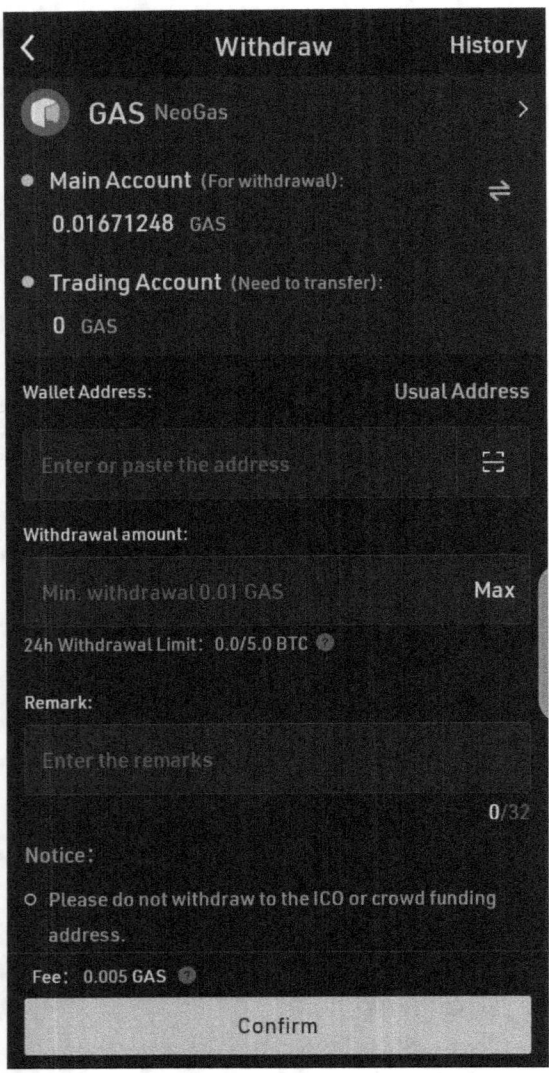

Withdraw funds from your KuCoin account

7. You will be required to type your trading password, click a verification link sent to your email and also provide the 6 digits passcode from your 2FA app. These are all security measures to ensure that only you can withdraw funds from your account.

These are some of the features and tips you need to know in your KuCoin app. Make out time to check around the app. You will learn more by doing so.

Guide to KuCoin Spot Trading

There are some things you need to know about spot trading.

- You can only buy a coin that is worth the balance you have in your trading account, unlike in margin and futures trading where you enjoy leverages.
- You can fund your account by buying BTC, USDT or any other base pair with your credit card, or pay a friend or third-party site to deposit a cryptocurrency equivalence of the cash you paid them.
- You only make profit if the price of the coin you bought goes up, else you lose a part of your capital.
- If you need to withdraw more than 2 BTC within 24 hours, then you must complete your KYC.

With these in mind, you are now ready to spot trade. For a step by step guide on KuCoin spot trading, check this article at https://support.kucoin.plus/hc/en-us/articles/360015207073-How-to-Make-a-Trade-on-KuCoin.

How to Trade Margined Futures with KuCoin App and the Web Version

The USDT-Margined Futures takes USDT as margin to exchange bitcoin or other popular Futures. For BTC-Margined Futures, it takes BTC as margin to exchange BTC Futures.

NOTE: Futures in the USDT-margined market are settled in USDT. While Futures in BTC-margined market are settled in BTC.

The table below will help you understand the difference between USDT-margined market and BTC-margined market.

Type	Margin	Pnl & Settlement Coin	Max Leverage	Supported Futures	Price Fluctuation
USDT-Margined	USDT	USDT	100x	Bitcoin Futures	Stable, will not be influenced by USDT price fluctuation
BTC-Margined	BTC	BTC	100x	Bitcoin Futures	Will be influenced by BTC price fluctuation

USDT and BTC futures trading

Below are the summary of the steps involved in KuCoin Futures Trading via KuCoin App:

- **Enable Futures Trading** on your KuCoin app.
- **Account Assets:** You can get cryptocurrencies via three methods on KuCoin App - Transfer, Buy Cryptos and Deposit.
- **Trading Futures:** There are three steps involved in Futures trading - Place an Order, Check Positions and then Close Positions. You can also Check Futures Portfolio and Check Orders.

For step by step guide on how to trade KuCoin futures via your KuCoin app, check out this article at https://support.kucoin.plus/hc/en-us/articles/360037940573. For guide on how to trade KuCoin Futures Pro (Website Version), check out this article at https://support.kucoin.plus/hc/en-us/articles/360039738293.

How to Use Binance Exchange App

Binance app is very easy to use. But there are some important features and tips you need to know in the app in order to trade successfully and securely with the app.

Mastering Binance App Home Interface

When you first login to your Binance exchange app, you will see the home page. Here, you will see the current prices of some popular cryptocurrencies like BTC, ETH and BNB in USDT. You will also see the top gainer and top loser lists.

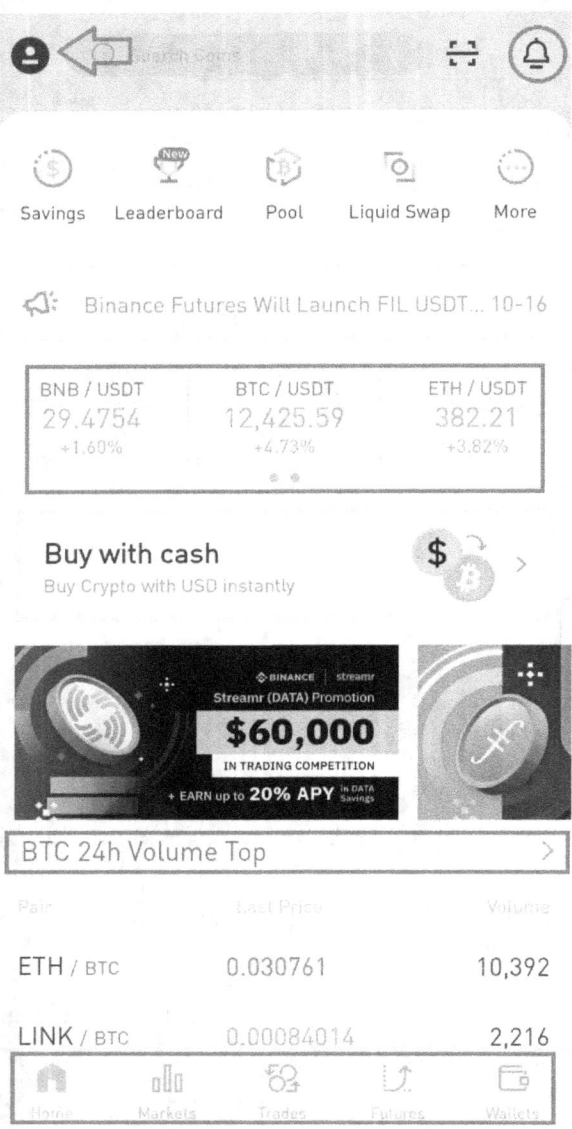

Binance home page

Binance App User Profile

At the top left corner of the Binance app home page, you will see the user profile link. When you click on the link, you will see some other important features like Using BNB to pay for fees (25% discount), Referral ID, Identity Authentication, Security, Payment Methods, Settings, etc.

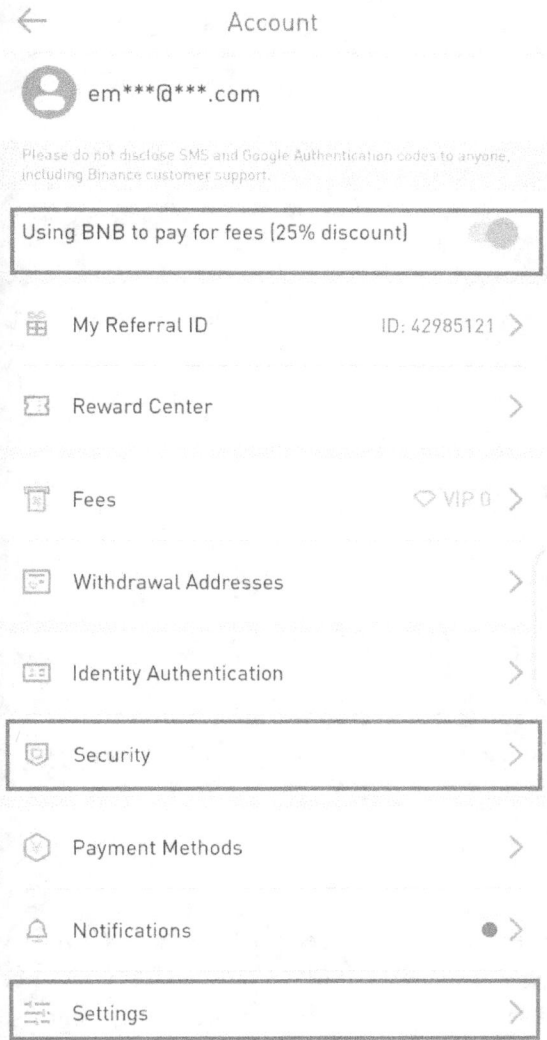

Binance user profile

Binance App Security Set Up Guide

Before you start trading with your Binance app, there are some security settings you need to setup. You can access Binance security settings from the home page, then click on the **user profile link > Security**. The important security settings you need to put in place are **Email Binding**, **Unlock Pattern** and **Google Authenticator**.

Before you can login to your Binance app for the first time, you are required to verify the email address you used in signing up with Binance exchange. That is email binding.

Like I said earlier in this book, Google authenticator provides a more trusted security than SMS authenticator.

NOTE: One key difference between KuCoin and Binance app is that Binance app does not have trading account and passwordas seen in KuCoin exchange app. So you need to tighten up your security in Binance app.

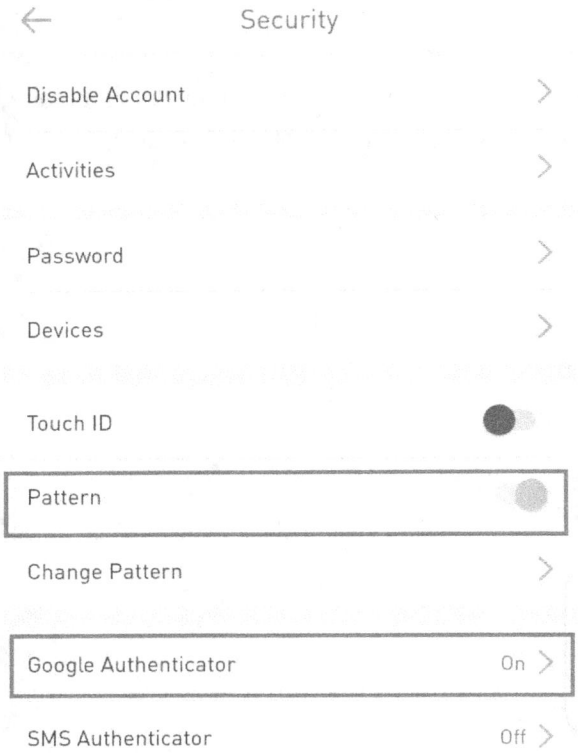

Binance security setup

I explained how to setup Google authenticator for any mobile app in this book. Follow the guide to setup Google authenticator for your Binance exchange app.

Also, create a unique unlock pattern for your exchange app. Don't use the same pattern used for unlocking your phone. But make sure you don't forget it.

How to Use the BNB Pay 80% Fee Feature

When you click on the user profile link at the top left corner of the home page, you will see the "Using BNB to pay for fees (25% discount)" function. Once you toggle it ON, the trading fee of any coin you purchase on Binance will be charged from your BNB token balance. For any crypto coin traded on the Binance platform, if you choose to use BNB to pay the trading fees, you will enjoy a 25% discount on the trading charges. This means that you need to have enough BNB token in your Binance account to enjoy this discount.

Important Binance Pages

At the bottom section of Binance home page, you will see 5 important tabs: **Home, Markets, Trade, Futures** and **Wallets**.

Markets

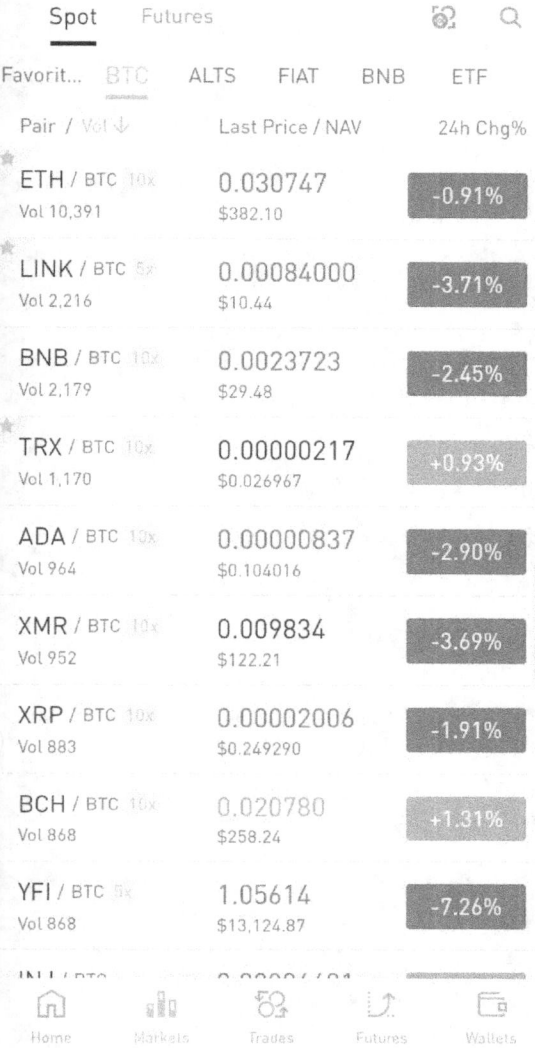

Binance markets

The second tab is the Binance "Markets". This is where you see all the tokens and coins that are featured on Binance with their available trading pairs like BTC pairs, ETH pairs, BNB pairs, etc. You will also see the list of all the trading pairs you marked as "favorites" here.

By default, the app displays the **Spot** market. But if you are a margin trader, you can click on the **Futures** tab.

Trades

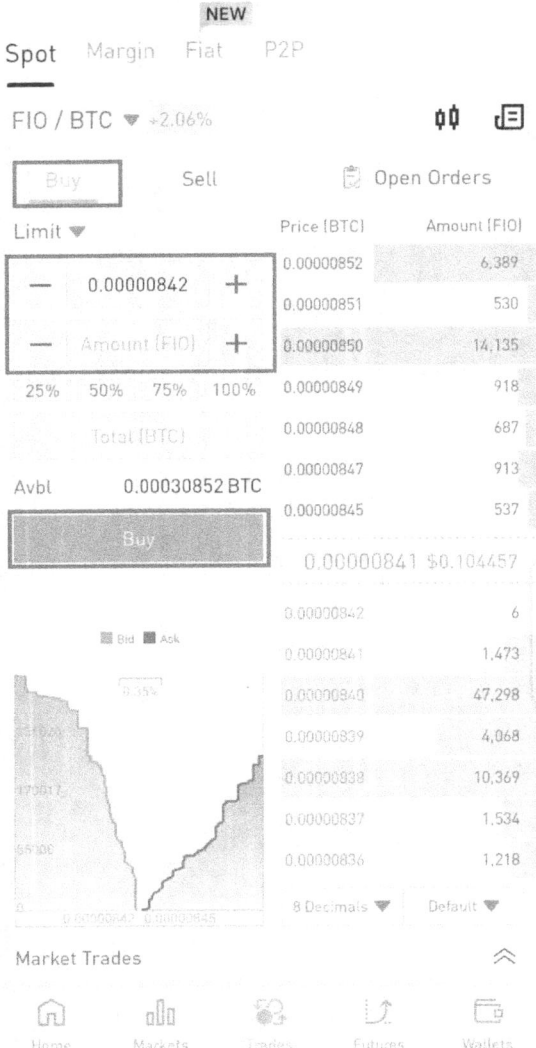

Binance trades

This is where you buy and sell your coins. Now, you will see the order book for the crypto pair to guide you. On the right side pane, both **Buy** and **Sell** orders are visible. The orders in **Red** are the Sell orders while the ones on Green are the **Buy** orders.

To buy a coin, you activate the **Buy** tab. Next, you input your choice unit buying (cost) price in the **Limit** box and the number of units of the coin you wish to buy in the **Amount** box and then click the green **Buy** button.

To sell a coin, you activate the **Sell** tab. Next, you input the unit price you wish to sell in the **Limit** box and the number of units of the coin you wish to sell in the **Amount** box and then click the red **Sell** button.

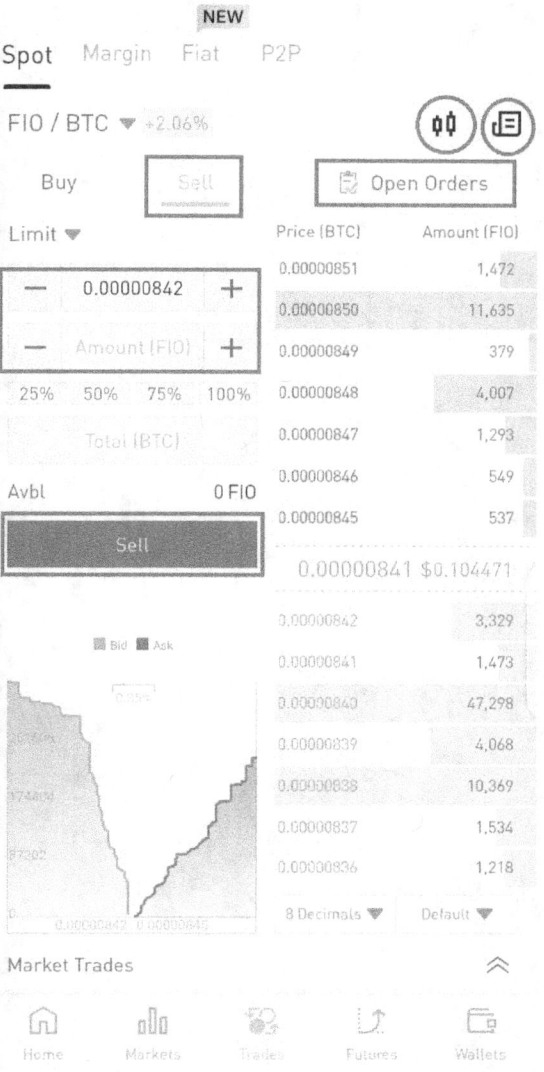

Binance sell

To see all your orders that have not been filled, click on the **Open Orders** from the **Trades** page.

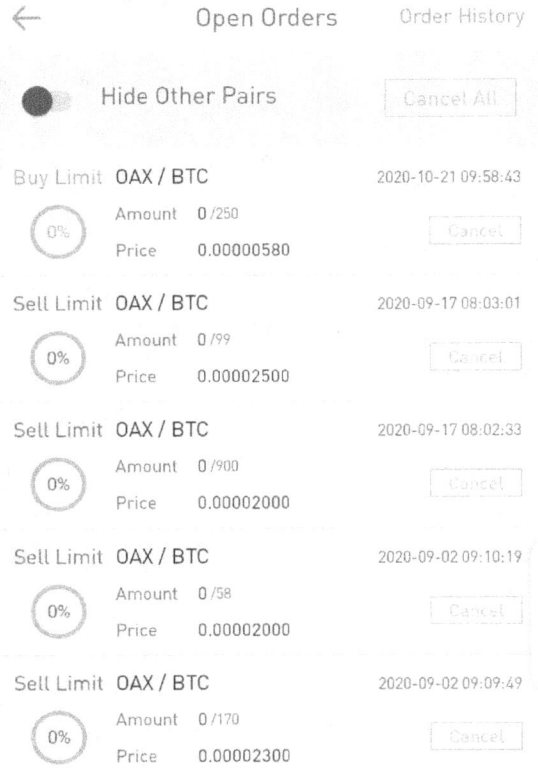

Binance open orders

To see your order history, click on the icon next to the **chart** icon on the **Trades** page.

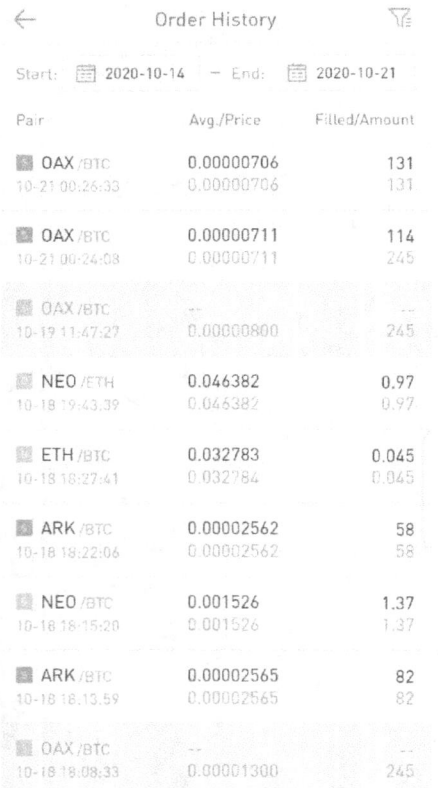

Binance order history

To access Binance technical analysis tools, click on the **chart** icon at the top right corner of the **Trades** page. This will show you the price charts. You can select any chart you wish to study, such as 8 hours, 1 day, 1 week, etc. by clicking the drop down arrow under **1 D**. To see more chart options click on **More**.

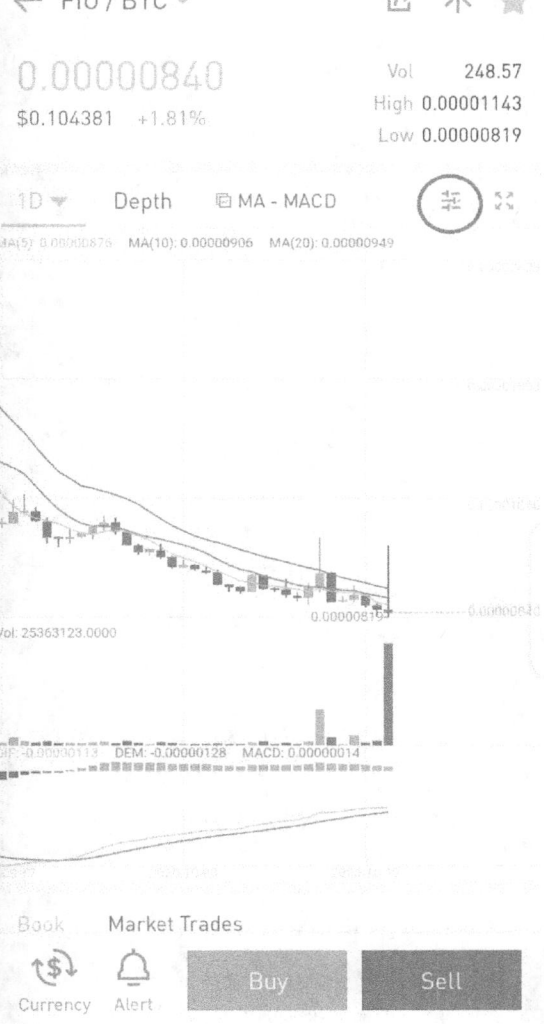

Binance chart

To see all Binance available indicators, click on the **Index Setting** icon and then select the indicators you wish to use for Technical Analysis.

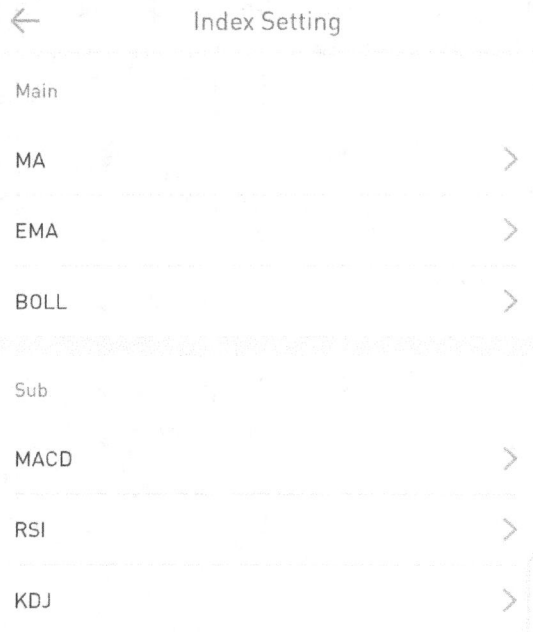

Binance indicators - TA tools

Binance Futures

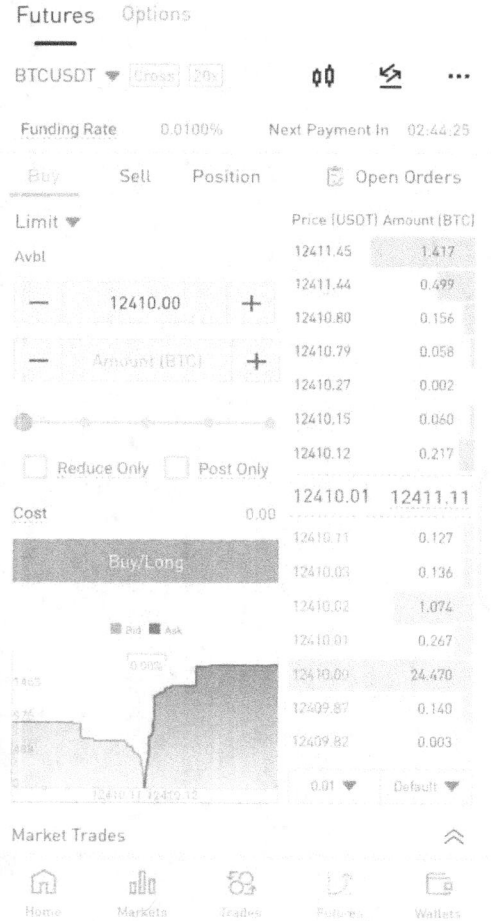

Binance futures

In Binance futures trading, you can participate in market movements and make a profit by going long or short on a futures contract.

By going long, a trader buys a futures contract with the expectation that it will rise in value in the future. On the other hand, a trader sells a futures contract to go short, to bet on prices to decline in the future.

On Binance Futures platform, you can go long or short with leverage to reduce risk or seek profits in volatile markets. You can check out this article on Beginner's Guide to Futures Trading at https://www.binance.com/en/support/faq/360039304272 for more details.

Wallets

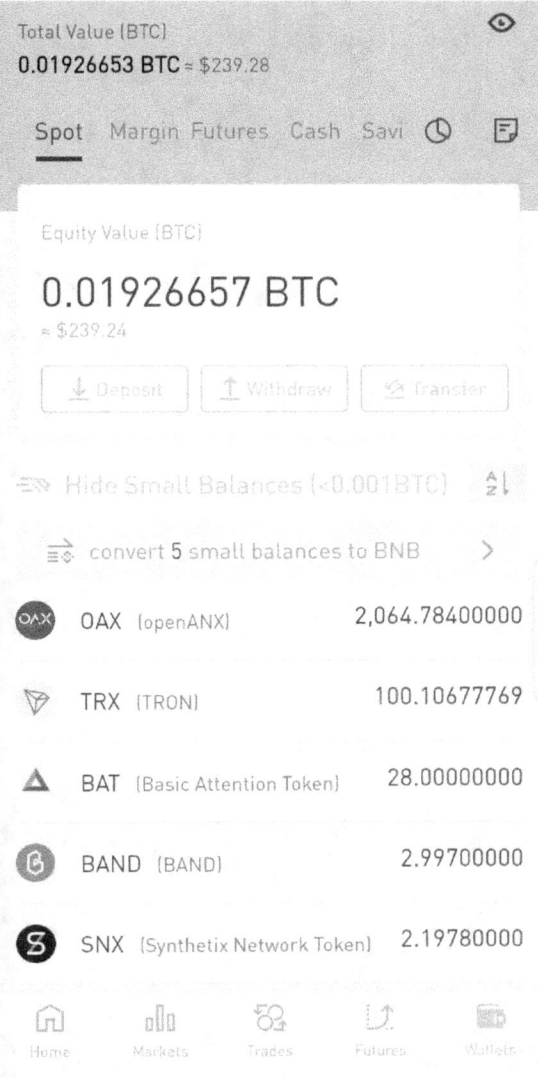

Binance wallets

This is where you see all your Binance assets; the coins you bought and the current value of the amount invested in each coin.

From this page, you can deposit funds to your account, withdraw funds from your account and also transfer funds from your spot trading account to your margin trading account.

How to Deposit Funds into your Binance Account

To deposit a coin into your Binance account, you need to copy the wallet address of that coin.

1. On the **Wallets** page, click on **Deposit**.
2. Select the coin you wish to deposit. You can simply search the coin.
3. Binance will display the wallet address of the coin. Copy the wallet address to your clipboard and then send it to the person who will send you the coin.

Binance deposit funds

NOTE: If you send the wrong wallet address to the fund sender, you will never recover the fund. So make sure you are copying the right wallet address. For example, if it is BTC, copy your BTC wallet address.

How to Withdraw Funds from your Binance Account

1. On the **Wallets** page, click on **Withdraw**.
2. This will take you to the withdraw page. Now select the coin you wish to withdraw.
3. Paste the recipient's wallet address. Make sure it is the wallet address of the same coin, else your coin will not reach the destination address and will be lost forever once you withdraw it.

4. Specify the amount you wish to withdraw.
5. Optionally, you make a remark.
6. Then click on **Withdrawal**.

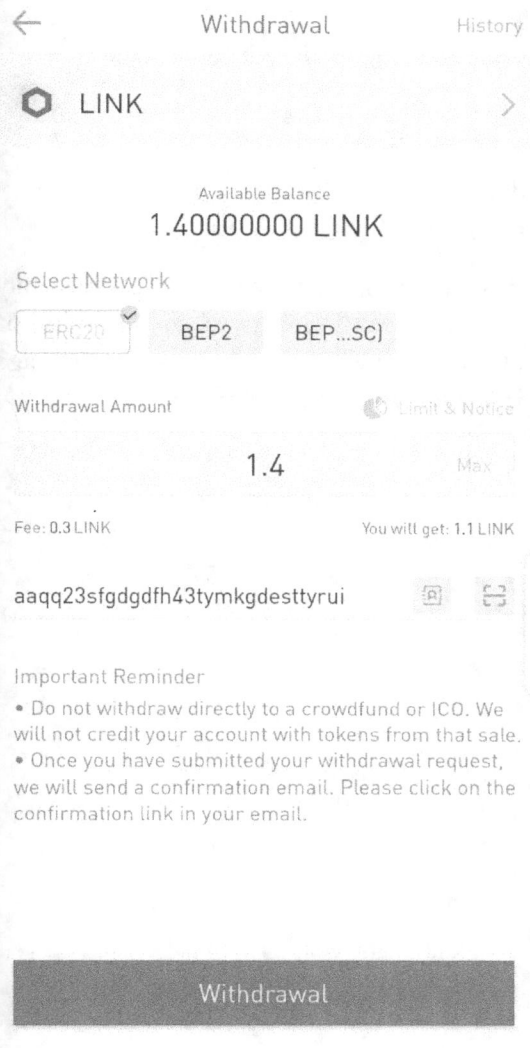

Binance withdraw funds

7. You will be required to provide the 6 digits passcode from your 2FA app and also click a verification link sent to your email. These are all security measures to ensure that only you can withdraw funds from your account.

These are some of the features and tips you need to know in your Binance app. Make out time to check around the app. You will learn more by doing so.

Guide to Binance Spot Trading

With all the Binance app tips revealed in this section, you can easily spot trade with Binance app once you follow the guide. But if you wish to spot trade via Binance website, then check out this guide at https://www.binance.com/en/support/articles/115003765031.

Guide to Binance Features Trading

Here are the basic steps to start trading on Binance Futures platform:

1. Deposit USDT/BTC into your futures account as margin.
2. Select the level of leverage you wish to use. You can choose leverages up to 125X with hedge mode.
3. Choose the appropriate order type (buy or sell).
4. Indicate the number of contracts you wish to own.

Check out this article for a step by step guide to tracing on Binance futures at https://academy.binance.com/en/articles/the-ultimate-guide-to-trading-on-binance-futures.

NOTE: The main difference between spot and futures crypto trading is that in spot markets, traders can only profit when the value on an asset increase. While in futures contracts, you can profit in both ways as the value of an asset rise or falls. But note that there are more risks in futures trading. Only experienced traders that can manage a high level of risk can trade futures contracts. If you are a beginner or a trader with little experience, stay away from futures trading. You can start with spot trading.

DECENTRALIZED CRYPTO EXCHANGE TRADING GUIDE

In this section, you will learn the basic things to help you trade successfully and securely on decentralized exchange apps and how to setup decentralized wallet apps. We will illustrate with Uniswap, Trust wallet app, Imtoken wallet app and metamask (PC version). Once you understand how to use these apps, then you can easily trade on any decentralized exchange app and also use any wallet of your choice.

NOTE: Before you can trade on any decentralized exchange platform, you need to setup and secure a decentralized wallet like trust wallet, imtoken wallet and metamask.

Private Key vs. Recovery Phrase

The private key of a wallet is different from its recovery phrase. You need to know the difference between the two.

Private Key

A private key is the most important information in crypto. Without your private key, you cannot access your crypto. You can compare it with the PIN of your debit card. Unlike the bank system where you can easily get a new PIN or debit card by calling your bank's customer care or visiting the bank, in the crypto world, nobody can issue you a new private key for a particular wallet.

For every public address, there is always a Private Key that is paired to it. These private keys give you full control over the public address (wallet address). So with your private key, you can send crypto or sign transactions. If you have the private key of any wallet address, then you basically have control of the specific address. And that is why, it is the most important thing you have to keep safe if you are handling your own funds.

Recovery/Mnemonic Phrase

The private key for every coin and token that is supported by the wallet is derived from its Recovery Phrase; a 12 to 24 word phrase. As soon as you start creating a wallet, you will be presented by the 12-word Recovery Phrase. So make sure to backup as this will be helpful if you need to restore your wallet.

Compared to a private key, a recovery phrase is easier to read for humans. Also, the use of recovery phrases enables crypto wallets apps to store multiple private keys with one recovery phrase. For example, you have a Ledger Wallet with Bitcoin, Bitcoin Cash and Ethereum on it; and each of these coins has its own private key. It is not necessary to save their private keys individually because by making a backup of your Ledger Wallet recovery phrase, you make a backup of all private keys on the Ledger Wallet.

There might still occasions where you need to backup the private key of a particular wallet address, especially if you have huge funds stored in it and wish to retrieve only that wallet address in another wallet app that is not Ledger wallet app, like ImToken app or trust wallet app.

NOTE: Always create an offline backup of your recovery phrases. Write them down and keep it secure.

How to Use Trust Wallet App

Trust wallet is one of the popular multi-chain decentralized ERC-20 wallet and DApp (Decentralized Application) browser. It is very easy to use.

Here are some of the amazing features of Trust wallet app:

- Fully functioning Web3 browser that can be used to interact with any DApp.
- Meticulously crafted tool that provides a seamless, simple and secure connection between you and any decentralized application (DApp) on Binance Smart Chain, or the Ethereum network.
- Integrated interface that is fully optimized for mobile so you can enjoy the content designed specifically for your device.

You need to download and install the trust wallet app in your mobile device. Go to https://trustwallet.com/dapp/. Scroll down and then click on the link to download the app from apple or google play store depending on your phone's OS.

How to integrate your DApp into Trust Wallet

Trust Wallet's DApp browser provides a simple API for DApp developers to create multi-chain applications. Currently, our API allows you to get accounts and sign transactions with both iOS and Android.

Learn More

Download trust wallet app

NOTE: Clicking the app download link from Trust wallet official website will ensure that you don't download the fake app from play store.

How to Setup a Private ERC20 Wallet using Trust Wallet App

1. Now go ahead to download and install the Trust Wallet app on your mobile device if you have not done so. After successful installation, launch the app on your mobile phone.
2. You will be required to create a new wallet or import a wallet if you wish.
3. If you click on **I already have a wallet**, you will be asked for the 12 recovery phrases. Once you provide it, it will be successfully imported.

4. If you don't have any wallet, click on **Create a new wallet**.

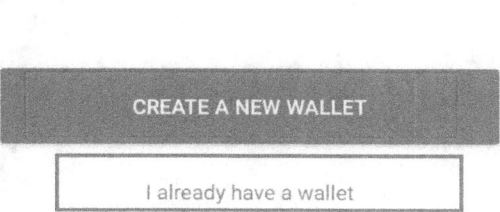

Create a new wallet or import existing wallet

5. Accept Trust wallet terms and click **Continue**.

Accept trust wallet terms and continue

6. In the next screen, your secret 12 words recovery phrase will be revealed to you. Write down the recovery phrase in the same order they appear on the screen and keep it in a safe place. Do not screenshot them. Make sure you don't lose it, else the funds in your wallet will be gone forever. Don't save it in your phone or online for security purposes.
7. Next, you will also be required to verify that you have backed up your recovery phrase, by providing the randomly asked recovery phrases. Once you are done with the verification, you will see Trust wallet home page. You will see the wallet name you created. Your new privately owned wallet address is under the name.

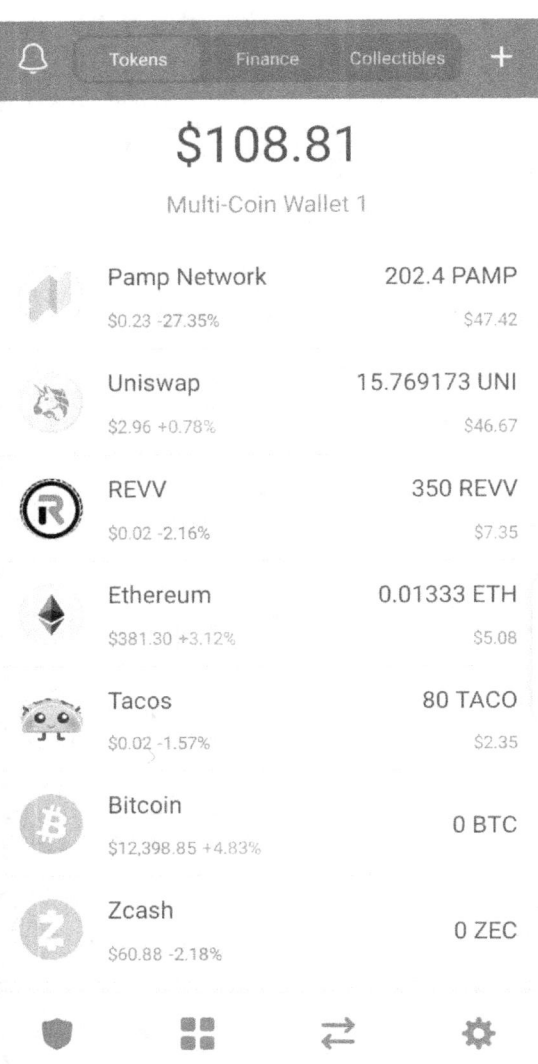

Trust wallet app home page

At the bottom section of trust wallet home page, you will find links to some of the important pages of the app like the DApp, Swap/Exchange and Settings.

How to Secure your Trust Wallet App

The first thing you should do when you install any app is to setup the security features, so that an unauthorized user cannot have access to your funds.

You need to setup a passcode for your Trust wallet app. So that anytime you launch the app on your mobile device, you will need the passcode or your fingerprint to unlock the app.

To setup trust wallet passcode:

Click on the **Settings** icon (the last icon on the bottom section of trust wallet home page). Then click on **Security**.

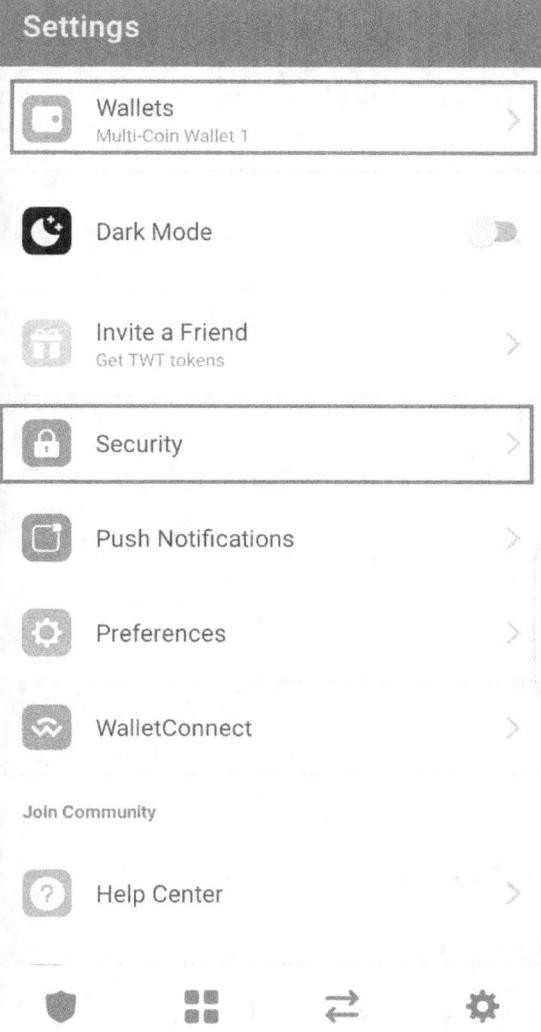

Trust wallet security

Toggle **Passcode** ON. You will be asked to add a 6-digit passcode and may also be required to verify your mobile device finger print.

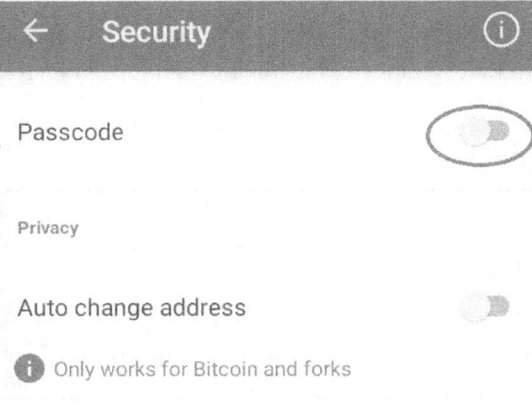

Setup trust wallet passcode

How to Import/Create Multiple Wallets in Trust Wallet App

Trust wallet allows you to create, import and manage multiple wallets from a single app.

To import/create another wallet in trust wallet app:

1. Click on the **Settings** icon (the last icon on the bottom section of trust wallet home page). Then click on **Wallets**.
2. You will see all the wallets you created or imported to trust wallet app. To create add a new wallet, click the + sign.

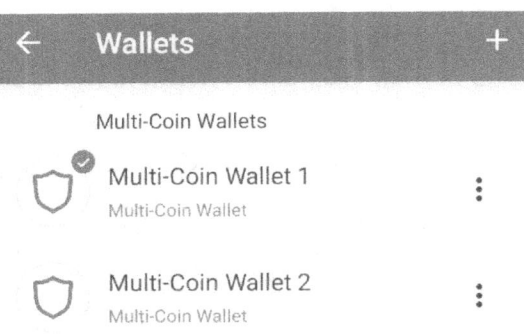

Import or create multiple wallets in trust wallet app

3. Specify if you wish to create a new wallet or import an existing wallet. Then follow the screen to screen guide to import/create another wallet.
4. Also note that each wallet has its unique 12 words recovery phrase. So make sure you distinguish these recovery phrases while safe-keeping them.

How to Add/Remove a Token from Trust Wallet App Home Page

1. To add a token to your app home page, click on the + sign at the top right corner of the app home page.
2. You can search for the token by name or by contract address.
3. Once you find the token, toggle it ON. It will automatically be listed on your app home page.

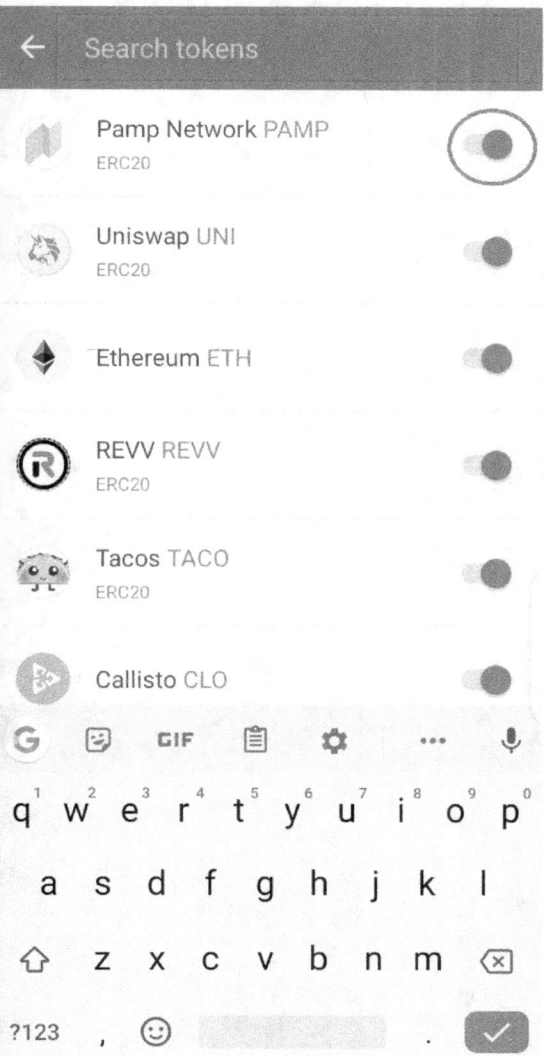

Search for the token and toggle it ON

4. To remove a token from the home page, simply search for the token and toggle it OFF.

How to Deposit and Withdraw Tokens with your Trust Wallet App

You can easily send and receive tokens with trust wallet app.

To deposit tokens:

1. You need to copy the wallet address of the token you wish to receive and then send the wallet address to the sender.
2. Add the token you wish to receive in your app home page. Now click on the token from the home page.
3. Specify if you wish to send or receive the token. In this case, you are receiving, so click on **Receive**.

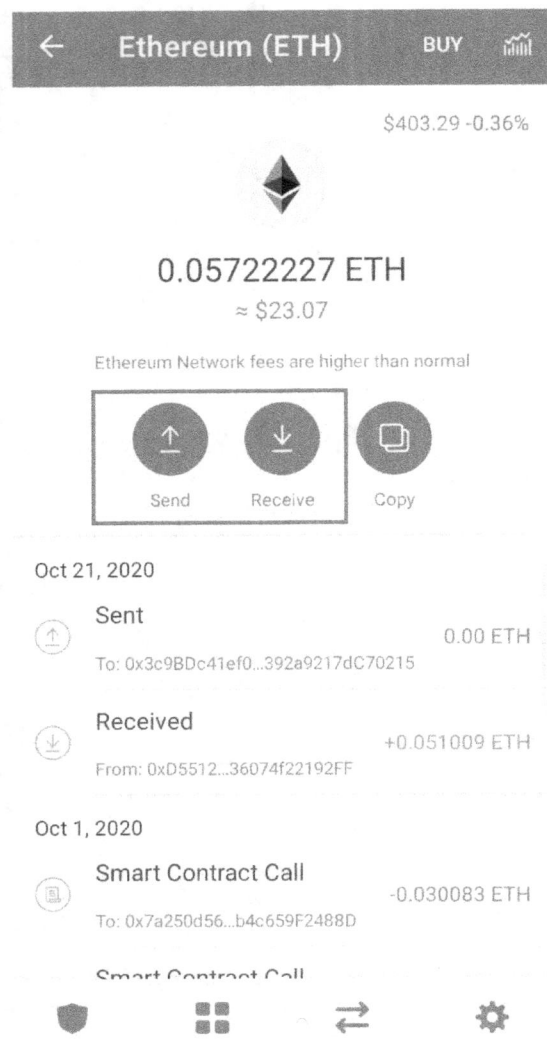

Specify if you wish to send or receive the token

4. You will now see the wallet address of the token. Click on **Copy** to copy it to your clipboard. Send the copied wallet address to the sender.

Copy the wallet address

After the sender has sent the token to your address the crypto network of the token verifies the transaction, trust wallet will notify you and the token will reflect in your balance.

To send a token:

1. You need to first get the token wallet address of the receiver. Copy it to your clipboard.
2. Add the token you wish to receive in your app home page. Now click on the token from the home page.
3. Next, click on **Send**.
4. Paste the receiver's token address and then specify the amount you wish to send. The miner fee will be displayed. Then click on **Next**.

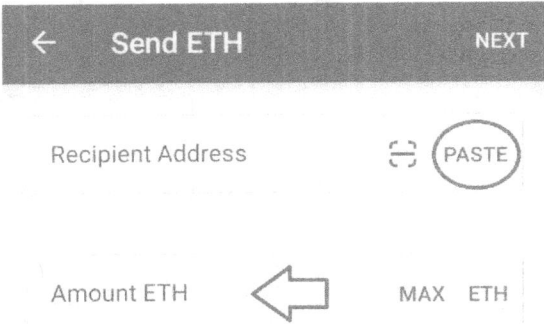

Paste the wallet address of the receiver and specify the amount

5. Next, confirm that you wish to send the amount to the receiver. The amount you sent plus the miner fee will be deducted from your balance. Once the transaction is verified, the receiver will be notified and the amount you sent will reflect in the receiver's balance.

How to Trade with Trust Wallet Built-In DEX

Trust wallet app has a built-in DEX you can use to **exchange** and **swap** tokens. The exchange section of the DEX resembles the trade section of centralized exchange apps.

The Token Exchange Section

Trust Wallet connects directly to Binance DEX (https://www.binance.org) in order to process your trades in the built-in DEX. Note that the **Exchange** option is only available for BNB to BEP2 tokens trading. Also note that for each transaction you make on the Exchange, you pay a network fee.

To use the Exchange section:

1. Launch your trust wallet app. At the bottom section of the home page, click on the **Swap/Exchange** tab.
2. Now click the **Exchange** tab to activate it.

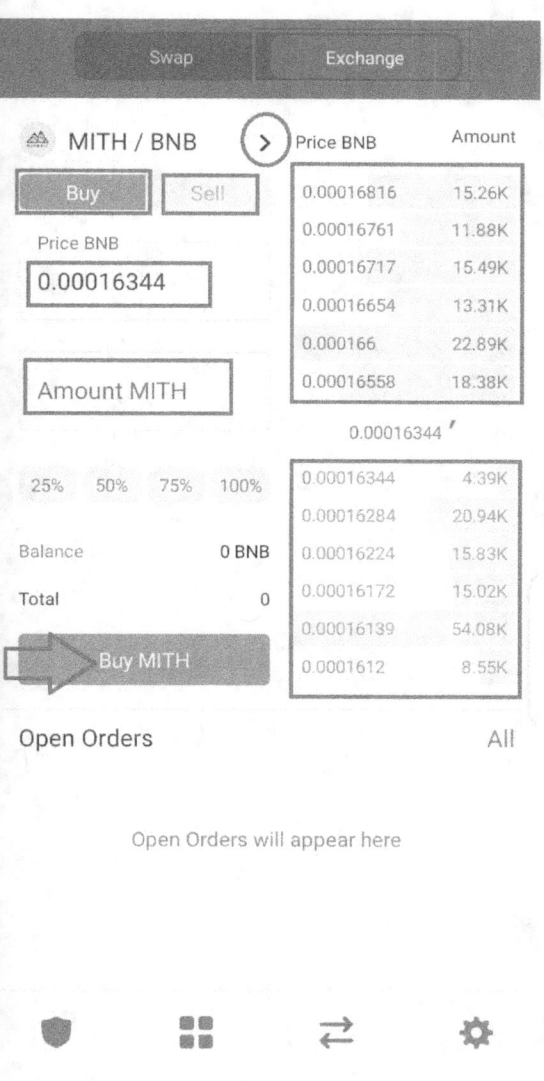

Click the Exchange tab

3. Next is to select a trading pair. Tap the arrow beside the default trading pair on the upper left, which is usually MITH/BNB. Search for the pair you wish to trade in the available markets and select it.

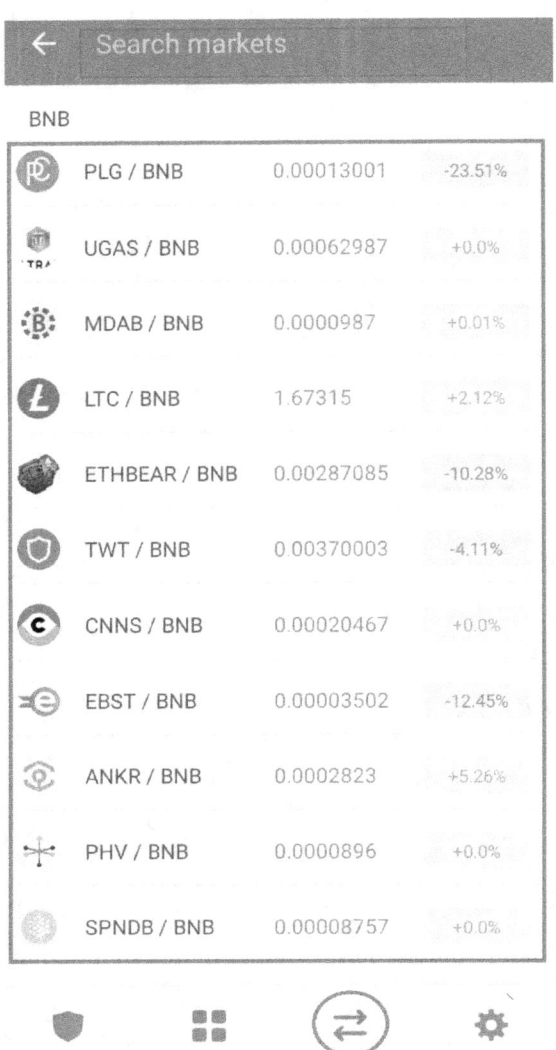

Select a trading pair

Note that if you did not see the trading pair you searched, then it means that it is not yet listed on the DEX.

4. Now, you will see the order book for the crypto pair to guide you. On the right side pane, both **Buy** and **Sell** orders are visible. The orders in **Red** are the Sell orders while the ones on Green are the **Buy** orders.
5. Next is to create a buy order. The Buy order section. If you do not intend to buy the lowest Sell order, just indicate the price per token and the amount on their fields. Tap any existing Sell order to automatically use the order price.
6. For sell order, tap on the **Sell** tab under the desired trading pair. Indicate the price per token and the amount on the space provided. You can also tap on an existing Buy order to automatically indicate use the order price.
7. Now, after specifying the order price and amount to buy or sell, tap the **Buy** or **Sell** button as the case may be.
8. Next, confirm the transaction. You will then be notified that the transaction is successful.

The Token Swap Section

The Swap section provides a more simplified method of buying and selling tokens from trust wallet app. ETH Swaps go via the Kyber Network integration, while the BNB Swaps go via Binance DEX. Also note that you can do swaps to any token of the same chain. All Swap transactions require a network fee.

To use the Exchange section:

1. Launch your trust wallet app. At the bottom section of the home page, click on the **Swap/Exchange** tab.
2. The **Swap** tab is usually activated by default. If it is not, click on it to activate it.

Activate the Swap tab

3. Next is to set these two parameters: **You Pay** and **You Get**. **You Pay** is the token that you currently have. While **You Get** is the token you want to receive in exchange with the one you have.
4. Now select the **You Pay** and **You Get** tokens by clicking the small arrow pointing to the right of each.
5. Next is to set the **You Pay** amount. You can decide on how much tokens you would like to swap, but there will be an automatic conversion rate that will give you an estimate of how much tokens you will receive.

Note that there are limits on the amount you can buy or sell. You can only buy in multiples of 10, 100, etc.

6. After setting the **You Pay** amount, tap on **Next**. Now confirm the transaction by clicking on **Send**. The confirmation time will depend on the swap you did. ETH swaps usually need confirmation from the miners. While BNB swaps are almost instantly. Trust wallet will notify you once the swap is complete. The token will also reflect in your wallet balance.

You can see more details on how to use trust wallet built-in DEX at https://community.trustwallet.com/t/how-to-trade-with-the-built-in-dex/169.

How to Use ImToken Wallet App

ImToken wallet app is a multi-chain asset management, decentralized exchange and DApp browser, an alternative to Trust wallet app. It is also very easy to use.

Here are some of the amazing features of ImToken wallet app:

- **Multi Coin Wallets Management:** Manage your BTC, ETH, EOS, ATOM, BCH, TRX, LTC, CKB tokens.
- **Built-in Token Exchange:** Enjoy the secure, reliable and seamless mobile trading experience.
- **Carefully guarding your assets:** Offline signature is more secure with imKey Pro hardware wallet.

You need to download and install the trust wallet app in your mobile device. Go to https://token.im/. Then click on the link to download the app from apple or google play store depending on your phone's OS.

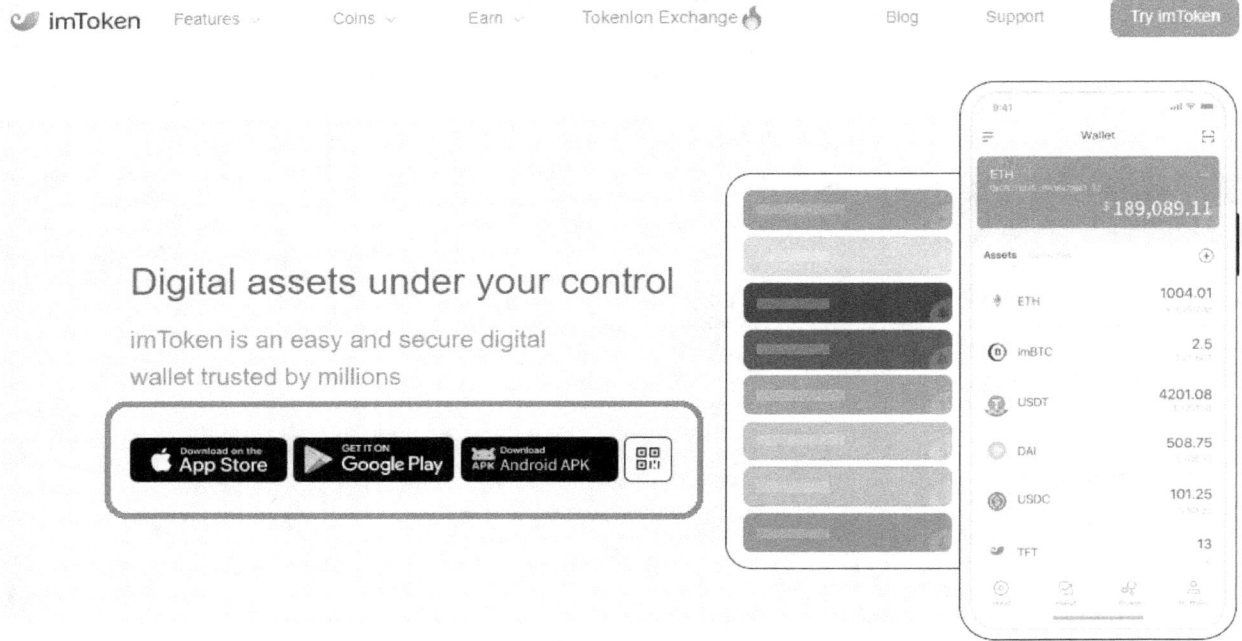

Download ImToken wallet app

NOTE: Clicking the app download link from Trust wallet official website will ensure that you don't download the fake app from play store.

ImToken Security Tips

ImToken offers some security features that are not available in most multi-chain wallet apps like Trust wallet.

- Each wallet created or imported into ImToken has a password which is required before you transact with any wallet address in that wallet. So make sure you create a very strong password when creating or importing a wallet.
- Also, ImToken gives you access to both your private key and recovery phrase. This means you can easily recover both in case you lose where you backed them up, but still have access to the wallet through ImToken app. It is recommended that you backup both your private key and recovery phrase.

How to Setup a Private ERC20 Wallet using imToken App

1. Now go ahead to download and install the ImToken app on your mobile device if you have not done so. After successful installation, launch the app on your mobile phone.
2. You will be required to create a new wallet or import a wallet if you wish.
3. If you click on **Import**, you will be asked for the 12 recovery phrases, mnemonic phrase (or private key). Once you provide it, it will be successfully imported. You will also need to create a password for the wallet, which will be required before you can perform any transaction with the wallet.
4. If you don't have any wallet, click on **Create Wallet**.
5. Type a name for your wallet. This can be any name you choose.
6. Type a password for your wallet. The password will be required before you can perform any transaction with the wallet. So create a very strong password that you don't use anywhere else, and don't forget it. Optionally, you can type a password hint, but make sure it does not reveal your password.
7. Accept ImToken Terms of Service and Privacy. Then click **Create Wallet**.
8. Next is to back up your recovery phrase. Click on **Next** and **Understood**.

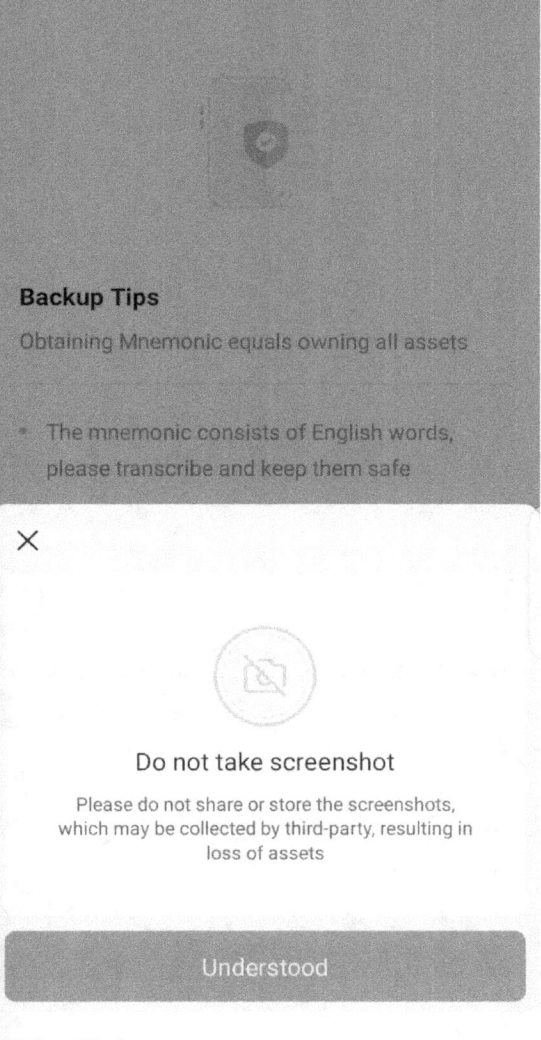

Click on Understood

9. In the next screen, your secret 12 words recovery phrase will be revealed to you. Write down the recovery phrase in the same order they appear on the screen and keep it in a safe place. Do not screenshot them.

Make sure you don't lose it, else the funds in your wallet will be gone forever. Don't save it in your phone or online for security purposes.

10. Next, you will also be required to verify that you have backed up your recovery phrase, by providing the randomly asked recovery words. Click on **Confirmed backup**.

Confirm the mnemonic phrase backup

11. Once you are done with the verification, you will see ImToken wallet home page. You will see the wallet name you created. Your new privately owned wallet address is under **Assets**.

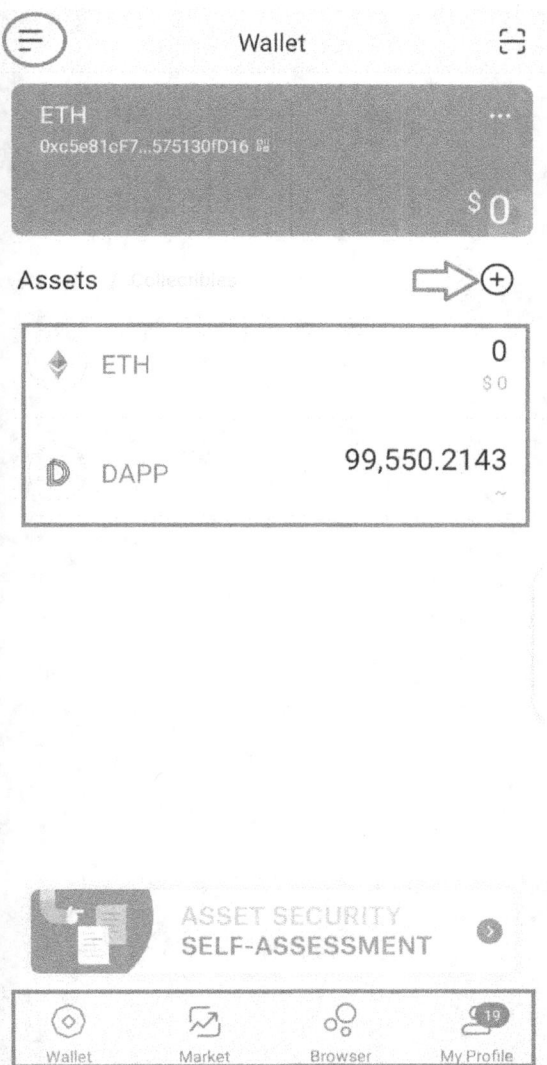

ImToken app home page

At the bottom section of trust wallet home page, you will find links to some of the important pages of the app like Wallet (home page), Market, Browser and My Profile.

When you create an ETH wallet in ImToken, you can activate some other wallet addresses. To see the available wallet addresses under your wallet, click on the **Select wallet** link at the top left corner of the ImToken home page.

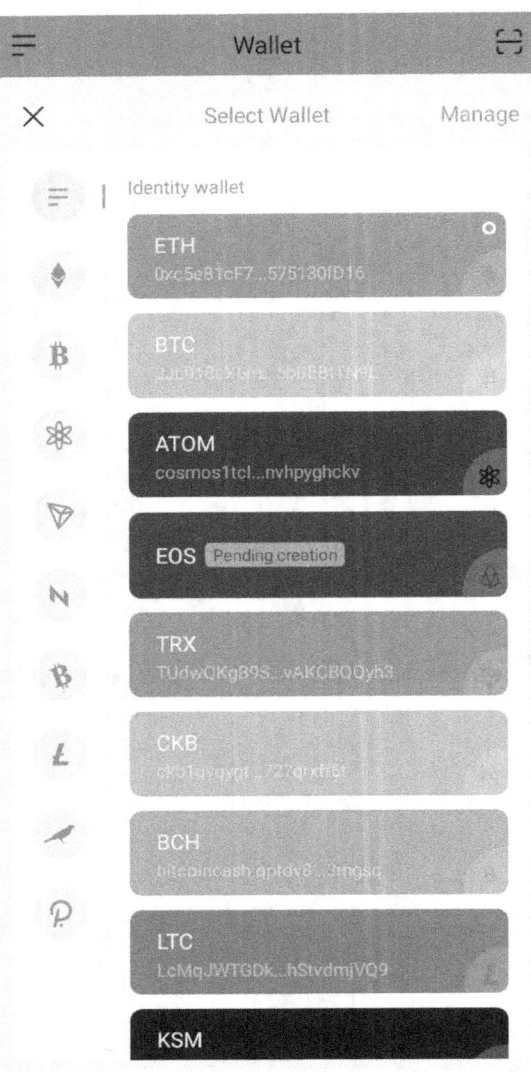

The available wallet addresses

The first wallet you created or imported in ImToken is called *Identity wallet*. Any other wallets you create or import later can be seen when you scroll down.

NOTE:

- You can only recover the mnemonic phrase of wallets you created with ImToken. You cannot recover the mnemonic phrase of imported wallets.
- You will also notice that EOS token is listed by default, but has a pending creation label. This is because EOS utilizes an account system with a resource staking mode, any actions executed on the EOS blockchain consumes resources, including the creation of EOS accounts. To complete the EOS account creation process, another EOS wallet with sufficient EOS is required to pay for the required resources. Check out the step by step guide to create EOS account and wallet in ImToken app at https://token.im/hc/en/articles/360006465214-How-to-Create-an-EOS-Wallet.

How to Import/Create Multiple Wallets in ImToken Wallet App

ImToken wallet allows you to create, import and manage multiple wallets from a single app.

To achieve this:

1. Tap on the **Select wallet** link at the top left corner of the ImToken home page. Then tap on the **Manage wallet** tab.
2. Next, tap on **Add Wallet**, located at the bottom right of the screen.

Tap on add wallet

3. Select the wallet you wish to add. For example, ETH, BTC, ATOM, EOS, etc.

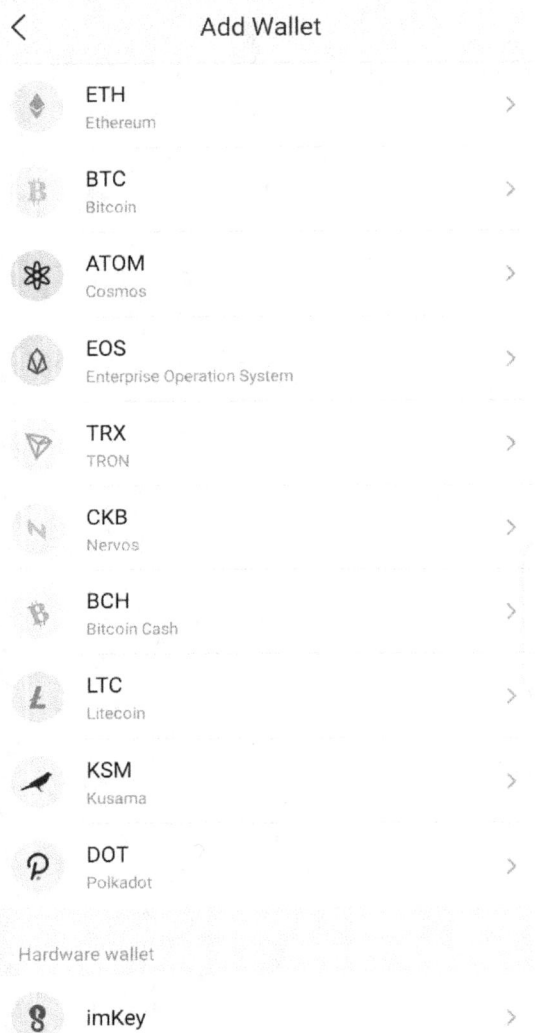

Select the wallet you wish to add

4. If you wish to create a new wallet, click on **Create**. But if you wish to Import another ERC-20 token wallet, click on **Import**.

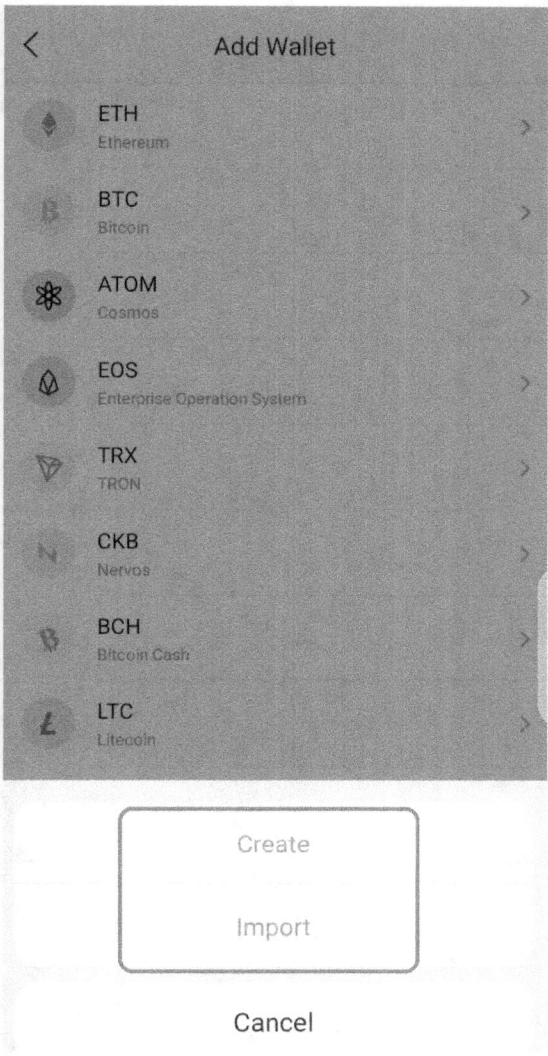

Specify if you wish to create or import another wallet

5. Type a name for your wallet. This can be any name you choose.
6. Type a password for your wallet. The password will be required before you can perform any transaction with the wallet. So create a very strong password that you don't use anywhere else, and don't forget it. Optionally, you can type a password hint, but make sure it does not reveal your password. Then click on **Create**.

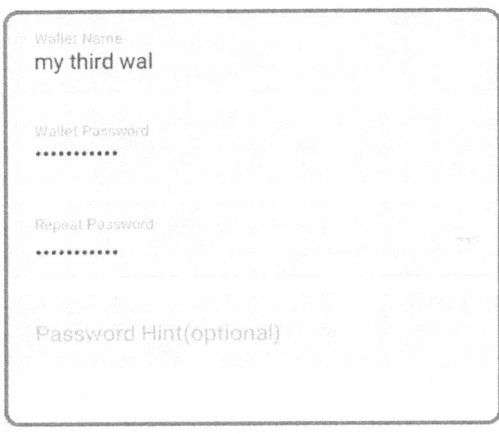

Click on create

NOTE: If you clicked on **Import**, you will be asked for the 12 recovery phrases, mnemonic phrase (or private key). Once you provide it, it will be successfully imported. You will also need to create a password for the wallet, which will be required before you can perform any transaction with the wallet.

7. If you are creating another wallet, a new 12-word mnemonic or recovery phrase will be generated. Write down the recovery phrase in the same order they appear on the screen and keep it in a safe place. Do not screenshot them. Make sure you don't lose it, else the funds in your wallet will be gone forever. Don't save it in your phone or online for security purposes.

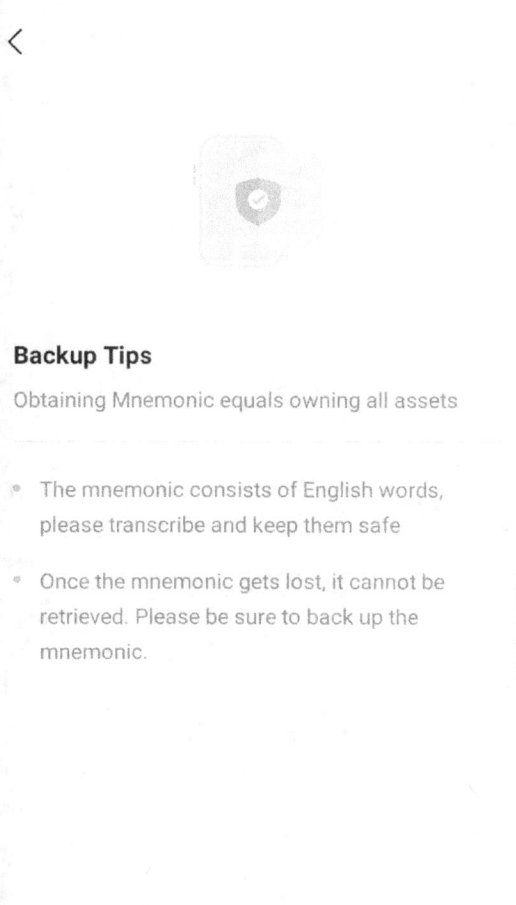

Click on next

8. Next, you will also be required to verify that you have backed up your recovery phrase, by providing the randomly asked recovery words. Click on **Confirmed backup**.
9. Once you are done with the verification, the wallet will be successfully created or imported as the case may be. On the home page, you will see the wallet name you created. Your new privately owned wallet address is under **Assets**.

How to Add/Remove a Token from ImToken Wallet App Home Page

You can choose to add tokens so that they appear under **Assets** in your ImToken app home page once you activate the app. You can also remove some any token so that it does not appear under Assets in your ImToken app home page when you activate the wallet.

To add a token:

1. Click the small circled **+** sign from the home page.
2. Now search for the token using its name or contract address. If you don't see the token, it means you need to add the token manually using the contract address.
3. Once you see the token, click on the small circled **+** sign at the right hand side.

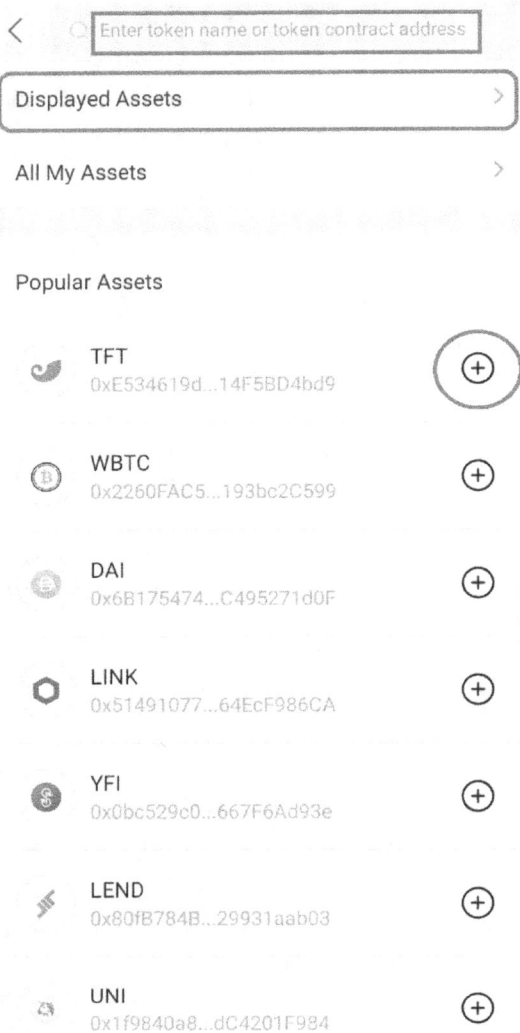

Search the token either by name or by contract address

The token will appear under Assets when you go to the home page.

To remove a token:

1. Click on **Displayed Assets**.
2. Then click the red remove button beside the token name.

Click the remove button

The token will not appear under **Assets** when you go to the home page.

How to Deposit and Withdraw Tokens with your Trust Wallet App

You can easily send and receive tokens with ImToken wallet app.

To deposit tokens:

1. You need to copy the wallet address of the token you wish to receive and then send the wallet address to the sender.
2. Add the token you wish to receive in your app home page. Now click on the token from the home page.
3. Specify if you wish to send or receive the token. In this case, you are receiving, so click on **Receive**.

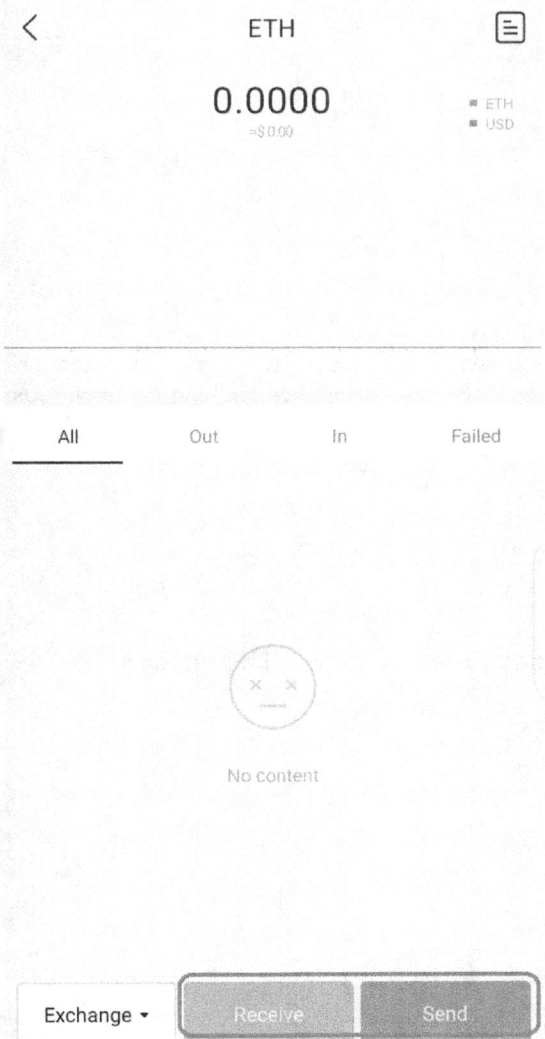

Specify if you wish to send or receive the token

4. You will now see the wallet address of the token. Click on **Copy** to copy it to your clipboard. Send the copied wallet address to the sender.

Copy the wallet address

After the sender has sent the token to your address the crypto network of the token verifies the transaction, trust wallet will notify you and the token will reflect in your balance.

To send a token:

1. You need to first get the token wallet address of the receiver. Copy it to your clipboard.
2. Add the token you wish to receive in your app home page. Now click on the token from the home page.
3. Next, click on **Send**.
4. Paste the receiver's token address and then specify the amount you wish to send. The miner fee will be displayed. Then click on **Next**.

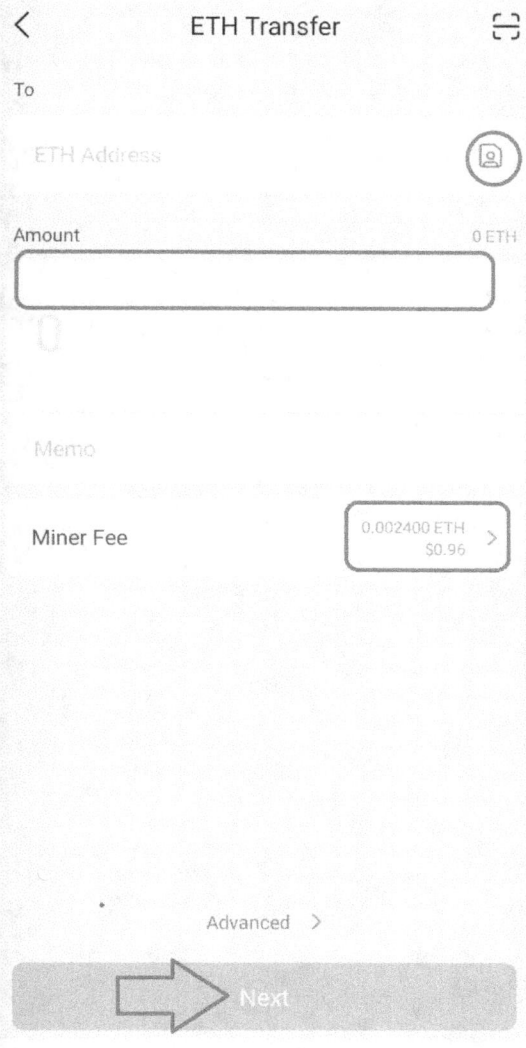

Paste the wallet address of the receiver and specify the amount

5. Next, confirm that you wish to send the amount to the receiver. You will be asked to provide the wallet password.

The amount you sent plus the miner fee will be deducted from your balance. Once the transaction is verified, the receiver will be notified and the amount you sent will reflect in the receiver's balance.

How to Swap Tokens with ImToken Built-in DEX

ImToken wallet app has a built-in DEX you can use to swap tokens only. This provides a very simplified method of buying and selling tokens from ImToken wallet app. Note that all swap transactions require a network fee.

To swap tokens:

1. Launch your ImToken wallet app. At the bottom section of the home page, click on the **Market** tab.
2. The **Trade** tab is usually activated by default. If it is not, click on it to activate it.
3. Next is to set the swap tokens: The token on the left hand side is the token that you currently have. While the token on the left hand side is the token you want to receive in exchange with the one you have. In the screenshot below, we wish to use to exchange our ETH to get USDT.
4. Now select these swap tokens by clicking the small arrow pointing to the right of each. Then click on **Exchange** button.

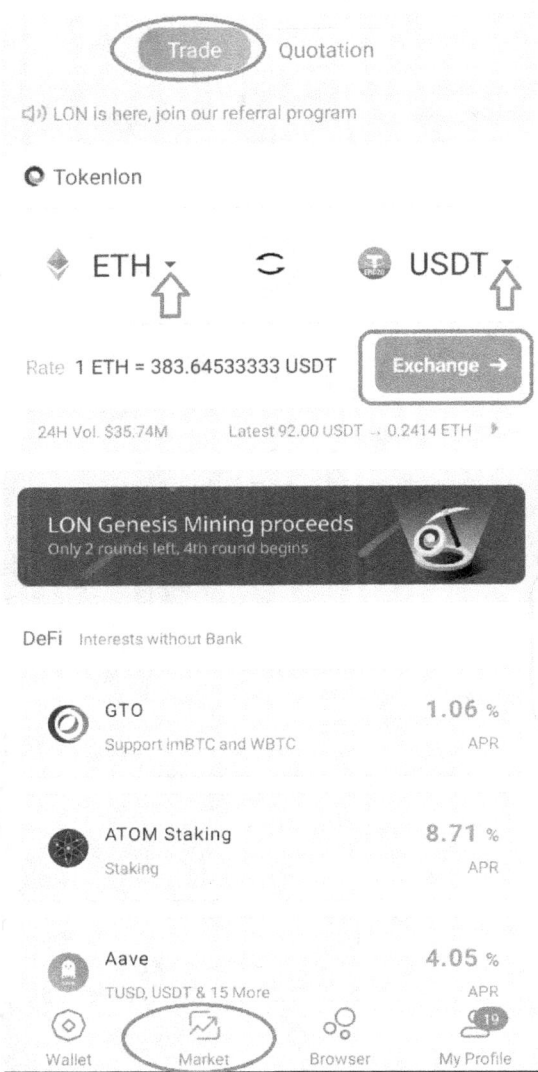

Click the exchange button

5. Next is to set the swap amount. You can decide on how much tokens you would like to swap, but there will be an automatic conversion rate that will give you an estimate of how much tokens you will receive.
6. After setting the swap amount, tap on **Next** Now confirm the transaction. The confirmation time will depend on the swap you did. ImToken wallet will notify you once the swap is complete. The token will also reflect in your wallet balance.

NOTE: There are limited number of tokens you can swap with the ImToken built-in DEX. If the token pair you wish to swap is not available, you can connect your ImToken wallet to an external DEX like Uniswap which has more swap tokens. Simply paste the external DEX swap URL in the ImToken DApp browser. Connect your wallet and swap the token. I explained **How to Use the DApp Browser of any Decentralized Wallet App to Trade with any DEX** in a later section of this book.

How to Access the Recovery Phrase and Private Key of your Wallet in ImToken

To access the private key and recovery phrase of any wallet you imported or created with ImToken:

1. From the home page, click on the ImToken app **My Profile** icon (the last icon at the bottom section of the app home page).
2. Then click on **Manage your wallet**.

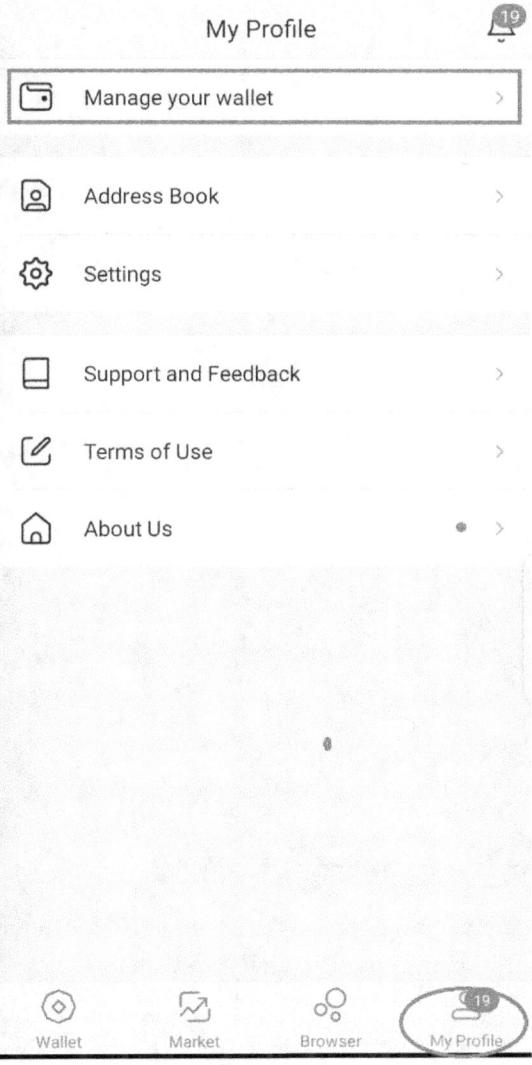

Click on manage your wallet

3. From the **Manage** page, you can see the wallet address and also edit the wallet name if you wish. You can also backup your wallet recovery phrase in case if you have lost the backup copy you did previously.
4. Toggle the **Advance** button ON to see two more features; **Export keystore** and **Export private key**.

To access the recovery phrase of that wallet:

1. Click on **Backup wallet**.
2. Type the password of that wallet.
3. Then you can access the recovery or mnemonic phrase of that wallet. Back it up offline.

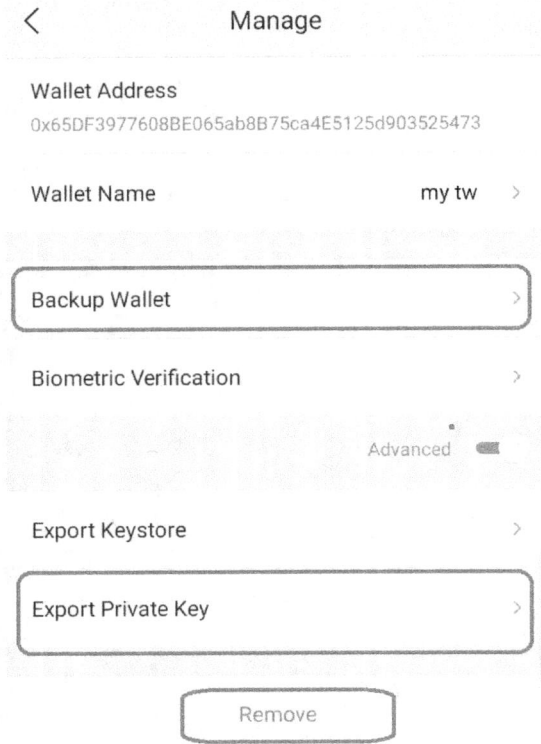

Access your wallet recovery phrase and private key

To access the private key of that wallet:

1. Click on Export private key.
2. Type the password of that wallet.
3. Then you can access the private key of that wallet. Copy it and back it up offline.

NOTE: You can also remove or delete the wallet from ImToken app, by clicking **Remove**. Make sure you have backed up the private key and recovery phrase of the wallet, else you can never recover it again.

How to Use WalletConnect with Trust Wallet and ImToken App

WalletConnect is an open protocol for connecting desktop DApps to mobile wallets using end-to-end encryption by scanning a QR code. This enables a user to use a mobile app like Trust Wallet and ImToken to connect to websites (DApps) and carry out transactions securely without revealing any secret information.

Assuming you have a Trust Wallet or ImToken app setup on your mobile phone and wish to do a quick trade via your PC web browser without revealing any secret information about your Trust wallet or ImToken wallet, the end-to-end-encryption of WalletConnect makes it possible.

To illustrate how WalletConnect works, we will access Binance DEX and do a quick trade. You will need your Wallet app and another device to access the Binance DEX website (preferably a desktop browser). For this example you will see how to access WalletConnect from Trust Wallet app and ImToken app.

To achieve this:

Open your desktop browser, and then go to the official website of Binance DEX at https://www.binance.org.

NOTE: Make sure you trust the website that request you to connect your wallet. Double check the URL before connecting your wallet.

Click on **Connect Wallet** located at the top right of the page. Choose the **Wallet Connect** option for unlocking your wallet.

A QR code will be displayed. You need to scan the QR code with your Trust wallet app or your ImToken app or any other wallet app that supports WalletConnect as the case may be.

WalletConnect QR code

To scan the QR Code with Trust Wallet App:

On the Trust Wallet app, go to **Settings** > **WalletConnect**.

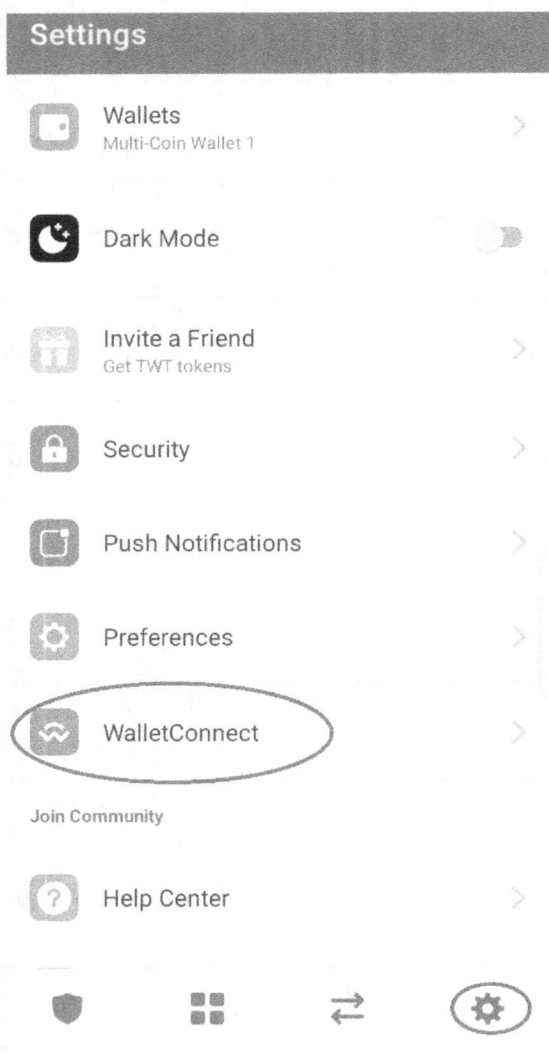

Click on WalletConnect

To scan the QR Code with ImToken Wallet App:

Click on **ImToken scan QR code** icon located at the top right corner of the app home page.

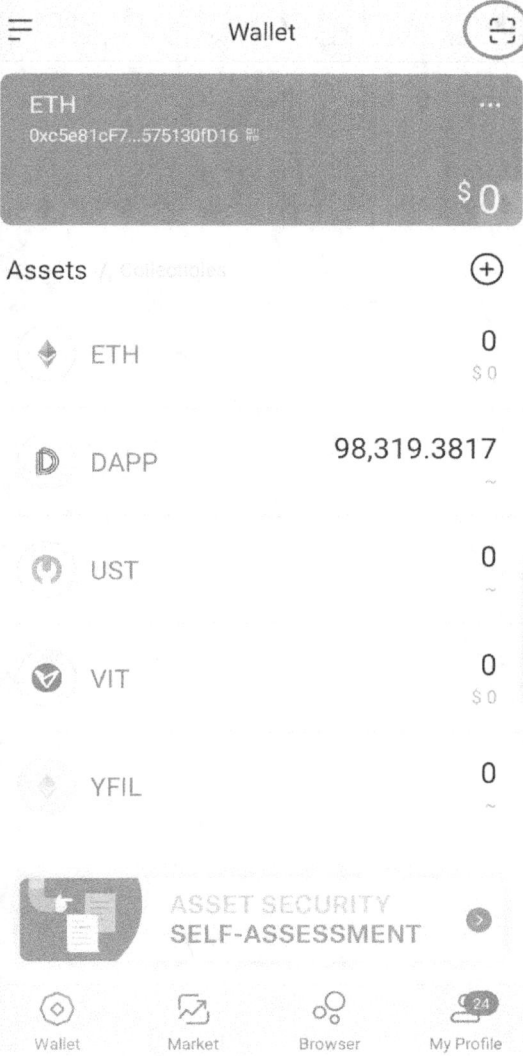

Click on ImToken scan QR code icon

Scan the QR code that is on the desktop browser. As soon as the QR code is scanned, the app will automatically recognize that you are trying to connect your wallet to the exchange platform. Next is to tap the **Connect** button to confirm.

Next is to browse the DEX and make a trade. You will see on the upper right corner of the page your Wallet status and the address that is currently in use.

Once you submit the transaction on the Binance DEX page, your wallet app will automatically recognize this and give you a prompt to either confirm the transaction by tapping **OK** or reject it by tapping **Cancel**. Confirming the transaction completes the trade on the DEX and the balances on your wallet will be updated automatically. Congrats!

How to Use the DApp Browser of any Decentralized Wallet App to Trade with any DEX

There are some cases where the crypto pair you wish to swap is not available in built-in DEX of youe decentralized wallet app like trust wallet. You can use the DApp browser to connect your wallet to any external DEX like Uniswap and swap your token.

Simply type the swap URL of the DEX you wish to connect to in your DApp browser. For example, if you wish to trade swap your ETH for PAMP token via a DEX like Uniswap, type https://app.uniswap.org/#/swap.

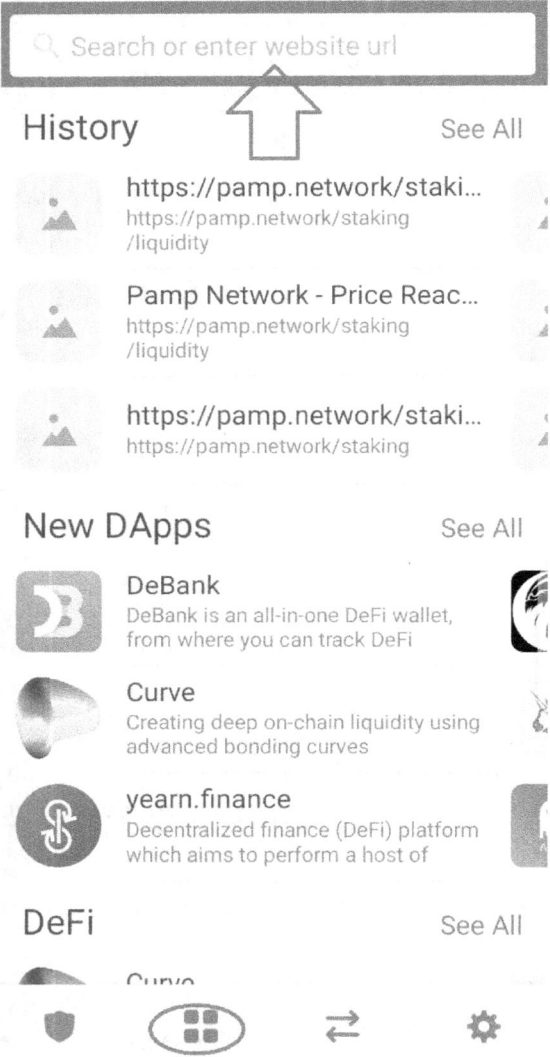

Type the DEX swap URL here

This will load Uniswap swap page. Specify the swap source token and the token you wish to receive. In the above example, the source token is ETH and the token we wish to receive is PAMP. Once you have specified the swap source token in the **From** section, click the **Select a token** button in the **To** section. To add PAMP, I need to get its *contract address*.

Contract address refers to the address location of the actual token contract that manages the logic for the tokens. This does not refer to the address that holds your own personal tokens.

NOTE: You can get the contract address of any token by searching it on Coingecko.com and checking the **Info** tab.

Specify the swap source and destination tokens

Make sure you have copied the contract address of the destination token before clicking the **Select a token** button. Now paste the contract address in the search bar. This will show you the token that has the contract address. Check the logo to ensure it is the token you wish to swap to. Now click on **Add**.

Paste the contract address and add it to the swap page

Specify the swap amount in the **From** section. It will display the equivalent in the **To** section. Now click the **Swap** button.

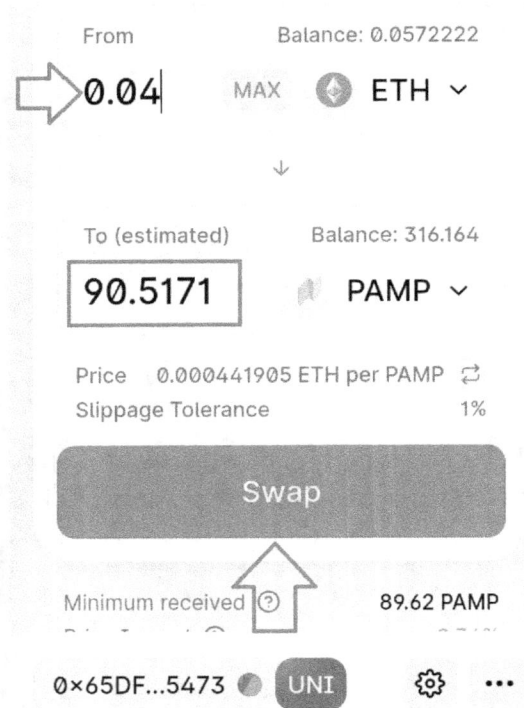

Specify swap amount and then swap

Also click on **Confirm Swap**. Trust wallet will ask you to approve the transaction request to your wallet. Both trust wallet and Uniswap will charge you gas fee.

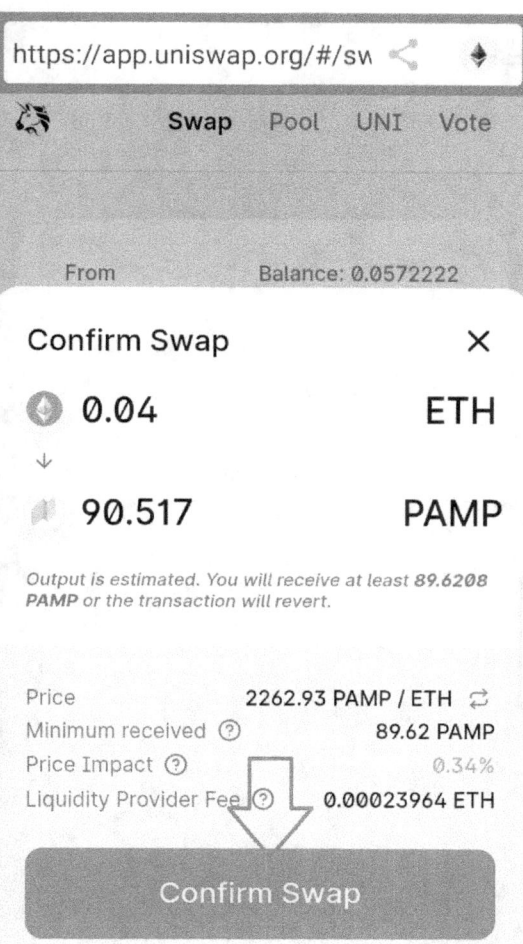

Confirm the swap

Once the swap request is processed and verified, trust wallet will notify you and the destination token will be added to your wallet balance.

How to Setup and Use Metamask Wallet

If you need a good wallet to use on your PC, then Metamask is a good option for you. It also has a mobile app.

How to Install Metamask on PC

1. You can install Metamask here: https://metamask.io
2. Click "Add to Chrome" to Install MetaMask as Google Chrome extension.
3. Click "Add Extension" to confirm and MetaMask will be added.
4. You can see that MetaMask is added by the little fox logo that shows up on the top right corner when you click the Chrome extension icon on your browser.

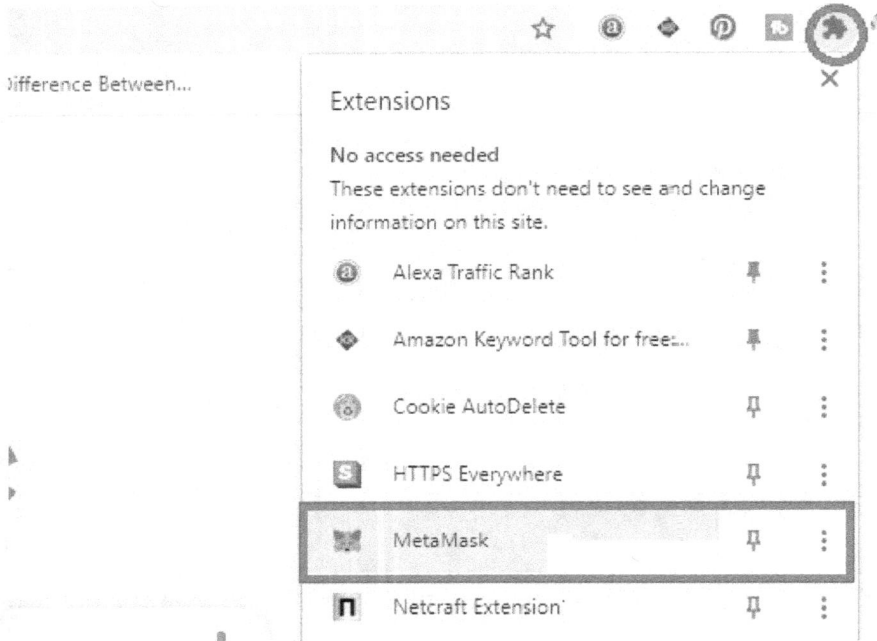

Metamask Chrome extension

Creating a Wallet

1. Click on the Metamask logo (the little fox logo).
2. Read and agree to the MetaMask terms and Conditions.
3. Click "Create a new vault", or "Create new wallet". This depends on your browser.
4. Enter a strong password and click "OK"
5. Metamask will now show you your seed. It is very important that you copy and store those 12 words, without them you cannot restore your wallet.
6. Congrats! You now have a Metamask wallet.

NOTE: If you already have a decentralized wallet which you wish to use, you can easily import it to Metamask instead of creating a new one.

Uniswap Trading Guide

Uniswap is one of the most popular decentralized exchanges in the form of two smart contracts hosted on the Ethereum blockchain. It's a 100% on-chain market maker allowing the swapping of ERC20 tokens, as well as ETH to an ERC20, and vice-versa.

In a layman's term, Uniswap is a set of computer programs that run on the Ethereum blockchain and allow for decentralized token swaps. It works with the help of unicorns. It is an automated liquidity protocol. There is no order book or any centralized party required to make trades. Uniswap allows users to trade without intermediaries, with a high degree of decentralization and censorship-resistance.

Traders can exchange Ethereum tokens on Uniswap without having to trust anyone with their funds. Meanwhile, anyone can lend their crypto to special reserves called liquidity pools. In exchange for providing money to these pools, they earn fees.

We explained how to swap token using Uniswap DEX with Trust Wallet app in this book.

Below are two comprehensive article that will explain more about Unswap and also guide on how the DEX.

- **All About Uniswap and How it Works:** https://academy.binance.com/en/articles/what-is-uniswap-and-how-does-it-work
- **Step by Step Guide on How to Use Uniswap DEX:** https://defitutorials.substack.com/p/the-ultimate-guide-to-uniswap

CONCLUSION

If you have read this guide from start to end, you have a strong foundation in Bitcoin and other cryptocurrencies, and can take this forward to start making sound investments. This is just the start for you, so we urge you to track the trends with Bitcoin and other cryptocurrencies, and to keep abreast of all new developments with cryptocurrencies.

There have been fortunes made through cryptocurrencies investing and trading. But it is not a get rich overnight business. You need to develop an investment plan and only make investments that you can afford lose. Initially we strongly recommend that you approach Bitcoin investing as a long term investment.

With more and more businesses realizing the power of Bitcoin, you will be able to use yours in more places to make purchases in the nearest future. If you have a business yourself, then we strongly recommend that you provide your customers with the choice of making Bitcoin payments. If you are concerned about the future of Bitcoin then there is no need for this. It is growing and here to stay. The fact that you can now purchase Bitcoins from ATM's speaks volumes.

The blockchain technology that supports Bitcoin is now considered to be the future of online financial transactions and supply chain management. So now it is over to you. You need to take action and follow the advice in this guide. Reading this guide will make you smarter, taking action has the potential to make you richer.

Remember to start small and use reputable cryptocurrency exchanges like Coinbase, Binance, Kucoin, etc. Also get a secure wallet to transfer your long term cryptocurrency investments and keep them safe. If you see a cryptocurrency offer that looks too good to be true then it probably is. Avoid anything that claims to sell Bitcoins at way below market value or will guarantee returns. This are all scams. Nobody can double your Bitcoins either, so steer clear of this as well.

Also, pay special attention to the cryptocurrency security tips in this book.

We hope that you found this cryptocurrency trading and investment guide helpful. Get started today with your cryptocurrency investments and trading. We wish you every success on your cryptocurrency journey. Remember that you always need to keep learning. Work smartly because the smartest investors are the ones that make the highest profits!

Please if you found this guide helpful, don't hesitate to drop your testimony at the Amazon page of this book. **Good luck!**

OTHER BOOKS BY THE AUTHOR

1. The Passionate Entrepreneur's Strategies: Learn how to discover business ideas that will be successful, grow multiple online income streams, make money from home, attract new & retain customers, applications of SWOT analysis in any business, skills that will help you succeed as an entrepreneur, self-discipline, etc.

Click to see more about the book: https://www.amazon.com/dp/B089YV65TM

2. How to Make Money from Blogging & Affiliate Marketing: Learn the Step by Step Guide Creating, Growing & Optimizing your WordPress Blog from Scratch for Search Engines (SEO) & How to Make Money through Google AdSense, Affiliate Marketing & Other Strategies for Earning Passive Income Online.

Click to see more about the book: https://www.amazon.com/dp/B08GQG96V4

3. How to Make Money Self-Publishing Books for Beginners: Learn the Step by Step Guide to Self-Publish a Best Selling Book on Amazon KDP, How to Design Book Covers with Adobe Photoshop, Format, Edit & Proofread your Book Manuscript with Microsoft Word, Promote your Book on Various Online Platforms & Earn Monthly Passive Income Online.

Click to see more about the book: https://www.amazon.com/dp/B08GXXVSGM

4. Google Classroom & Zoom Meeting for Beginners: Learn the Step by Step Guide with Screenshots on How to Use Google Classroom as a Business Owner, Teacher or a Student. Also Learn how to Use Zoom for Online Meeting, Web Conferencing, Video Conferencing & Webinars in Mobile Devices, PC & Mac. Make Distant Teaching & Learning a Fun!

Click to see more about the book: https://www.amazon.com/dp/B08JPC9NS1

Buzzer Joseph

CRYPTOCURRENCY INVESTMENT BONUS

All About Bitcoin: https://academy.binance.com/en/articles/what-is-bitcoin

All About Bitcoin: https://academy.binance.com/en/articles/what-is-ethereum

Ultimate Guide on How to Read Crypto Charts: https://blockgeeks.com/guides/learn-how-to-read-crypto-charts/

A Guide to Cryptocurrency Fundamental Analysis: https://academy.binance.com/en/articles/a-guide-to-cryptocurrency-fundamental-analysis

5 Essential Indicators Used in Technical Analysis: https://academy.binance.com/en/articles/5-essential-indicators-used-in-technical-analysis

How to Apply Technical Analysis to Cryptocurrencies: https://swissborg.com/blog/how-to-apply-technical-analysis-to-cryptocurrencies

15 Best Secured Cryptocurrency Exchange Platforms for Trading: https://www.buzzingpoint.com/2020/09/secured-cryptocurrency-exchanges.html

How Bitcoin Mining Works: https://www.investopedia.com/tech/how-does-bitcoin-mining-work/

A Complete Guide to Cryptocurrency Trading for Beginners: https://academy.binance.com/en/articles/a-complete-guide-to-cryptocurrency-trading-for-beginners

Cryptocurrency Market Cap - The Ultimate Investor's Guide: https://blockgeeks.com/guides/cryptocurrency-market-cap/

A Beginner's Guide to Day Trading Cryptocurrency: https://academy.binance.com/en/articles/a-beginners-guide-to-day-trading-cryptocurrency

How to Make a Trade (Spot Trade) on KuCoin: https://support.kucoin.plus/hc/en-us/articles/360015207073-How-to-Make-a-Trade-on-KuCoin

Beginner's Guide of KuCoin Futures: https://support.kucoin.plus/hc/en-us/articles/360039172094-Beginner-s-Guide-of-KuCoin-Futures

How to Trade Futures on KuCoin App: https://support.kucoin.plus/hc/en-us/articles/360037940573

How to Trade KuCoin Futures Pro (Website Version): https://support.kucoin.plus/hc/en-us/articles/360039738293

Learn About Futures Margin Trading: https://www.thebalance.com/all-about-futures-margin-on-futures-contracts-809390

KuCoin Security Guide: https://support.kucoin.plus/hc/en-us/articles/360015207473-KuCoin-Security-Notice

The Ultimate Guide to Trading on Binance Futures: https://academy.binance.com/en/articles/the-ultimate-guide-to-trading-on-binance-futures

How to Spot Trade on Binance Website: https://www.binance.com/en/support/articles/115003765031

How to Restore a Multi-Coin Wallet: https://community.trustwallet.com/t/how-to-restore-a-multi-coin-wallet/43

How to Trade with Trust Wallet Built-In DEX: https://community.trustwallet.com/t/how-to-trade-with-the-built-in-dex/169

How to Use WalletConnect with Trust Wallet: https://community.trustwallet.com/t/how-to-use-walletconnect-with-trust-wallet/36247

How to Trade on SushiSwap: https://community.trustwallet.com/t/how-to-trade-on-sushiswap/68574

How to Peg-In ERC20 and TRC20 tokens to Binance Smart Chain: https://community.trustwallet.com/t/how-to-peg-in-erc20-and-trc20-tokens-to-binance-smart-chain/73243

How to Monitor Transactions on Your Wallet: https://community.trustwallet.com/t/how-to-monitor-transactions-on-your-wallet/28110

How to Create EOS Account and Wallet in ImToken App: https://token.im/hc/en/articles/360006465214-How-to-Create-an-EOS-Wallet

All About Uniswap and How it Works: https://academy.binance.com/en/articles/what-is-uniswap-and-how-does-it-work

Step by Step Guide on How to Use Uniswap DEX: https://defitutorials.substack.com/p/the-ultimate-guide-to-uniswap

OTHER FREE HELPFUL RESOURCES

5 Best Digital Marketing Types and Tips You Should Know - https://www.buzzingpoint.com/2019/07/best-digital-marketing-types-tips.html

20 Best Udemy Online Courses for Personal Development - https://www.buzzingpoint.com/2019/06/best-udemy-online-courses.html

125 Inspiring Business Quotes & Advice from Successful Entrepreneurs - https://www.buzzingpoint.com/2020/04/business-advice-for-entrepreneurs.html

5 Best High in Demand Programming Languages to Learn - https://www.buzzingpoint.com/2019/07/best-programming-languages.html

12 Best Ways to Raise Funds & Save Money for Young Businesses - https://www.buzzingpoint.com/2020/03/ways-save-money-young-business.html

30 Best Worldwide Small Business Grants and How to Secure Them - https://www.buzzingpoint.com/2020/04/best-worldwide-small-business-grants.html

25 Best Lucrative Online and Offline Business Ideas for Students - https://www.buzzingpoint.com/2019/11/lucrative-students-business-ideas.html

5 Best Lucrative Skills You Can Learn Online for Free - https://www.buzzingpoint.com/2019/07/best-online-free-lucrative-skills.html

7 Steps to Help you Start DropShipping Business Online Successfully - https://www.buzzingpoint.com/2020/04/how-to-start-dropshipping-business.html

Tips to Help You Choose the Best Antivirus Software for Your PC - https://www.buzzingpoint.com/2020/04/how-to-choose-best-antivirus-software.html

15 Best Websites You Can Learn Online Skills for Free - https://www.buzzingpoint.com/2019/07/best-websites-learn-skills-free.html

6 Legitimate Simple Ways to Make Money Online for Free - https://www.microsofttut.com/2017/12/6-legitimate-simple-ways-to-make-money-online-free.html